THE VARIETIES OF NONRELIGIOUS EXPERIENCE

The Varieties of Nonreligious Experience

Atheism in American Culture

Jerome P. Baggett

NEW YORK UNIVERSITY PRESS

New York

NEW YORK UNIVERSITY PRESS
New York
www.nyupress.org
© 2019 by New York University

References to Internet websites (URLs) were accurate at the time of writing. Neither the author nor New York University Press is responsible for URLs that may have expired or changed since the manuscript was prepared.

Library of Congress Cataloging-in-Publication Data
Names: Baggett, Jerome P., 1963– author.
Title: The varieties of nonreligious experience : atheism in American culture / Jerome P. Baggett.
Description: New York : NYU Press, 2019. | Series: Secular studies | Includes bibliographical references and index.
Identifiers: LCCN 2018030573| ISBN 9781479874200 (cl : alk. paper) | ISBN 9781479884520 (pb : alk. paper)
Subjects: LCSH: Atheism—United States.
Classification: LCC BL2747.3 .B243 2019 | DDC 211/.80973—dc23
LC record available at https://lccn.loc.gov/2018030573

New York University Press books are printed on acid-free paper, and their binding materials are chosen for strength and durability. We strive to use environmentally responsible suppliers and materials to the greatest extent possible in publishing our books.
Manufactured in the United States of America
10 9 8 7 6 5 4 3 2 1
Also available as an ebook

For Sheri, to whom I say, "Yes!"

CONTENTS

Several years ago I designed and then taught for the very first time a new graduate-level course titled "The 'New Atheism' in American Culture." At the risk of seeming immodest, I must say that it was a terrific course. We read material on secularization and religious change, historical accounts of irreligious notables and movements, and a number of more polemical works by both forthrightly atheist authors and their unimpressed critics. Who could ask for more? The students, I am happy to report (again, with apt modesty), also appreciated the course, and, all things considered, it turned out to be quite the academic success that semester.

But there was this one sticking point. Especially upon discussing some of the recently published books by best-selling atheist polemicists, many of my students divulged that they did not see their own experience reflected in these works. I had expected to hear this from the majority of these students who considered themselves to be religious, some of whom were actually preparing for careers in ministry of one sort or another. And sure enough, at times many of them did get pretty flummoxed by what they took to be wildly off-the-mark depictions. They were not scriptural literalists, they pointed out. Indeed many were, or were in the process of becoming, very sophisticated in the critical interpretation of religious (and other) texts. They also insisted that they were not irrational or in any way anti-science, a response made most vociferously by one of my master of divinity students who also happened to have previously earned a doctorate in molecular biology. Nor, they seemed to guffaw in unison, did they think their religious beliefs should be imposed upon other citizens or that the crucial "wall of separation" between church and state should be allowed to falter in any way. Nor did they condone any form of religiously inspired violence. Nor were they blind to the multitude of perfectly legitimate religions other than their own. Nor could they somehow not tell the difference between what people generally consider to be knowledge and, alternatively, what believers hold to as matters of faith. Nor could . . . well, you get the idea. Let's just say that this admittedly small sample of well-educated, self-consciously religious graduate students did not recognize themselves within the pages of these anti-religion best sellers.

Far less expected, though, was that the two self-described atheists in the class also did not recognize themselves with respect to the attitudes and overall tone displayed by their fellow-atheist authors of these books. They sometimes grimaced when, rather than accurately writing about people of faith, these authors seemed content to smugly write them off for being, as suggested above, uniformly fundamentalist, anti-science, theocratic, violent, and judgmental people of dogmatic proclivities. In contrast, neither of these two students was particularly exercised about religion as a phenomenon, nor did they care much about what religious, or secular, people believed, just as long as they behaved in ways that did not harm others. Given their own perduring uncertainties related to befuddling questions about human existence and meaning, they were also not quick to reproach religious people for arriving at whatever answers seemed most credible to them. In short, they felt that these authors represented a more religion-fixated and religion-bashing, tip-of-the-iceberg subset of atheists instead of the less visible, significantly larger mass of American atheists among whom they included themselves. One of these students, Steven (whose name, like the names of all respondents introduced in this book, is a pseudonym) was especially irritated by the cocksure militancy of one of these writers. He learned a good deal and, he took pains to mention, considered this author's voice to be an important one to hear within a class on atheism in the United States. Yet, Steven asked, referencing his own as well as certain friends' and family members' decidedly less polemical experience of leading lives that just happened not to include believing in God, "Where the hell's everybody else?"

That was a good question. Since, as I could tell from the look on Steven's face, it was also a nonrhetorical one, I explained to him that the atheist "everybody else" would get heard from later in the course when we addressed sociological studies of nonreligious Americans. As it turned out, while valuable, these studies were mostly survey based and thus did not give everyday atheists the full hearing that Steven and other students wanted. More in-depth, qualitative works would be published after that first year I taught this class—and incorporated into the course syllabus thereafter—but they are only a start. The truth is that, from about the very moment he posed it, Steven's question gnawed at me.

Eventually deciding to address it head on, I began to do what any good sociologist does: I went to where I thought "everybody else" was. I started showing up at various atheist "meet-ups"—especially those of the pub-based, "Beer Not God" variety—sponsored by atheist organizations throughout the San Francisco Bay Area, where I live. I also went to more than a few atheism-related lectures, usually sponsored by these same organizations or packaged together for such special events as the SkeptiCal conference I attended in Berkeley or the annual Freethought Day I checked out in Sacramento. I listened, I took notes, I chatted with people, I drank beer. It was all very interesting, and I discovered much about a subculture that had been largely unknown to me. Yet, a particularly important insight came to me during a long day at the Atheist Film Festival held in San Francisco's iconic Roxie Theater. I watched six of the seven films shown that day (missing only the one about the life and work of Charles Darwin) and, between screenings, mingled among the approximately 120 people in attendance. Then it occurred to me: even after just a few months of doing this firsthand research, I knew by name, by reputation, or just by face nearly half of them. This "it's a small world, after all" feeling was only reinforced later on when I realized that several of the people who appeared in the festival's showing of *Hug an Atheist*, a documentary film aimed at dispelling myths about nonbelievers, were also in attendance. That's when Steven's question truly became *my* question. I definitely enjoyed exploring this milieu of dyed-in-the-wool atheists for whom disbelief in God and often the denigrating of religion are core to their identities. Nevertheless, I found myself asking, a bit more intently this time, "Where the hell's everybody else?"

So, at that juncture, I did what all somewhat pigheaded sociologists do: I expanded the scope of my study. I spent a day visiting the Center for Inquiry in Los Angeles and, later that evening, was allowed to sit in on a secular AA meeting held on the premises. I attended the three-day, fiftieth-anniversary conference of American Atheists in Austin, Texas. I even hung out for a couple of days at the Northern California chapter of Camp Quest, a secular summer camp for kids. From all this, my next real insight came not from doing participant observation at these institutions and events, all of which I considered to be fascinating. Instead, it emerged from casual conversations with some of my atheist friends who, on those occasions when I happened to recount some of what I saw and heard, seemed much less enthralled than I was expecting. What's going on? I asked myself. Were they distracted? Was I not the relentlessly intriguing raconteur I had always imagined myself to be?

The answer came one evening when I was about to drive to San Jose to experience my very first Sunday Assembly gathering. Sometimes known as the "atheist church," on its website it prefers to call itself a "secular congregation that celebrates life" and aims to help people, as stated in its mission, to "live better, help often and wonder more." I was all in. Anyone would be into checking this out, I thought—until I asked Daniel, a longtime friend (and neighbor) and appreciably longer-time atheist, if he would like to join me. "No thanks, man," he shot back before I finished inviting him and informing him that I would even pay for dinner. "I moved past all that a long time ago." I proceeded to tell him how Sunday Assembly was initially organized by two British comedians, that it was supposedly very intellectual and fun, and that it would be a good place to hang out for a while with like-minded people. Nothing. He was having none of it. Finally, just as I was about to play the free dinner card again, he interrupted me. "Nope," he said, and then repeated with a distinct emphasis, "I moved past *all* that a long time ago."

That's when I got it. Daniel was actually where "everybody else" is. Beyond simply belief in God, he also moved past whatever desire he may have once had to associate with fellow nonbelievers. Past the need to participate in any organized retort to religious ritual. Past the urge to consolidate and label his worldview. Past thinking of atheism as the defining feature of his identity or as some kind of lifelong job description. Now past all of this, Daniel was coming from a place that, while densely occupied by American atheists, is very seldom heard from within both public conversations and the pages of books written by and pertaining to nonbelievers.

But I wanted, as they say, to "go there," to listen to what people like Daniel—who months later actually became my very first interviewee for this project—had to say, and then share what I would hear with readers. So, consider this book a majority report, not a minority report. It pays attention to lots of voices from the rank-and-file center, not just from the film-festival-attendee margins. Rather than recapitulating arguments first articulated by best-selling "somebodies" of the atheist firmament, it attempts to capture the workaday cacophony of commonly drowned-out viewpoints that could well be described by the phrase, which James Joyce waggishly used in *Finnegans Wake* to describe Catholicism, "here comes everybody."

As readers will see in the final section of chapter 1, I operationalize "everybody" as the 518 respondents for this study. That's a lot. It includes people who have been sometimes profoundly influenced by such atheism-related books as the ones we read in my class years ago. It also includes people who, to varying extents, are likely to attend events like the Atheist Film Festival, participate in such initiatives as SkeptiCal and Freethought Day, and count themselves among the members of local atheist organizations or communities like Sunday Assembly. Important to emphasize, it also includes the majority of American atheists, people like Steven and Daniel, who rarely or, more likely, never attend, participate in, or consider themselves members of any manifestation of public atheism.

With so many people taking part in this study, presenting what I have discovered obviously requires some organization and selectivity. Hence, in part 1, "Getting the Lay of the Land," I begin in the first chapter by clearing away six commonplace presuppositions about atheism and American atheists, and then introduce the sociological methods used for this study. Next, I present in chapter 2 the ways in which respondents describe what it felt like for them to first identify as atheists and then, in chapter 3, how they do the ongoing work of maintaining their atheist identities by situating themselves within an "imagined community" of fellow nonbelievers.

In part 2, I start "Digging a Bit Deeper" by showing that four distinctive roots of atheist thinking (introduced in chapter 1), even though they reach back two and a half millennia to ancient Athens, continue to inflect atheist discourse presently. Not different types of atheism, these roots instead represent styles of atheist thinking that have long histories and also go a long way toward assuring atheists today that their identities, though often deprecated within the broader society, are actually legitimate and worthwhile. As we will see in chapter 4, atheists rely upon the *empirical* root in framing religion as the antithesis of science and, at the same time, using the language of personal meaning and sometimes even of spirituality to stand clear of scientism. The epitome of this root is the so-called science versus religion "conflict myth," which functions to naturalize three sets of oppositional categories that respondents deploy in order to highlight and hone key dispositions they claim to be features of their identities as atheists. For instance, especially when they specifically address the topic of religion, they rely upon the *critical* root to accentuate their rejection of religion's comforts in preference to what they experience as their own lives of greater integrity. I focus on this topic in chapter 5. Then, in the following chapter, I show how respondents draw upon the *agnostic* root when attending to certain "big questions" and perennial matters of faith and, in doing so, privilege their own openness over the purported closed-mindedness of believers. Finally, in chapter 7, I explain how, when the issue of morality is raised in conversation, atheists typically display the discursive style of the *immanent* root in demonstrating that, compared to the regressive nature of religion-based moralities, their more this-worldly ethical sensibilities are both superior and far more precipitous of societal progress.

In the process of my getting the lay of the land and then digging deeper, I happened upon some intriguing nuggets scattered about, some key themes I consider well worth the trouble of excavating. The first has to do with variety. In their important book *American Secularism: Cultural Contours of Nonreligious Belief Systems*, sociologists Joseph Baker and Buster Smith situate atheists among a broader swath of secular Americans, which also includes agnostics, nonaffiliated believers, and the nonpracticing "culturally" religious. My work contributes to this conversation by complementing Baker and Smith's wider gaze with one that explores the variations *within* that subset of secular Americans who identify as atheists. Second, while only a minority of the 518 people I spoke with are members of atheism-related organizations or small groups, in one way or another, nearly all of them draw symbolic boundaries between themselves and religious believers, and thus participate in an "imagined community" of the putatively like-minded. A third nugget is the salience of nonbelief's affective dimension. Whereas atheists are generally known for their critical thinking and intellectualism—leaving many observers to focus on the cognitive dimension[1]—I argue that feelings are essential to many atheists insofar as they provide a kind of affective confirmation that they are living authentic, meaningful lives and are indeed part of the aforementioned imagined community of others endeavoring to the same. Fourth, as Steven, my former student, already knew, nonbelievers often voraciously read about, learn from, and find support for their own perspectives within the works of popular atheist authors. But that does not mean they parrot them. In fact, as we will see, their views are significantly less prone toward scientism and, in some ways, far more nuanced in their assessment of religion than what appears within the pages of best-selling books. The final and perhaps most important nugget concerns the revalorization of atheism itself. Here I mean something more than moving from a stigmatizing perception of atheists—which, after all, is based upon erroneous stereotypes—to a more accurate one. This, too, is essential. Yet, beyond even that, I also mean moving from envisioning atheism in terms of a rejection (abandoning religion) or a negation (not believing) or an absence (without faith) to seeing it in more positive terms—as an active and affirmative embrace of convictions and dispositions that are, to use sociologist Lois Lee's preferred term, quite "substantial" in their own right.[2] As much as the arcs of their lives have taken them *from* belief, as we will see in the chapters ahead, they have also directed these 518 respondents *toward* new, wholly desirable ways of being in the world that deserve to be approached in an equally new, interpretively capacious manner.

People often say lots of uninformed, untrue, and oftentimes quite unsavory things about atheists. And it has only been recently that the voices of atheist writers, bloggers, organizers, celebrities, and other public figures have added important rejoinders that have been heard by more and more of their fellow citizens. Now, lest those voices come to be thought of as expressing the totality of what is on nonbelievers' minds, it is time for "everybody else" to also chime in and be heard. This book is intended to facilitate that process.

While working on it, I was sometimes struck by the irony of a sociologist writing about nonbelief being so thoroughly inspired by a non-sociologist's expressed belief. But so be it. In his own preface to the now classic *The Varieties of Religious Experience* (1902), the great American psychologist and philosopher William James informs his readers of his guiding "belief that a large acquaintance with particulars often makes us wiser than the possession of abstract formulas."[3] I could not agree more. So, in the pages ahead, I aim to introduce readers not to some abstract, formulaic thing called "atheism" but instead to as many particular, flesh-and-blood people as possible—in all their varieties—in order to provide a granular sense of what they think and how they go about living both *without* God and very much *with* a purposefulness of their own design. If, in making their acquaintance, readers consider themselves the wiser for it, then I will consider this work, while perhaps not destined to be a classic, to at least have been worth the effort to write.

PART I

Getting the Lay of the Land

Identifying as Atheist

1

Well, I'll Be Damned!

Considering Atheism beyond the "Popular View"

In the absence of any serious investigations, what has been believed about irreligion is whatever constitutes the "popular view," and on a subject such as this the opinions of the general public are notoriously unreliable. In general, opinions about irreligion were forged in the white-hot furnace of emotion surrounding the great religious debates of the late nineteenth century. At the time both sides were capable of believing almost anything to the disadvantage of the other, and although now the furnace has burnt very low, underlying attitudes linger on.
—Colin Campbell, *Toward a Sociology of Irreligion* (1972)

Considering American Atheism in the Twenty-First Century

It has been nearly half a century since the distinguished British sociologist Colin Campbell first directed his colleagues toward atheism and other species of irreligion as topics worthy of serious consideration. Relatively few, however, especially those living and working in the United States, have followed his lead.[1] Both "push" and "pull" factors have likely swayed them from doing so. American sociologists' frequent lack of interest in matters pertaining to religion has been the primary push factor. Considerably more secular than the public at large, they also score lower on most measures of religiosity than their scholarly peers from other academic disciplines.[2] Many have also subscribed to a particularly strong version of the secularization thesis—prominent among the highly influential founding generation of social scientists—that tends to equate increasing modernization with decreasing levels of piety and, in many colleagues' estimation, renders the empirical exploration of religion- or irreligion-related topics scarcely worth the effort. Plenty of researchers, including those advocating subtler versions of this thesis, have disagreed with this assessment, certainly.[3] After all, the zero-sum model that equates more modernity with less religion and vice versa, while alluringly simple, does not correlate especially well with the more complicated reality of religion's persistence in contemporary society.[4]

Yet, the lion's share of those who have acknowledged this reality and have been indeed interested in such topics have long found themselves pulled in other directions. At about the time Professor Campbell was writing his ground-breaking book, many sociologists were being drawn to such "new religious movements" as Scientology, Hare Krishna, and the Unification Church (the "Moonies") as fascinating venues for research. Shortly thereafter, the equally unexpected emergence of traditionalist piety, especially the politically active "Religious Right," commanded scholars' attention. Next came what was dubbed "New Age" religion as well as the newfound visibility of those who, bristling at denominational labels and other group-based religious identifiers, took to calling themselves "spiritual but not religious." Then the focus turned to the new institutional "carriers" of people's religious commitments that included small groups, community organizations, social movements, and the like. And so it went. With each passing decade, Americans' ever-churning religious marketplace supplied observers with more than enough new products to draw their attention away from the nation's minority of religious nonconsumers.

Things seem to be changing, though. Scholarship in this area has been growing as, within only the last decade or so, public expressions of atheism have become ever more visible. Comic performances such as Bill Maher's film *Religulous* and Julia Sweeney's one-woman show exploring her *Letting Go of God* have found large audiences and stirred much media interest. The same goes for a number of documentaries, the most notable being *The God Who Wasn't There*, *The Atheism Tapes*, and *The Unbelievers*. The Church of the Flying Spaghetti Monster (also known as Pastafarianism), a spoofing of religion prompted by the Intelligent Design movement's influence within public schools, has become an Internet sensation. The number of atheism-related online support networks, forums, podcasts, blogs, and videoblogs is dizzying, and seems to grow daily. And this groundswell of discourse is increasingly complemented by important voices from on high. In his 2009 inaugural address, President Barack Obama spoke to what he hailed as "a nation of Christians and Muslims, Jews and Hindus, and non-believers."[5] Even Pope Francis, in a lengthy editorial printed on the front page of the Italian newspaper *La Repubblica*, responded to questions about atheism by telling readers that "God's mercy has no limits" and, he continued, "the question for those who do not believe in God is to abide by their own conscience."[6]

Adding to this enhanced visibility are local atheist organizations that, due mostly to the cultural contretemps that often ensue when publicizing themselves, are also finding their way onto people's "radar screens." In one instance we hear about the Los Angeles United Atheists adopting a local strip of highway and then complaining publicly when vandals, theists presumably, etched out the A on their sign.[7] In another, the Colorado Coalition of Reason created a brouhaha when, during the Christmas season, they sponsored eleven billboards bearing such messages as "Don't believe in God? You are not alone" and "Why believe in God? Just be good for goodness sake."[8] In yet another, we read in the *New York Times* that a Habitat for Humanity affiliate would not allow volunteers from a South Carolina secular humanist group to build houses while wearing their "Non-Prophet Organization" T-shirts.[9]

Despite the pushback they can receive, local initiatives like these are proliferating, often in conjunction with nationally organized ones doing the same. For decades the American Atheists, founded by Madalyn Murray O'Hair in 1963, was virtually the only national-level atheist advocacy organization known to the public. Now many others, almost all founded within the past decade or two, are coming onto the scene and expanding. For example, Camp Quest—a network of secular-themed summer camps for children—is currently in over a dozen locations across the country. The Secular Student Alliance, the national umbrella organization for campus-based atheist and humanist groups, had fewer than fifty affiliates in 2007; now it has nearly four hundred established at colleges and universities from coast to coast. Held on the National Mall in Washington, D.C., the 2012 Reason Rally, the so-called Woodstock for atheists, was able to attract an estimated twenty thousand people and also publicize the event to many more, mainly because of the coordinated effort of nearly twenty distinct national organizations. Running the gamut from the United Coalition of Reason to the Freedom from Religion Foundation, from the American Humanist Association to the Skeptics Society, from the Congress of Secular Jewish Organizations to the Military Association of Atheists and Freethinkers, and everywhere in between, a full description of such organizations could fill the remaining pages of this book. Suffice it to say that they, along with the events they sponsor, the magazines they publish, and the websites they maintain, have all helped American atheism go public.

Maybe the best indicator that atheism is finding a place within the wider culture is the unexpected popularity of four books—all best sellers at some point—that take aim at religion: Sam Harris's *The End of Faith: Religion, Terror and the Future of Reason* (2005); Richard Dawkins's *The God Delusion* (2006); Daniel C. Dennett's *Breaking the Spell: Religion as a Natural Phenomenon* (2006); and Christopher Hitchens's *God Is Not Great: How Religion Poisons Everything* (2007). These books are generally regarded as comprising the vanguard of what has come to be known as the New Atheism. This term is misleading in that neither atheism in general nor these books' arguments in particular are without precedent. What is new for the American context, in addition to their appealing to a large readership as well as augmenting (sometimes inspiring) additional works by both lesser-known atheists and theistic critics alike,[10] is their offensively defensive quality. In other words, rather than trying to *understand* religion (presumed to be almost wholly nefarious) or religious people (presumed to be almost uniformly fundamentalist)—or even bother to engage religion scholars who do—they take the offensive and seek to explicitly *eradicate* religion. This posture is compounded by a kind of defensiveness that would be unfamiliar to an earlier, more secularly triumphant generation of atheists that includes such familiar figures as Karl Marx, Sigmund Freud, and Friedrich Nietzsche. Unlike these and other "old" atheists, their present-day counterparts express a call-to-arms urgency and conviction that, rather than being on the ascendancy, secular ways of thinking and living are in fact being assailed by religious publics from seemingly all sides.

Why these authors, commonly known as the "four horsemen" of the New Atheism, have become such well-known intellectuals and why their books have sold so briskly are enquiries that beg the larger, more encompassing question of why a cultural space for public expressions of atheism opened up when it did. No doubt a confluence of factors was at play here. Two of these—the emergence of Islamic terrorism and the political traction the Intelligent Design movement has gained within America's public schools—have been highlighted by each of the New Atheist authors. The fact that Sam Harris began writing *The End of Faith* the day after 9/11 provides some grounds for speculating that this event may have had a comparable anti-religion effect among the broader populace. And while Richard Dawkins and Daniel Dennett are distinctive for each having written important books on Darwinian theory, many Americans have no doubt shared their fed-up-with-faith reaction to the imposition of a religious agenda that Creationism (among other political initiatives advanced by religious conservatives) represents.[11] A third factor facilitating atheism's greater visibility is the emergence of what one scholar calls a widespread "societal cynicism concerning organized religion."[12] One wonders, for example, if Christopher Hitchens's subtitle, "How Religion Poisons *Everything*"—not just *some* or even *many* things—would seem so plausible to Americans were it not for their all-too-vivid awareness of certain televangelists' financial misdealings; former National Association of Evangelicals president Ted Haggard's troubles concerning drugs and male prostitutes; the Catholic Church's pedophile scandal; religious organizations' opposition to stem-cell research and same-sex marriage; and so on. Fourth, even if it were the case that a proportion of Americans have perennially deemed the influence of religion to be unvaryingly poisonous, the end of the Cold War seems to have made it easier to actually voice this opinion. With the fall of "Godless Communism," expressions of irreligion, while still often stigmatized, no longer smack as alarmingly unpatriotic as they once did. Finally, these expressions are being heard and corroborated to a previously unimaginable degree with the emergence of the Internet. Given that atheists have long been a scant, often "closeted" segment of the population, it would be difficult to overemphasize this as a factor in helping people to connect with intellectually compatible others, consolidate their identities as atheists, and then "come out" in ways that feel appropriate to them. Thanks to the Internet, observed David Silverman, the current president of American Atheists, "there is no way that a person who is an atheist can think they're alone anymore."[13]

They can, however, rightly think of themselves as being misunderstood by the majority of their fellow citizens. Filling the void left by sociologists' (and others') chronic inattention to contemporary atheism has come what Professor Campbell called the "popular view," which, as when he first reflected upon it, remains "notoriously unreliable." This viewpoint is unreliable because it is largely reductionist. In the course of their everyday thinking, in other words, people tend to reduce the complicated and multifaceted reality of atheism to something they cursorily presume to be simple and clear-cut.

Before exploring this tendency in greater detail, it is worth noting that reductionist thinking is a two-way street, and it has been well travelled by both cursory and critical observers of religion. On the most basic level, discussion about, critiques of, or dismissiveness toward this thing called "religion" all neglect the reality that no such thing truly exists. There are actually many religious traditions throughout the world, and these all have complex histories and hand on quite disparate teachings and practices that influence adherents' lives in equally disparate ways. This might be obvious to most readers. Nevertheless, even more analytically minded treatments of religion can fall prey to this reductionist tendency. A classic sociological example is Karl Marx's eminently disdainful harrumph that religion functions primarily as the "opium of the people," an ideological bromide that lulls the exploited masses into a listless state of political quiescence when, in his view, they ought to mobilize themselves and surmount the forces oppressing them.[14] Neglected here is the reality that, while some manifestations of religion function in the very manner Marx described and surely witnessed throughout much of mid-nineteenth-century Europe, this is hardly true of all. Just as often, as innumerable studies of the long-standing connection between religion and political engagement have shown, religiously derived ideas and networks can function as a kind of "amphetamine of the people," stirring them toward collective action of all kinds. This too may be obvious to readers, especially in light of the role that American religious institutions and publics have played in sustaining broad-based political initiatives that range from the civil rights movement decades ago to the pro-life movement today.

Still, reductionism has not necessarily gone out of style. All four of the aforementioned New Atheist writers, for example, depict religious faith as belief without evidence and, in doing so, reduce religion to intellectually vapid propositions about the natural world. To Richard Dawkins, religious faith, which he describes as a "persistently false belief held in the face of strong contradictory evidence," is really nothing more than shoddy science.[15] "Thanks to the telescope and the microscope," exults Christopher Hitchens in agreement, "[religion] no longer offers an explanation of anything important."[16] Approaching religion this way, though, is tantamount to a confusion of genres. It is something akin to disparaging Franz Kafka's *The Metamorphosis* for being an extremely poor entomology textbook or to carping about certain astronomical in-accuracies charted in Vincent van Gogh's *The Starry Night*. The fact is that most religious people in the United States see little overlap or con-flict between religious and scientific claims, and since they think of faith as being about connecting them to something *super*natural, they often find discussion about confirming or disconfirming evidence discerned within the natural world to be missing the point.[17]

Getting Beyond the "Popular View"

There are, of course, additional points to be missed when heading along reductionism's two-way street in the other direction, in the direction of atheists. Drawing attention to these and thus giving readers a clearer, more full-blooded view of contemporary American atheism is largely what this book sets out to do. This task is complicated—and, I would add, particularly pressing—because so many Americans, believers and sometimes even nonbelievers, do travel this street with great regular-ity and carry with them stereotypes in place of actuality, conjecture in place of true understanding. As a result, their perspective on the matter, the "popular view," has become egregiously skewed in that it generally reflects widely held, though erroneous, presumptions concerning both atheism as such and atheists themselves. Allow me to give three exam-ples of each.

Presumption One: Atheism as Simple

Things taken to be simple frequently turn out, upon closer inspection, to be merely simplified. This is certainly true of Americans' typical conception of atheism. From the Greek *atheistos* (*a* for "without" and *theos* for "god"), atheism fundamentally refers to any worldview that does not include God (or gods).* Notice that the term is negatively defined. Rather than necessarily denoting an expressed belief in the nonexistence of God, it is a residual construct based upon the far-ranging presumption of theism itself. This is significant. Few of us would use the terms *a-leprechaunists* or *a-Sasquatchists* to label those who do not believe in little people guarding pots of gold or in an apelike humanoid roaming the forests of the American Northwest—simply because belief in the existence of such creatures is not taken for granted among the general public. No such cultural category signifying dissent is necessary. Others, such as the anti-polygamist or the abolitionist, can largely fall out of use as society changes. Who among us feels the need to describe ourselves in these ways at a time in the United States when multiple marriage and chattel slavery are so roundly opposed among its citizenry? This is not the case with the atheist. That people do feel the need to describe themselves or others as atheists, however, says far less about them or about this category of people than it does about the extent to which religious conviction of some sort is held to be normative within American society today. Looked at more closely, then, the term tells us vanishingly little about those to whom it purportedly refers.[18]

Things do not get much clearer when, as is routine, people hamhandedly reduce atheism to being necessarily antithetical to religion. This makes little sense when you consider that, while some versions of atheism certainly espouse an aggressively anti-religion stance, other versions display a kind of "live and let live" attitude and evince little concern about how one's God-fearing neighbors might be spending their Friday nights or Sunday mornings. Also, just as atheism can actually get along relatively well with religion, it can be constitutive of it as well. I do not mean that atheism is a kind of religion, a contention one sometimes hears from within theological circles and that, when one thinks about it, is about as analytically useful as considering *not* playing ice hockey to

---

*Many of those who responded to my questionnaire in writing use an uppercase *G* in "God" when referring to the Western notion of a monotheistic deity and a lowercase *g* to denote other understandings or intentionally pejorative construals, and I have followed this practice in this book. This decision is for the sake of style and consistency, and is not meant to convey a normative position on my part.

be a kind of sport. No, here I direct readers to the converse reality that religions can be atheistic. God concepts, in other words, are obviously key features of many religions, but not of all of them. Anthropological studies of "traditional" religions are informative in this respect. Many of these religions uphold the existence of nature spirits that are said to inhabit certain plants or animals, geographical locations, natural phenomena, and the like. Others focus on revering and interacting with ancestor spirits. Still others accept the reality of a nonpersonal, supernatural force ("mana," "chi," etc.) that is believed to animate the world. Adherents are said to be capable of accessing these spirits and forces at specified times and places, but they are clearly not taken to be gods in the sense that divinity is generally thought of in the West.[19] A similar observation can be made about important strands of Buddhism, Confucianism, and Jainism, which are clearly nontheistic.[20]

Another simplification of atheism is that it is persistently cast in terms of what sociologists call an "achieved status," a dimension of personal identity that, like educational attainment or political affiliation, one acquires during the course of one's lifetime. One is presumed to become an atheist much like one becomes a college graduate or a registered Democrat. The problem here, as each of the previously discussed New Atheist writers mention, is that people are actually born atheists, and even the majority of Americans who get socialized into religious faith actually remain atheistic toward at least other people's gods (Zeus, Osiris, Thor, Quetzalcoatl, and the rest). Moreover, increasing numbers of people, those raised in nonreligious households, are coming to their atheism via nonreligious socialization rather than turning to atheism after many years of being reared in a religious tradition.[21] All this notwithstanding, at present most atheists in the United States are essentially apostates in that they indeed have *become* atheists after receiving some degree of religious upbringing. Yet, as sociologist Phil Zuckerman points out, even this process is not as simple as it sounds because the context and meaning of people "achieving" this new status as nonbelievers vary enormously.[22] For example, stage of life is a key variable. Some people become atheists later in life after a significant period of religious belief and affiliation. Much more common, though, are those who do so in their teens or twenties in conjunction with their individuating from the direct influence of their families. A second variable is how transformational becoming an atheist is for people. Some reject a religious faith in which they have had little investment, whereas others may have been deeply religious, and thus their becoming atheists is experienced as a more life-altering enterprise, which may have significantly affected (or even ended) relationships with family and friends. Still another variable has to do with how clean a break people make with religion. Some atheists have made a complete break and may even consider themselves to be unabashedly irreligious. Others do not go as far. They may be among the approximately one-third of American atheists who attend religious services from time to time.[23] They may consider themselves "spiritual but not religious" or convinced that there is "something out there." Or perhaps they take a pass on the more militant-sounding "atheist" label and prefer "agnostic," "freethinker," or "secular humanist."

As with becoming an atheist, *being* an atheist also tends to be unduly simplified in the public's mind. It is almost uniformly depicted, to use another bit of sociological jargon, as a kind of "master status," as absolutely central to one's self-identity. This is understandable. A key strategy among many atheist writers, bloggers, activists, and advocacy organizations is to use the framework of "identity politics" as a means for portraying atheists to the wider public as a unified and aggrieved minority pursuing a shared agenda of securing rights and social recognition.[24] Consequently, many Americans have come to think of atheism as being an inevitably core feature of selfhood about which atheists themselves have similar attitudes. But this, too, is a gross simplification. Rather than experiencing it as a master status, many people are relatively indifferent toward their atheism.[25] What may be true of impassioned, self-consciously atheist writers, bloggers, activists, and advocates is often much less true of others who just "happen to be" nonbelievers. Growing numbers, it seems, would agree with the sentiments expressed by avowed atheist Denis Diderot in a letter to his fellow *philosophe* Voltaire (June 11, 1749): "It is very important not to mistake hemlock for parsley," he confided, "but to believe or not to believe in God is not important at all."[26]

Even people for whom religious issues do indeed fall within the more important "hemlock versus parsley" category have varying attitudes toward their atheism. Some, espying the promise of human progress, look eagerly forward to a world without God in which reason supplants superstition. "Civilization will not attain to its perfection," declared novelist Émile Zola, "until the last stone from the last church falls on the last priest."[27] Others can be quite wistful about God, feeling an acute sense of loss or disappointment about exiting a putatively secure realm of belief into which they feel they can never reenter. In the play *Endgame*, one of Samuel Beckett's characters captures this mood precisely: "The bastard! He doesn't exist!"[28] Others, the vast majority of American atheists, actually, equate their rejection of faith with feelings of being freed from religion's strictures and, consequently, with being responsible for living meaningful lives in whatever ways they choose. In sum, scratch the surface of this seemingly simple concept, atheism, and one discovers that the complexities, while persistently overlooked, are really quite striking.

Presumption Two: Atheism as New

Not usually one to name-drop, I mention these luminaries from the past to help advance my aim in confuting the popular conceit that atheism is a relatively new phenomenon. This presentist reduction is evident within various quarters. Many secular activists and organizations, for instance, rely upon it as a means of highlighting the degree of success and momentum the professedly burgeoning atheist "movement" has already achieved within a brief span of time. Meanwhile, more than a few religiously inclined detractors seem to rely upon it, consciously or not, as a way to minimize the long-standing and substantive nature of atheism's challenge to faith. Linking atheism to such recently emergent phenomena as the cultural shift that occurred in the sixties (legitimating "doing your own thing"), the expansion of higher education (problematizing traditional verities), changes in family structure (undermining religious socialization), and the ubiquity of consumerism and the mass media (distracting the citizenry from life's "big questions") all functions to make nonreligion seem more of an unintended and nouveau consequence of something else than as something that is deeply rooted and truly consequential in its own right.

Both the secular and religious versions of this presentist outlook are mistaken, however. What is new about the New Atheism may be its offensively defensive tenor, its spate of newly published books, and its newfound hearing within the public square, but it is not at all new with respect to its atheism, which is very probably as old as religion itself.

Providing a satisfactory account of this history is clearly impossible here. Yet, two points are essential. The first is that the roots of an intellectually sophisticated tradition of atheism in the West are remarkably deep. They reach back as far as the pre-Socratic Milesian philosophers of the sixth century BCE who, among other things, endeavored to replace mythological explanations of the world around them with ones based on the rational assessment of facts and arguments that were available for all to consider.[29] We see this again and again among the classical thinkers whose work has survived, although often in fragments and sometimes in secondhand accounts, to the present. The second point is that these roots are surprisingly variegated. When it comes to matters pertaining to religion, one can detect in these philosophers' writings four main intellectual roots that, as we will see in later chapters, continue to anchor and nourish nonreligious sensibilities to this very day.

The first of these is what we can call Western atheism's *empirical* root. The representative voices here are thinkers whose explanations of the natural and social worlds privilege observable and publically accessible evidence over religious conviction. For example, the earliest historical figure known to actually have been indicted for atheism was Anaxagoras (b. 510 BCE), who is remembered for his investigations of rainbows, the sun, and eclipses. He was even the first to explain that the moon shines because it reflects the sun's light. Nonetheless, he ran afoul of the Athenian establishment when a meteorite fell to the ground in 467 BCE and, after close examination of it, he concluded that, rather than being deities, the sun and other stars were more likely to be fiery lumps of metal. This inference was not well received. After his trial, Anaxagoras was exiled from Athens and a new law was promulgated to ensure that citizens would "denounce those who do not believe in the divine beings or who teach doctrines about things in the sky."[30]

As with what came to be known as the natural sciences, a similar commitment to empiricism occurred within the study of history as well. Whereas Herodotus's *Histories* are filled with divine interventions and moral lessons and, like the earlier works of Homer and Hesiod, were frequently recited at festivals as sources of public entertainment, something new appears only a generation later with Thucydides's *History of the Peloponnesian War*. Here one sees a much stricter standard of evidence gathering and an attempt to present history as a series of factual and dated events, the causes of which are carefully explained in explicitly nonmythological terms.[31]

If scientists, historians, and others of an empiricist bent tended to overlook the Olympian deities, still others attempted to look at them more closely and then explain them in rational terms. This second intellectual preoccupation, what I am calling atheism's *critical* root, represents an early attempt to think through the origins of religious beliefs in ways that led either directly to atheism or at least to the style of analytical critique that put conventional religious views into question. Democritus of Abdera (b. 460 BCE) took the first of these routes. Best known for his materialism, whereby, he claimed, the universe was comprised of countless "atoms" that interacted randomly and hence left no room for teleology or divinity, he wondered why religious ideas would enter people's minds in the first place. He responded with two theories, versions of which would come to be espoused by scholars (and bloggers) for more than two millennia.[32] The first, more psychological, theory held that the gods have long appeared in dreams that arise from people's guilty consciences and, in time, they have been accepted as divine beings linked to moral obligations of various sorts. The second, more anthropological, theory founded the origin of religion upon people's tendency to assign gods to those wonders of the natural world that instilled in them the most fear and awe.

Although neither an atheist nor strictly a philosopher, the poet Xenophanes of Colophon (b. 570 BCE) undoubtedly belongs within this critical tradition as well. For one thing, he initiated the long-standing, essentially "deconstructivist" approach to religion as a culturally relative human projection. If oxen, horses, and lions could paint, he mused in one famous stanza, they would depict the gods in their own image. "Ethiopians say that their gods are snub-nosed and black," he observed in another, "Thracians that they are pale and red-haired." He was also unwaveringly dismissive of the all-too-venial Homeric gods, themselves mere projections of Hellenic society. This in turn led him to a more constructivist approach: He began to reason carefully about what divinity must actually be like. God must be one, he concluded, and must govern the universe through mind (*nous*)—"One God, greatest among the gods and men, in no way similar to mortals either in body or in thought."[33] Some have claimed that his bringing reason to bear in reflecting on how

God must necessarily be different from humans and lesser gods establishes Xenophanes's place as the West's first theologian. In any case, he also contributed to an intellectual style that, while culminating in monotheism for him, has led generations of others to more secular positions.

There is another position that regularly gets overlooked in conversations about religion in antiquity. This is largely because the term "agnosticism" (in Greek, *a* for "without" and *gnosis* for "knowledge") was not in usage until first coined by the English biologist Thomas Huxley in the mid-nineteenth century. Frustrated with polemicists of all kinds who reliably confused "a conjecture with a certainty," he invented the word to denote those who, like himself, "confessed themselves to be hopelessly ignorant concerning a variety of matters, about which metaphysicians and theologians, both orthodox and heterodox, dogmatise with utmost confidence."[34] For Huxley, a sincere agnosticism was born of both this very sort of epistemological humility and a dedication to incessant questioning, which were two qualities that, even in the absence of his neologism, were evident in the Athens of old.

Perhaps no one represents this *agnostic* root better than the self-proclaimed "Sophist" philosopher Protagoras (b. 490 BCE), who began his treatise *Concerning the Gods* with what has to be one of the more memorable opening lines in the history of religion scholarship. "Concerning the gods, I have no means of knowing whether they exist or not or of what sort they may be," he confessed, "for many things prevent knowledge including the obscurity of the subject and the brevity of human life."[35] This line is so resounding not simply because it is the sole surviving fragment of his text, the remainder of which has been lost to history. Nor is it due to his acknowledgment of the brevity of human life, a topic about which he would become all too familiar. (Legend has it that this treatise eventually got him indicted for blasphemy, which led to his attempting to escape his impending trial by crossing the sea to Sicily and subsequently drowning.) Rather it is because Protagoras embraced his own unknowing with great honesty. He acknowledged religious matters to be uniquely obscure and suggested that the typical "means" for attaining knowledge about them—adhering to religious tradition for the populace, engaging in contemplation for the next generation of Athenian philosophers (most notably Plato and Aristotle), and so on—seemed unconvincing to him. Socrates (b. 469 BCE), his near contemporary, shared this epistemological humility. On his dying day, he said, regarding what wisdom he possessed, "I do not think I know what I do not know."[36] He did, on the other hand, advocate and exemplify an important means for discovering whatever degree of truth was possible to attain. He questioned everything and, in doing so, assiduously cultivated doubt as a way to arrive at greater understanding. More than simply *answering* questions, his now-called "Socratic method" is actually more about *questioning* the established answers about how to think and live that have been handed down from one generation to the next.

The ideas we have been considering were sowed during the roughly two-hundred-year period that is now referred to as the Hellenic age of classical Greece. The following period, known as the Hellenistic age, is customarily demarcated as the three centuries between the deaths of Alexander the Great (323 BCE) and Queen Cleopatra (31 BCE). As the term "Hellenistic" (more Greek-ish than Greek) suggests, this was a transitional, even chaotic, time. With their conquest by Philip of Macedon, the Greek city-states were no longer able to provide citizens with the strong sense of individual purpose and collective identity they once had. When Philip's son Alexander created a vast empire, which brought different cultures—primarily Greek, Egyptian, and Persian—into contact, this destabilized long-held assumptions about the good life, about politics, about the nature of the cosmos, and about seemingly everything. Amid this gathering uncertainty, many people began to recognize the parochial character of their polis-based deities and then turned to new empire-wide cults, such as those dedicated to the Eleusinian Mysteries and the goddess Isis, for a restored sense of meaning. Other people were drawn to what one contemporary scholar calls the secular "graceful-life philosophies" that emerged as attempts to make sense of the culturally eclectic and indeterminate world that had come into being.[37]

What unites these philosophies is their intent to guide people toward living meaningful and happy lives within the workaday world and, at the same time, attaining a contented peace of mind, which the Greeks called *ataraxia*. Together they represent atheism's *immanent* root in the sense that, negatively speaking, they reject all notions that one should aspire to connect with or live according to some transcendent realm, and more positively, they advocate that this world is quite enough. There is enough beauty to be found, enough pleasure to be had, enough good to do, they tell their adherents, such that there is no need for more than the world can give.

Different schools, of course, presented this appreciation of immanence in different ways. The Cynics argued that happiness was found in living according to what came most naturally to humans. Thus they often slept outdoors and inevitably rejected conventional desires for fame, power, and even personal possessions. For the Stoics, happiness came from freeing oneself of destructive emotions and contributing to the broader good by performing one's roles in life to the best of one's ability. Probably the most influential graceful-life philosophy was Epicureanism. Its founder, Epicurus (b. 341 BCE), taught that happiness came from neither renouncing worldly goods (contra the Cynics) nor necessarily engaging in public affairs (contra the Stoics) but instead from appreciating the pleasures of everyday existence. The acquisition of knowledge, the company of good friends, a sense of inner tranquility, and the enjoyment of good food and drink: these are to be savored, as they provide happiness aplenty. The chief obstacles to doing so were three universal fears. The fear of pain, he argued, made little sense because intense pain tends to be short-lived, and long-term pain tends to be mild. The fear of death made just as little sense because in dying we basically revert back to our prior nonexistence. Death, he wrote in a passage that remains a favorite among today's atheists, "is nothing to us, seeing that, when we are, death is not come, and, when death is come, we are not."[38] Lastly, fear of the gods also made little sense because, even if they do exist, he reasoned, they appear not to be involved in the quotidian, immanent world where people may live in peace, find some measure of pleasure, and truly thrive.

Presumption Three: Atheism as Extrinsic

As deep and variegated as atheism's roots are in the West, they did not produce significant yields until the modern period. For sure, there was no shortage of talk about atheism. But for centuries the term was used derisively, more as an accusation against those denying a particular conception of divinity than of divinity per se. Famously, this was Meletus's meaning when he publicly reproached Socrates for being an "atheist" philosopher—notwithstanding the fact that he received his vocation from an oracle—who corrupted the city's youth by turning them away from the gods of the Athenian establishment.[39] Early generations of Christians were also often accused of atheism, in their case for refusing to participate in pagan rites, especially the cult of the Roman emperor. Responding to his second-century critics, the apologist Justin Martyr confirms this perennial use of the term, complaining that Christians like himself "were even called 'atheists'—which we are in relation to what you consider gods, but are most certainly not in relation to the Most High God."[40] This was the dominant pattern for many centuries. In fact, since they were generally believers in natural religion apart from any divine revelation, it was not uncommon for Deists, in both Europe and the colonies that would become the United States, to be denounced as atheists well into the eighteenth century.[41]

What shifted this pattern and made atheism, as we understand the term today, a conceivable option for more people had to do with important developments that dramatically altered the cultural ecology of the West. Many of these developments, which we now associate with modernity, are quite well known. The Scientific Revolution undermined the time-honored cosmology of the Middle Ages and drew people's attention from the Good Book to the Book of Nature as a source for discovering and verifying truth. The invention of the printing press effectively ended the Church's regulation of learning and facilitated the exchange of new ideas. The creation of modern secular states introduced new *raison d'etat* principles of governance and a new basis for collective identity that no longer relied upon religious warrants for legitimacy. Something similar occurred with the rise of capitalism, which as Marx noted more incisively this time, "melts all that is solid into air and profanes all that is holy."[42] In other words, as with the newly autonomous institutional spheres associated with science and the state, the capitalist economy inculcated certain rationalized practices, competitive norms, and pecuniary values that were often inimical to religious convictions. All these changes—and more, of course—meant that, during the daily round of their lives, people increasingly came to interact with institutions steered by rationalized logics that seemed at odds with a religious mindset.

Obviously, this is hardly an exhaustive account. The main point is that nonbelief as a thinkable option for people was not the product of some extrinsic cultural influence. To suggest otherwise would be to reduce atheism to something alien and perhaps ephemeral, and it would cast a blind eye to the fact that its emergence was very much connected to the ongoing developments of Western consciousness. The rationalization of public institutions and, as the sociologist Max Weber memorably put it, their accompanying "disenchantment" created a cultural terrain amenable for atheism, given its previously discussed deep cultural roots, to finally, although sparingly, burgeon forth.[43] What is more, to add a distinctly religious irony to the fire, contemporary *atheism* is also inextricably caught up with the manner in which *theism*—and here we will focus on Christianity in particular—has itself been conceived and consolidated in the West, a reality that has theological, confessional, and apologetic dimensions.

Theologically speaking, as trite as it might initially appear, modern atheism is founded upon a modern conceptualization of God.[44] Previously, throughout much of the Middle Ages, theologians were tremendously concerned with highlighting the transcendence of the divine in an effort to underscore God's utter inscrutability and radical difference from the world. For instance, recognizing that language was developed by human beings in reference to worldly things, the thirteenth-century theologian St. Thomas Aquinas advocated his broadly influential doctrine of analogy whereby, he insisted, one could apply language to God only in a highly qualified, analogous fashion. Statements like "God is good" or "God created the world," he explained, were true in a provisional sense but were also quite misleading insofar as God is not delimited by human conceptualizations of goodness or by human experiences with creating things. Even to say that "God exists" was for Thomas and other prominent theologians problematic since God could not "exist" in the same way as did other beings because God, they held, is Being itself from which all existence emanated.[45]

Especially with the advent of modern science, this emphasis on analogy came to seem less precise and definitive, and over time, theological thinking began to emulate the elevation of the "clear and distinct" ideas so lauded by René Descartes. Concerned with securing the place of victorious Reason in articulating matters of faith, theologians increasingly claimed that all such ideas, and the language that expressed them, were "univocal"—that is, had the same meaning whether applied to things human or divine. God's transcendence, therefore, came to be conceived less as an ontological difference between humanity and divinity, and more as a matter of degree. Understood univocally, God's "being" was deemed to be of the very same quality as human "being" such that God's transcendence came to be thought of in quantitative terms, as infinitely good, infinitely powerful, and the like. This theological move, while making God accessible to reason, was not without its consequences. As yet another being (although an infinitely good and powerful one) in the world, this modern and considerably domesticated God could eventually appear to many to be superfluous as the scientific method rendered the natural world ever more self-sufficient and explainable. With the dethronement of analogical thinking, then, theological language could more easily be dismissed as referring to a deity that, rather than being far beyond the capacity of human conceptualization, was in fact no more than a hypostatization of human images and ideals. The appearance of atheism as a thinkable option for modern people was thus nearly inevitable in light of the changes in the conceptualization and articulation of theism itself.

Its appearance had a confessional dimension as well. The role of the Protestant Reformation cannot be overstated here. In establishing various and vying religious confessions—and thus undermining the long-standing claims to unity, sanctity, catholicity, and apostolicity of *the* Church—the Reformation also diminished a widely held confidence in the universality of religious truth in general. In addition, since contending religious confessions were the source of so much intellectual disagreement as well as, arguably, of the fratricidal wars that ravaged much of Europe for a century after Martin Luther first broke with Rome, they also helped to incite and legitimate a reaction whereby people turned toward new, nonreligious ways of thinking about and living in the world.[46] In this sense, the Reformation greatly facilitated the previously mentioned differentiation of institutional spheres—science, the state, the capitalist economy, and so forth—each operating in accordance with its own, increasingly secular imperatives.[47] This process was further augmented by governments that, in the aftermath of so much religious warfare, sought to reestablish peace and ensure religious toleration by significantly reducing the churches' authority and range of activity within these other institutions.[48]

Competing religious confessions also contributed to atheism's appearance in another, far more subtle way. It slowly but relentlessly objectivized the life of faith. Consider, for instance, the category of religion

itself. It was not until the Reformation that the word began to be accompanied by an article ("a" religion, "the" religion) to designate a system of expressed beliefs distinguishable from and often in competition
with others.[49] Before then, "religion" was thought of in a more subjective mode—as one's participation in communal rituals, one's fidelity to
certain practices, and one's overall sense of piety. In time, though, the
Reformation era's incessant theological disputes shifted the emphasis toward doctrines, and "a religion" came to be construed as a discrete body
of creedal formulations exacting adherents' collective assent.[50]

This in turn altered the meaning of a second religious category. From
time immemorial, religious "belief" signified something more subjectively affective than objectively propositional. For instance, when, at the
turn of the fifth century, St. Jerome translated the Bible from Greek into
Latin, he used the word *fides* ("loyalty") for faith. But since this word
has no verbal form, he settled upon the Latin verb *credo*, a word derived
from *cor do* ("I give my heart"). It apparently never even occurred to
him to use *opinor* ("I hold an opinion"). When the Bible was eventually
translated into English and *credo* became "I believe," this verb was generally understood in a manner similar to its correlates in Middle English
(*bileven* for "to hold dear") or German (*belieben* for "to love").[51] This is
precisely the sensibility that has been lost. Rather than giving one's heart
to a life of piety and giving one's loyalty to the person and teachings of
Christ, belief indeed began to be understood as holding opinions—lots
of them. In short, belief became much more rationalized with the Reformation, much more thought of in terms of one's intellectual concurrence
with "clear and distinct" theological propositions.

In quickening this urge to objectivize the categories of religion and
belief, the Reformation ensured that the life of faith would become a
divisive one. This discrete religion could now be set against that religion,
these beliefs deemed orthodox (from the Greek for *orthos*, "right," and
doxa, "opinion") set against those denounced as heretical. The ensuing
and seemingly interminable arguments and condemnations that came
from such distinctions went a long way toward both discrediting all religion in many people's eyes and facilitating the appearance of atheism on
the modern scene. The English philosopher and scientist Francis Bacon
undoubtedly reflected a pervasive sentiment when he observed that "the
causes of atheism are divisions in religion, if there be many."[52]

His tract "Of Atheism" was one of the many written on the topic in the decades after the Reformation. This is not because atheists abounded. They did not. The eighteenth-century skeptic and empiricist David Hume, in fact, once claimed never to have met one. It was instead intellectuals' and especially religious leaders' fear of atheism that abounded. They grew increasingly aware of the challenges the new sciences posed to contemporary understandings of God, and like Bacon, they worried about the effects that the disunity of the churches would have on the faithful over time. Importantly, their defense of Christianity was as pivotal for what it did not entail as for what it did. It did not entail their trying to recapture aspects of faith that had been depreciated in the modern era. Participation in rituals, a sense of unknowable mystery, pious practices, and mystical experiences: these critical and long-esteemed aspects of the faith were generally not held up as ways of connecting with the sacred. Neither was there an effort to reemphasize the transcendent otherness and ineffability of God. Rather, their apologetics took on a decidedly this-worldly tone. Church leaders of the time responded to what they perceived as the threat of atheism in ways that both brought God closer to human experience and, ironically, made that God much easier to reject as a consequence.

No one chronicles this apologetic dimension of how atheism became culturally possible, specifically within the United States, better than historian James Turner.[53] Throughout the nineteenth century, he explains, theologians and clergy attempted to stem the tide of atheism by enacting two basic strategies, both of which tried to sidestep doctrinal disputes but, in doing so, relied upon a domesticated and ultimately dismissible conceptualization of divinity. Their first strategy, under the rubric of "reasonable Christianity," was to insist that the truths of science and religion are entirely consistent because the workings of nature's laws, discernible through reason, simply reflect God's providential wisdom as inscribed within the natural world. Depicting God in these terms, however, made religious belief more vulnerable to scientific disconfirmation than it would otherwise have been, as new discoveries—Darwinism is the exemplar here—seemed to contradict notions of divine agency at work in nature. Under the rubric of "heightened moralism," their second strategy, which made sense especially as secularized public institutions pushed religion into the private sphere, founded the reality of God in personal ethics. Just as the natural world revealed God's reason, so too, the argument went, did human nature and especially the vigilant conscience reveal God's moral law written upon the human heart. The problem here was that, in conflating the divine will with human values and purposes, it became much easier for people to do away with God and simply live morally by subscribing to a more secularized version of humanism.

In both cases, Christian leaders' apologetics, especially their arguments aimed to combat atheism, actually made living without God more conceivable to more people. "The natural parents of modern unbelief turn out to have been the guardians of belief," writes Turner in full appreciation of this irony. "They committed religion *functionally* to making the world better in human terms and *intellectually* to modes of knowing God fitted only for understanding this world. They did this because, trying to meet the challenge of modernity, they virtually surrendered to it."[54] This dimension, like the theological and confessional dimensions also discussed, caution us from envisioning atheism as coming from outside of either Western culture or the ongoing cultural project of expressing theism itself. On the contrary, in some significant ways, the emergence of atheism as a cultural possibility was very much, as they say in Hollywood heist films, an "inside job."

Presumption Four: From the Outside In—Atheists as Immoral Other

Shifting from atheism in general to actual atheists, the first thing one notices is that, at least in the United States, they are in no way representative of the public at large.[55] About seven in ten of them are male. They also tend to be quite young; half of them are age thirty or under, and only one in five are over fifty. Despite recent polling data showing increased secularity among people of color, the majority of atheists, still nearly seven in eight of them, are white. With 43 percent of them being college graduates, they are also better educated than the general population, among which only 27 percent have graduated from college. Twenty-one percent have earned some sort of postgraduate degree, about double the proportion for their fellow citizens. Geographically speaking, atheists are most concentrated on the West Coast and in the Northeast, whereas they are least abundant in the South. And with respect to their location along the political spectrum, the majority identify themselves as either liberal (about half) or moderate (about one-third), while only a minority (about 15 percent) think of themselves as conservative. In 2012, nearly three-quarters of them leaned toward or were affiliated with the Democratic Party, and only 18 percent claimed affiliation with or leaned toward the Republicans.

Even though they are not particularly representative of their fellow citizens, it is startling to discover just how stigmatized atheists are by the general public.[56] This, incidentally, is an old saw. More than two millennia ago, Plato discerned four distinct categories of atheists but then concluded that they all deserved a single fate: the death penalty.[57] At about the same time, the writer of the Bible's Psalm 14 declared that "Fools say in their hearts, 'There is no God,'" and, putting a still finer point on the matter, attested, "They are corrupt, they do abominable deeds; there is no one who does good."[58] Pretty harsh views here! Fortunately, attitudes have softened since then—but not as much as one might think.[59] Versions of the psalmist's accusations of foolishness, corruption, and unwillingness to do good get repeated with great frequency. The most recent national surveys continue to show that the majority of Americans have an unfavorable opinion of atheists.[60] In a recent Gallup poll, 43 percent said they would be less likely to vote for a presidential candidate if that person were an atheist, which is more than the proportion who said this about a Muslim or homosexual candidate.[61] Things look similar closer to home: seven in ten Americans say they would be troubled if a member of their immediate family were to marry an atheist.[62] All in all, according to a careful and extensive study of Americans' attitudes toward various minority groups, atheists are the group most stigmatized and least accepted by their fellow citizens.[63]

One of the more interesting aspects about this generalized aversion is that it is directed toward a category of people marked by the very sociodemographic characteristics—predominantly white, male, and well educated—that are usually effective in helping to shield people from stigma. Also unusual is that the antipathy toward atheists does not seem to follow the same pattern of abating over time as seen with such previously deeply marginalized groups as Jews, African Americans, and homosexuals. This is because it is based on reductionist thinking that presumes morality to be equated with religiosity, and thus immorality with the nonreligious. This reductionism, in turn, is especially durable because, when people stigmatize atheists, they seldom have a *particular other* in mind. Unlike members of other minority groups, atheists can easily "pass" for everybody else.[64] They bear no discreditable features that single them out from the crowd. People seldom ask them about religious matters at the office or the local supermarket, and even if they were to do so, atheists are under no obligation to "come out" to those around them. In fact, according to one recent Pew study, roughly two-thirds of atheists seldom or never discuss their religious views with the people of faith in their midst.[65] So, the reality is that most Americans simply have no idea who the atheists are in their neighborhoods, families, or even churches, much less whether or not they are behaving immorally.

Instead atheists function as a *symbolic other* who, in being cast and castigated as the immoral outsider, assure the majority that, despite their ominously fractious cultural and political differences, decent Americans actually do share a belief in God and thus their society's moral foundations are strong.[66] Other religiously derived moral boundaries performed a similar function in the past. The one drawn between *moral* Protestants and the "Papist" other comes to mind. As the Catholic segment of the population grew and became more integrated into the mainstream, the one between the more encompassing *moral* Christians and the Jewish other followed. Then, by the mid-1960s, as anti-Semitism waned and, with the loosening of immigration laws, waves of adherents of other faiths arrived, the boundary between the still more encompassing *moral* Judeo-Christian citizenry and various religious outsiders (labeled religious "others" on most surveys) came next. Now, during a period of increasing religious tolerance toward people of nearly all faiths, this line has been redrawn yet again—this time between the *moral*, theistic public and the immoral, atheist other.[67]

Its functionality notwithstanding, the reason this "popular view" is so reductionist is that, when it comes to everyday morality, real atheists do not look very much like "symbolic" ones. The majority of them actually look a lot like their fellow citizens whose viewpoints lean toward the liberal/progressive end of the political spectrum. For instance, when compared to Americans who identify with various religious faiths, atheists and other secular people are more supportive of gender equality, gay rights (including same-sex marriage), stem cell research, physician-assisted suicide, government-sponsored initiatives aimed at protecting the environment, and progressive tax policies that redistribute wealth to poorer citizens. They are also less prejudiced and nationalistic, and considerably less supportive of the corporal punishment of children, the death penalty, and their government's use of torture.[68] One 2005 study found that fewer than one-third of self-described secular Americans considered the U.S. invasion of Iraq to be justified whereas 87 percent of Evangelicals, 84 percent of Catholics, and 73 percent of mainline Protestants did.[69] Another, more qualitative study of child-rearing within nonreligious households found that parents, rather than being seething nihilists, were remarkably intentional in "providing a coherent system of meaning and values" for their children.[70] All this is entirely impressionistic and delineates positions that many people of more conservative leanings would consider morally problematic. Yet, data like these reveal that atheists' lives are as morally serious as anyone else's. Despite the prevailing stigma presuming otherwise, they can be and, at least on the basis of their particular convictions, very commonly are, to quote the title of a recent book written by Harvard University's humanist chaplain, "good without God."[71]

Presumption Five: From the Inside Out—Atheists as Rational Other

For the most part, atheists are well aware of the stigma of atheism, and given that it is demonstrably unfounded, many are understandably irked by it. It is not unusual for them to push back. Many atheist organizations expend significant effort in trying to convey to a dubious public that they are as moral as other citizens. For instance, one local group created its "Ask an Atheist" project, for which members set up booths within public parks in the hopes of starting conversations with passersby. Its stated goal is "to show believers that as people we have more in common than not, and to show them we are, in fact, good people." Another initiative is Atheists for Humanity, a philanthropic organization that enables people to make donations to any of twenty-three well-known charities in the name of atheism. "Our goals are simple," reads a statement on the organization's website, "raise money and awareness for worthy charities and actively work to destigmatize atheists and atheism."[72] Individual atheists push back too. As we will see, rather than mirroring the polite claims to moral equivalence made by innumerable atheist groups and organizations, they typically mince no words in professing their moral superiority to most religious people.

Another way individuals, and some organizations, push back is by drawing a boundary of their own, this one between the rational atheist and their purportedly irrational fellow citizens. Interestingly, though, like the moral boundary atheists try to debunk, this rationality-based one they so often try to promote is also reductionist. At its most immodest, it tends to presume that atheists are all and always uniquely rational and thus capable of airily soaring above the inescapable biases, conformisms, and contradictions that once led the poet Dante to lament that reason has "small wings." Even when more restrained, this notion is still based on the supposition that atheists are capable of and largely defined by a capacity for critical thinking unmatched by those outside the "community of reason," a term one hears within certain atheist organizations quite often. As with the framing of atheists as an immoral other, the on-the-ground reality defies this rational other frame as well. In other words, despite philosopher Daniel Dennett's best intentions in coining the term "Brights" as a nonpejorative moniker for atheists, when it comes to reasoning, there is not nearly as bright a line between them and anyone else as he and many others seem to imagine.

To see this, consider a few examples from a subgenre of contemporary atheist books that deal with their authors' "conversion" from religious faith to atheism. The first, titled *Godless*, was written by Dan Barker, who says he received a "call to ministry" at age fifteen and eventually served for seventeen years as an Evangelical preacher. Like all these conversion accounts, his has much to say about the shortcomings of theistic arguments, contradictions within the Bible, how little one can actually know about Jesus, and so forth. Such topics, while often very illuminating and engaging to read, are all standard fare. So, too, is the linchpin of his particular conversion story: the trading of faith's un-thought-out assertions for atheism's commitment to reason. The distinction he repeatedly draws could not be more blatant:

> I finally realized that faith is a cop-out, a defeat—an admission that the truths of religion are unknowable through evidence and reason. It is only indemonstrable assertions that require the suspension of reason,

and weak ideas that require faith. Biblical contradictions became more and more discrepant, and apologist arguments became more and more absurd.[73]

"When I finally discarded faith," he concludes, "things became more and more clear." One would have no reason to gainsay the level of clarity he has achieved, and that he demonstrates throughout his book. There is, however, plenty of reason to doubt the excessively clear distinction he draws between atheists like himself who employ their rational faculties and believers who presumably do not.

If atheism is about using reason, this actually does very little to separate it from how actual, not stereotypical, believers generally think about and live out their faiths. As with other aspects of their lives, Americans tend to be "reflexive" about their religious identities and commitments in the sense that they critically interrogate them, continually revise them, and self-consciously situate them as being among a multitude of plausible others.[74] In short, rather than suspending reason, they sustain their faiths through a commitment to both reason and questioning not so unlike Barker's own. Only about half of Americans say that they "never" doubted their faith within the past three years, and a full three-quarters of them agree that questioning can actually strengthen one's faith.[75] With respect to the Bible, fewer than one in four agree that it should be "taken literally, word-for-word, on all subjects," whereas far more say it is inspired by God but should not be taken literally (28 percent); is open to multiple interpretations (28 percent); is a book of fables, legends, history, and moral precepts (18 percent); or simply have no opinion on the matter (4 percent).[76] Religious traditions are always changing, but now more people explicitly agree that they *should* change in accordance with what makes good, rational sense to them. One study found that 44 percent of religiously affiliated Americans told pollsters that their religion should preserve its traditional beliefs and practices, whereas many others said it should adjust to new circumstances (35 percent) or adopt modern beliefs and practices (12 percent).[77]

An atheist commitment to reason is also often displayed in these books by an author's critical thinking about religious institutions. This is central to William Lobdell's conversion account, which appears in his book *Losing My Religion*. In his twenties, after going through a number of personal problems, including a failed marriage, he became a born-again Christian. Also a journalist, he eventually landed a job as the religion reporter for the *Los Angeles Times*, an eight-year stint that acquainted him with some of religion's more unsavory realities. "God's institutions," he believed at the outset, "on average, should function on a higher moral plain than governments or corporations."[78] On the religion beat, though, this belief became increasingly difficult to hold:

> For a dozen years, I had been blessed with an unshakable faith that seemed to get deeper with each passing year. Now, my backstage pass to the world of religion had become a curse. I no longer gathered information about my faith from carefully written books, inspiring sermons, classes taught by and filled with fellow Christians, and well-choreographed church services. Starting with the Catholic Church scandal, I began to cover much less bright, shiny stories. I began to look behind the front of many bright, shiny facades. I didn't like what I saw.[79]

His investigations of religious corruption and hypocrisy were deeply disturbing to Lobdell, and more than anything else, they were the engines that drove his conversion.

What he saw, however, is not so dissimilar from what many churchgoing Americans see. Like someone who looks under an automobile's "bright, shiny" hood to discover a grimy, clanking motor, he cringes when others seem less fazed and more attentive to the task of simply not getting their hands dirty. This overall attitude, likely a product of their vaunted individualism, reflects Americans' distrust of all, not just religious, institutions. Fewer than one in five Americans report having "a great deal" of confidence in organized religion, which is actually about the same proportion expressing that level of confidence in banks and other financial institutions.[80] Even when acquainted with the disturbing realities that so shook Lobdell, other Americans are unlikely to be as affected as him. They are generally adept at enlisting their own critical thinking to distinguish the religious ideas and practices they often hold dear from the institutional vehicles for those ideas and practices, which they typically see as imperfect, if not deeply flawed. They also cede less of their own religious agency and feel less attached to religious institutions than in times past. A whopping four in five of them say they make up their own minds about faith, independent of any church or synagogue.[81] And should they find any one religious institution to be wanting, they feel perfectly free to "vote with their feet." More than four in ten of them have left the faith in which they were raised, usually to reaffiliate with another.[82]

Finally, sometimes atheism's fidelity to reason is presented in these books as a recognition of the provisional and pluralistic nature of truth claims. Compared to the best-selling New Atheist authors whose books he read with much interest, Lobdell confides, "I am not as confident in my disbelief as they are . . . I only know what is true for me." Such admissions are commonplace within this conversion subgenre. In *Why I Became an Atheist*, John Loftus, a former "Jesus Freak" as a young man in the 1970s and an Evangelical minister and apologist for many years thereafter, states the matter quite frankly: "I could be wrong, and I admit it." Then he continues by lifting up his awareness of religious pluralism— and thus his inability to accept any one faith as true—as the insight that most led to his becoming atheist:

> Many Christians seem absolutely confident that they are correct in what they *affirm*, and that's a huge difference between us. Given the proliferation of religious viewpoints separated by geographical location around the globe, the fact that believers have a strong tendency to rationally support what they were taught to believe (before they had the knowledge or capability to properly evaluate it), along with the lack of compelling evidence to convince people who are "outsiders" to the Christian faith, mine is the reasonable viewpoint to *affirm*; that's all.[83]

Atheists, the implied logic has it, are cognizant of the proliferation of religious traditions, which thus undermines the plausibility of them all.

Many religious Americans, though, have come to an alternative conclusion. Instead of undermining faith, the proliferation of traditions can just as often underscore for the faithful the complexities of the world, the mysteriousness of God, and the inability of any one tradition to capture the totality of what is ultimately true. Despite the "huge difference" Loftus sees between atheists and religious adherents, the reality is that believers often say things akin to "I could be wrong, and I admit it" and yet present this unknowing as a testimony to the inscrutability of what they hold sacred. Rather than necessarily reject them outright, religious pluralism typically forces people to instead rethink their faith traditions relative to credible others. For example, when sociologists Robert Lynd and Helen Lynd visited Muncie, Indiana (or "Middletown," as they pseudonymously called it), in the 1920s, they found that 94 percent of their respondents agreed that "Christianity is the one true religion, and all people should be converted to it."[84] Yet, when researchers returned to Muncie a little more than a half century later, they were shocked to discover that, although religious conviction and practice remained alive and well, only 41 percent of the city's inhabitants continued to agree with this statement.[85] Today, when asked which of two statements comes closest to their own views, only about one-quarter of Americans say "my religion is the one true faith leading to eternal life." Most of the rest, a remarkable seven in ten of them, prefer the statement "many religions can lead to eternal life."[86] Beyond mere tolerance, many Americans are now coming to embrace religious pluralism. Despite evidence of increased Islamophobia in the United States since 9/11, more than half of them say that "religious diversity has been good for America." More specifically, the vast majority (80 percent) of Christian church members think people should learn more about other religions, while far fewer (16 percent) say people should avoid doing so.[87]

Just as Joe and Josephine Atheist are no less moral than their religious neighbors, nor are they necessarily more rational—or at least no more rational in the ways that, illustrated by these three conversion books, they typically suggest. Like the one discussed in the previous section, this culturally constructed boundary demarcating believers from non-believers is simply not supported by the best data at our disposal. Undoubtedly born out in certain cases—since both irrational believers and less-than-impeccably upright nonbelievers can surely be found—when it comes to the bigger picture, it seems to be a presumption less based in fact than, ironically, taken on faith by many atheists themselves.

Presumption Six: Atheists as an Insignificant Minority

Compiling the most reliable survey data from the more than fifty nations for which this is available, sociologist Phil Zuckerman contends that, calculated quite conservatively, the number of people who say they do not believe in God or are not religious is somewhere between one-half and three-quarters of a billion worldwide. We do not know what proportion of this total would specifically label themselves as atheists. What we do know, unequivocally, is that nonbelievers make up a substantial slice of the global population. Turns out, if envisioned as a coherent worldview, they would actually constitute the world's fourth largest after Christianity (2 billion), Islam (1.2 billion), and Hinduism (900 million).[88]

Most would agree that these are impressive numbers. Still, when moving from the global to the national level, it is striking to learn how little impressed most Americans, especially people of faith, seem to be with the number of atheists among them. This may be due to their internalization of such cultural tropes as the United States being a "Christian country" or, more poetically, G. K. Chesterton's stamping of it as a "nation with the soul of a church."[89] It is probably also a function of their envisioning atheists as deviant. Many Americans, in other words, likely cling to the comforting presumption that the immoral other, those in defiance of such obviously beneficent social mores, must certainly be a miniscule out-group. Most of all, it seems to be a result of them mistaking the tip of the iceberg for the whole thing. They generally assume that the relatively few visible, in-your-face atheists they might know, whose books they have read, or whom they have seen via Internet podcasts constitute the totality of nonbelievers among them. In any case, the public tends to have a reductionist image of atheists, and consequently, they underestimate their numbers and significance within American society.

This is unfortunate because the total number of self-reported atheists is hardly minuscule. If we consider Gallup's recent (2017) finding that 12 percent of the American public tell pollsters they do not believe in God, then it would be difficult to write this grouping off as insignificant.[90] It shows, bracingly enough, that in the United States, the number of those who do not believe in God (even though most do not explicitly call themselves atheists) exceeds that of Mormons, Jews, Jehovah's Witnesses, Orthodox Christians, Muslims, Buddhists, and Hindus—*combined*.

While eye-opening, even this reality hardly captures the full picture. For one thing, we have reason to suspect a good deal of underreporting of atheists due to the so-called social desirability effect, respondents' reluctance to provide what they deem to be unpopular answers to certain questions. The fact that there tends to be a yea-saying bias when answer-

ing questions related to faith is a reflection of just how strong expectations of religiosity are in the United States. We see this, for instance, in
surveys that overreport the frequency of church attendance. The four
in ten Americans who claim to attend religious services weekly is, as
subsequent research has shown, actually true of about one-quarter of
them.[91] One would reasonably expect the opposite to occur—an appreciable nay-saying bias—with respect to self-reported nonbelief in God.
Even if the nonbelieving 12 percent is not actually larger than reported,
what of those among them who are indeed willing to use the "A-word" to
describe themselves? Only about 3 to 5 percent of Americans explicitly
identify as atheists on surveys, which is about double the proportion
from a decade ago. But especially in light of the persistent stigma against
them, one can reasonably infer that this percentage may in fact be considerably larger.

Second, not only do surveys almost certainly undercount atheists, but
also the way they are typically worded and reported on downplays the
seldom-discussed amount of uncertainty many Americans actually experience when thinking about God. This occurs with surveys that provide
people too few response categories—"Yes," "No," "No Opinion"—when
asking whether they believe in God. Or it happens when commentators,
for whatever reasons, "round up" by aggregating various intermediary
response categories that actually suggest far more religious indecision
on the part of the public than is usually acknowledged. We see this time
and again in reports trumpeting Americans' exceptional level of piety
(especially compared to most other Western nations) and announcing
that the vast preponderance of them believe in God.

Fortunately, there have been a number of thoughtful surveys that,
when examined closely, consistently indicate a considerable degree of
uncertainty about God among at least a full quarter of the population.[92]
One of the first of these was the 2005 Baylor Religion Survey. It por-
trays nearly three-quarters of Americans as being religiously certain;
63.4 percent of them say they "have no doubts that God exists," and an
additional 11.4 percent say they "believe in a higher power or cosmic
force." Every bit as worthy of our attention, though, are the intermediary
categories that point to considerable equivocation. The remaining one-
quarter of all American adults say they believe "with some doubts" (11.7
percent); they "sometimes" believe (1.8 percent); they "don't know and

there is no way to find out" (6 percent); they have "no opinion" (1.4 percent); or they agree with the statement, which rarely appears in surveys,
"I am an atheist" (4.2 percent).[93] Or consider the *Financial Times*/Harris
Interactive Poll conducted that same year. It found that once again more
than seven in ten respondents identify themselves as a "believer in any
form of God or any type of supreme being." Yet, others "would prefer
not to say" (6 percent) or are "not sure" (3 percent). The remaining claim
for themselves the survey-defined labels "agnostic (one who is skeptical
about the existence of God but not an atheist)" (14 percent) and "atheist
(one who denies the existence of God)" (4 percent).[94] Now fast-forward
to the aforementioned 2017 Gallup poll. It finds that 64 percent of Americans are "convinced God exists"—whereas 80 percent were just a dozen
years prior—leaving the rest to respond that God "probably exists, have
a little doubt" (16 percent); "probably exists, have a lot of doubt" (5 percent); "probably does not exist, but not sure" (6 percent); "does not exist"
(7 percent); and "no opinion" (2 percent). The point here is that, while it
is illuminating to focus our attention specifically on self-identified atheists, as this book endeavors to do, it is also important to keep in mind
that they are but one segment of a much larger grouping of Americans
who are openly uncertain about God and other religious matters.

Finally, there is plenty of reason to think that the numbers of people
who identify as atheist could be on the verge of growing in the United
States. After nearly two decades of no significant change, one of this
country's most dramatic religious shifts has been the sudden increase in
the proportion of "nones," Americans who do not identify with a religious tradition. From 7 percent in 1990, the percentage of those claiming
no religious preference jumped to 14 percent in 2000. The latest Pew
survey puts this number at 23 percent.[95] With only about a third of the
nones saying they do not believe in God, this shift more likely reflects
an increase in people's alienation from organized religion than it does
their wholesale rejection of God. Especially since this move toward no
religious preference has been mostly confined to religious moderates
and liberals, its timing suggests that it is at least somewhat a backlash to
the perceived political overreaching of the Religious Right.[96]

Nevertheless, there are features of this development that augur well
for atheism's expansion in the years ahead. One is that, with an additional two-thirds of a million people becoming nones each year, it is

now the nation's second largest (after Evangelical Protestants) and fastest-growing "religious" group. Another thing is that this growth comes at the expense of other religious groups. Since immigrants to this country are not exceptionally irreligious, and secular Americans actually have a birth rate of about half that of the religiously affiliated, this leaves only defections from other religious groups as the source of the nones' expansion. Also, because nones are disproportionately represented among younger generational cohorts and they now show a retention rate comparable to the nation's major religious traditions, this expansion is likely to continue in the years ahead. Needless to say, these observations about the nones do not tell the whole story, much less suggest an inexorable flowering of atheism in the United States. What we can say is that the number of atheists is not tiny; that the overused "very religious overwhelming majority versus deviant insignificant minority" frame for imagining their place in the national context is extremely deceptive; and that, with more and more nones distancing themselves from religious traditions, this could over time redound in Americans' waning adherence to the most central beliefs handed on by those traditions—including belief in God.

From Reductionism to *Verstehen*

To this point, I have taken something of a *via negativa* approach to the subject at hand. In my attempt to refute various reductionisms, I have essentially said, "No, atheism is not simple," "No, atheism is not new," and so on. This is a helpful first step. But additional—and more affirmative—steps are necessary to engage this subject to the extent it truly warrants. By this, I do not mean that I intend to advocate for atheism or, alternatively, for any number of theistic worldviews. Readers who would prefer otherwise should take a trip to their local bookstore where they will be pleased to discover plenty of polemical works that take definitive positions on whether or not God exists, whether religion is good or bad, whether one should or should not take faith seriously, and all manner of related questions. Many of these works produce, as they say, more heat than light, especially since a premium is so often placed more upon pontificating than actual understanding. That is not my goal here.

Instead of advocating for, arguing with, or merely talking about American atheists, my goal is to practice something Max Weber considered absolutely central to the sociological enterprise—*Verstehen*. German for "understanding," in Weber's distinctive usage it principally means resisting the temptation to impose one's own normative categories onto subjects' experience and, in doing so, trying hard to understand the other on the other's own terms.[97] Beyond polemics, beyond stereotypes, beyond, in other words, the "popular view" of atheists, to practice *Verstehen* in this context means paying close attention to atheists' view of themselves as well as how they think they ought to go about living in the world. More than anything else, this level of understanding requires careful listening. Lots of careful listening. I emphasize this point because, having taken more than a few trips to bookstores myself, I have been surprised at how few books on atheists have been grounded in actual conversations with many, or any, of them.

To remedy this situation—and, frankly, since I am garrulous by nature anyway—I embarked upon a series of conversations with atheists. I began in my own island town of Alameda, located just over the bridge from Oakland and, in the distance, across the bay from San Francisco. First, I invited a handful of neighbors, whom I knew from prior hobnobbing to be atheists, to my home for one-on-one interviews. Then I advertised on a few Internet websites specializing in local news and community forums, which garnered me several more participants whom I also invited to my home or met at local coffee shops, at bars, or at their homes for interviews. Things snowballed from there. Both my own contacts and the twelve Alameda-based people I eventually interviewed got me in touch with fifteen additional people living throughout the San Francisco Bay Area for a total of twenty-seven in-person interviews. I then contacted various atheist and humanist organizations. After explaining my project, a few generously agreed to post an invitation to participate in my study, which I also posted in a few Internet-based forums focusing on atheism-related topics. This resulted in approximately 150 more participants, a number that more than tripled once these people, via more snowball sampling, connected me with neighbors, friends, co-workers and relatives whom they knew or just suspected, usually correctly, to be atheists. All told, more than five hundred people (n = 518) participated in this project. Note that, because I did not want to include only group-based atheists in this study, after a few days I un-posted my online invitation to participate and recontacted those same atheist and humanist organizations to request that they do the same, which they were happy to do.

Along with the twenty-seven in-person interviews, I—actually "we" is more appropriate here since I hired two research assistants—conducted an additional eighty-five telephone interviews with people from our larger sample, about two-thirds of which I did myself. All 112 interviews were one to two hours in length; and all, both in-person and telephone-based alike, were recorded and transcribed in full. In addition to this, we employed two other data-gathering methods. First, all respondents also filled out a brief, closed-ended survey, which allowed us to collect demographic and other data presented throughout this book. Second, because we simply could not interview everyone who contacted us, we asked many people to participate by typing or, in a few cases, writing out their responses to the very same open-ended questions that also appear in our in-person/telephone interview schedule (see appendix A). Partly because of their higher-than-average educational attainment and partly, many made a point to mention, because atheists often have a lot to say without always having an accommodating public space for saying it, this was a very effective method. It yielded several hundred additional pages of reflections from 390 more people, many of whom took time to pro-duce extremely thoughtful and detailed responses, which they e-mailed (or occasionally just mailed) to me. These did not allow for the follow-up questions, interesting digressions, and back-and-forth exchanges that are the hallmark of semi-structured interviewing. Nevertheless, the basic themes and tensions expressed in these 390 e-mail interviews did not at all differ from those that emerged from the 112 in-person and tele-phone interviews we also conducted. An additional sixteen people chose not to reply to these open-ended questions and submitted completed surveys only.

Overall, as shown in the demographic snapshot in appendix B, this research sample reflects what we know about the broader population of American atheists reasonably well. Respondents come from forty-nine of the fifty states (sorry, Alaska!), and all of them say the term "athe-ist" describes them "very" (87 percent) or "somewhat" (13 percent) well. Note that, while the latter 13 percent usually voiced qualms about the atheist label, they all still identified themselves as atheists to some degree and, without exception, said they did not believe in God. Since the focus of this study is on atheists, people who primarily identified themselves as agnostics, seekers, secularists, or lapsed, or with any number of other interesting categories, were not included here. Despite sharing a common identity as atheists, respondents vary in other ways. They range from eighteen to eighty-six years of age. About two-thirds are male. The majority (80 percent) are Caucasian and, despite my effort to oversample people of other races, far fewer are Latino (7 percent), African American (6 percent), Asian (3 percent), or "other" (4 percent). About two-thirds are college graduates (nearly one-third have a graduate or professional degree), and more than nine in ten indicate that the term "politically liberal" describes them either "very" (60 percent) or "somewhat" (31 percent) well. Also, even though close to one-third of these respondents found out about this study from the website of an atheist or humanist organization, most said they only check out these groups "on occasion," "to see what other people are saying," or not infrequently, "just for fun." Rather than comprising atheism's dyed-in-the-wool vanguard, then, most of the people in this sample are actually the rank and file. They are people who identify as atheists and, at the same time, are typically more occupied with their families, jobs, hobbies, and other everyday pursuits than they are with matters pertaining to their being nonbelievers. In fact, as we will see, only a minority of them participate to any significant degree in online or in-person groups focused on atheism itself.

Two additional methodological points are important to make here. First, while this study is based upon a large and diverse cross-section of respondents, I got into contact with them through a nonrandom, snowball sampling method. Therefore, I cannot make statistically valid inferences about the overall population of American atheists or about differences among them based on the sorts of demographic variables mentioned above. As readers will discover in the chapters ahead, I do my best to make up for this by embedding my in-depth, qualitative data within the larger universe of other scholars' more broad-based and representative data whenever possible. Though I have been eager to incorporate this broader research, the fact is that my focus is less concerned with generalizability than with entering the cultural "sausage factory" of respondents' nuanced and, frankly, sometimes not-so-nuanced efforts at carving out nonreligious identities for themselves within a largely religious country.

Second, even as I was still collecting my data, I proceeded to the task of interpreting it, an inductive process that, as the "sausage factory" metaphor is intended to suggest, turned out to be enormously time-consuming and, at times, unglamorous. It entailed reading and rereading a few thousand pages of transcripts (derived from both in-person and telephone-based interviews) and e-mail questionnaires, and then coding these for emergent themes and subthemes.[98] Sometimes these themes would raise additional questions that I would then pose as follow-up queries during in-person and telephone interviews until, eventually, I reached a saturation point at which I seldom acquired new, unanticipated information from respondents.

Listening carefully, delineating key themes, attending to people's rationales and use of language, allowing people to tell sometimes very personal or even painful stories about their lives, and trying to understand them on their own terms—this practice of *Verstehen* requires a lot of time and effort. And it would have been well-nigh impossible if respondents were not so remarkably forthcoming. Some, when e-mailing to set up interviews, told me they wanted to participate in this project because, as one woman stated, "it's a noble endeavor." "I'm on board for anything," she continued, "that helps to open people's eyes and build bridges among different kinds of people." Others, apparently of a less optimistic temperament, hopped on board to help ensure that this book would not turn out to be yet another "slam piece" intent on perpetuating hackneyed stereotypes about atheists. "Basically, I just want to throw in my two cents so you'll get the story right," conveyed another woman. "Please don't tell the world that we murder kittens or anything like that!" Still others, it became clear to me, simply appreciated the opportunity to discuss a facet of their lives they could not bring up with friends and families. "I hope I haven't gone on too long, Jerome," sighed one man toward the conclusion of his interview, "but I really don't get to talk like this here in Arkansas too often."

That's too bad, I thought—and think still. The exchanges upon which this book is based were, to say the very least, candid and thoughtful. We asked people about their upbringings and about whether or to what extent religious faith had been a part of them. We asked about their experience as atheists, whether this was a source of division or connection with other people, whether they have ever been treated differently because of their atheism, and so on. We queried them about issues pertaining to faith, God, religion, spirituality—you name it. What's the foundation of your morality? Do you think children should be exposed to religion? Does the world have any meaning? Why do you think we're here? How do you think about suffering, injustice, and the inevitability of death? We did not hold back . . . and neither did they.

Big questions. An excess of five hundred atheists willing, to the best of their abilities, to provide answers. Candor. Thoughtfulness. *Verstehen*. This has proven to be an illuminating combination. As those who continue reading will see, it is certainly a combination that, contra presumption one, defies the simplifications wrought of a negatively defined category like "atheist." I cannot stress this enough. Most of us would not presume, for instance, that all noncombatants simply wile away their days *not* engaging in warfare, and do so in precisely the same manner. Nor would we suppose that all of the unemployed train the sum of their intellectual and imaginative faculties upon their present state of *not* participating in the paid workforce, and do so in precisely the same manner. So, too, with atheists. Lo and behold, they think about more and do more with their lives than merely *not* believe in God and, on those occasions when their focus turns to the matter—say, during a sprightly interview session—their viewpoints prove to be enormously variegated and nuanced.

Paying attention to this more complicated reality should go a long way toward disabusing readers of the "popular view" of contemporary atheism. As Professor Campbell contended, this is something that should be of interest to his fellow sociologists. Being one, I can certainly confirm this. Moreover, I think the conversations and analysis that follow will also be edifying for both American believers and nonbelievers more generally. Among the former, those who imagine religious faith to be the sole means by which people come to reflect deeply, behave morally, and live with integrity and purpose will need to think again. Whatever else might distinguish the life of faith from the lives discussed in the pages that follow, it is certainly not in bearing such fruits as these. Atheists already know this, of course. What they may not fully appreciate and what readers who also identify as atheist may be interested in discovering is the great diversity of opinion that exists among them. In any case, rather than reducing atheists (or atheism) to this or that on the basis of presumption, my goal has been to understand them on the basis of actual conversation. My hope, if I may express one here, is that if Americans, believers and nonbelievers alike, are to continue addressing such topics as God, truth, meaning, faith, and doubt, they learn to do so with the openness and honesty displayed by their fellow citizens in the pages ahead.

2

Acquiring Atheist Identities

Four Acquisition Narratives

Margaret Daly: The Religion "Graduate"

People sometimes think that because she makes her living as a medical researcher, it was her scientific training that turned Margaret Daly toward atheism. That is not true. Her skepticism began much earlier. The suburban Connecticut household in which she was raised was filled with family who were less what she calls devoutly "religious Catholics" than the merely going-through-the-motions type of "showing up Catholics." Fitting into this latter category herself, she underwent her share of religious education ("just memorizing a lot of stuff") and attended weekly or near-weekly mass ("the whole sit-stand-kneel rigmarole"), but even these core religious practices felt hollow for as long as she can remember. So, too, did even the notion of believing in God. "One of my earliest religious memories is of being in Sister Maria's fourth-grade CCD [catechism] class. It was a Saturday. We were talking about morality and how if you stole something and didn't get caught it was still bad because God knows you did it—something like that. And I remember asking her why she thought God even existed. It was such a memorable thing because she seemed so shocked that a nine-year-old would ask that, and she didn't know how to answer." "That question," Daly recalls, "just kept coming back over the course of time. I never found an adult who could answer it. And I remember asking a lot of them!"

The result of all these queries was not a once-and-for-all final verdict as, years earlier, it had been with respect to Santa Claus, the Tooth Fairy, and the Easter Bunny. Instead, she recounts, her belief-cum-inquisitiveness concerning God "just kind of dissipated; it just left my brain or something." As a matter of fact, by the time she was a high school senior, it was totally gone. That is what she told her parish priest in an exchange that "seems like just yesterday":

> I sat down with Father Bachman who interviewed all of us as part of our Confirmation preparation. And he said, "Why do you want to get confirmed?" and I said I didn't. So he told me, "Well, if you don't get confirmed, you can't get married in the Church," which seemed like a really odd response to me because I think he was assuming that would be some kind of motivator [laughs *loudly*]. . . . Anyway, I didn't think that was a problem, so then he told me that once I was confirmed, I'd be an adult in the Church. And I said, "Well, I just don't believe in any of it." Then he came back at me saying that I should just get confirmed and then make my decision later on. You know, I think he thought I'd grow out of it or that I was just being a petulant teenager. I don't know what he felt, but he didn't respond to my real situation. He just avoided it. So, I decided, "Okay, I'll get confirmed, but it'll be my last day in the Church—and then out I'll go." And that's what happened. That day was my graduation from religion.

That day, however, did not mark Daly's commencement of an explicitly atheist identity. As with many people, this would unfold much more slowly. For at least the next ten years, she referred to herself as a "genetic Catholic" or a "reformed Catholic." She did this partly to avoid offending people. In light of her growing "tolerance for ambiguity and the unexplained," it was also somewhat a reflection of her resolve to avoid simplicities and dogmatisms of any sort. It is her willingness to "live in a world of grey," then and now, that even makes her bristle at the few New Atheist books she has read over the years. "I've never been on some arduous search for the answer to whether or not God exists," she muses. "And some of the books I've read are so argumentative. It just seems like a self-serving debate—trying to prove who's right and who's wrong. There's no end to it, and I don't think there's much value in it either. I think the more interesting question is about how we should live together as a species."

As a high schooler, Daly was not quick to affix atheism's Scarlet *A* to her chest, even after her graduation from religion. Nor, years later, did she fervently come up with or subscribe to any particular refutation of God's existence that may have once and for all justified her atheist stance for herself and before others. On the contrary, she slowly came into her identity as a nonbeliever without at first noticing that she had arrived. She only became fully aware of her arrival when, in her forties, she was diagnosed with breast cancer. "It was a real struggle," she confides. During this time, she was truly touched by so many friends—including her best friend, a hospital chaplain—who assured her of their prayers. But, she notes with a conversational flourish, "it occurred to me that it had never even occurred to me to go to religion as a source of comfort and strength":

> I remember one point—it was a tough moment—I remember looking up at the sky, and it relaxed me. I looked up at the sky and thought that there's a big universe out there. And I'm just one little person, with this little hardship, living out this little story. I didn't look up and say, "God, help me," you know? It didn't occur to me. Nope, I looked up and said, "I can do this." That's the feeling I had, which, as I thought more about it, told me I really was an atheist. Deep down.

Huddled in one of life's little foxholes, Daly discovered at least one atheist therein—herself. As such, she presents herself as neither embattled by nor in any way antagonistic toward religion. Life is just too complex for that, she explains repeatedly. Although she does call herself an atheist now, she would never think to call her religious friends or her husband, Arturo, a practicing Catholic raised in Mexico, "complete idiots or anything like that." Her experience with breast cancer made her aware that, just as she finally turned away from belief in God, other people might have their own reasons for heading in the opposite direction. "Why wouldn't they look to their faith for strength?" she asks after describing how Arturo lost nearly sixty members of his extended family in a single devastating earthquake decades ago. She had this reaction again recently when she was present, along with three of her aunts, at her grandmother's deathbed. She did not disparage their assurances that their mother was in heaven. "To me she was just dead," she admits, "but that's not exactly the most profound answer either!" In short, despite having graduated from religion, she remains well schooled in the varieties of religious traditions and appreciative of the different ways they address key dimensions of human experience. "I don't believe in them literally, but myths that help us to understand questions like 'What is love?' 'How should we be in community together?' 'What should we value and not value?'—stuff like that. These are really important. It's fascinating how different religions come at these questions differently, and," she adds, "it's pretty humbling when I'm honest and acknowledge that I don't have better answers myself."

Joanne Cecchini: The "Reluctant Atheist"

At first glance, Joanne Cecchini seems to have a lot in common with Margaret Daly. A longtime resident of a Maine coastal town, she is a fellow New Englander. As a high school physics teacher, she, too, has a strong science background. Also like Daly, she did not become a self-acknowledged atheist until well into her forties. Yet, that is about where the similarities end. Far from being nominally religious, she was raised in an extremely devout "Christian household," which she tried to replicate once she had a family of her own. Along with her husband and three children, she attended church services and Sunday school each week "without fail." She taught Sunday school and Vacation Bible School for many years; she was very outspoken about her religious beliefs in public; and in short, she describes her faith as once being "a huge part of my everyday life."

This all came to an end when, in the midst of some undisclosed family troubles, she "turned to the Bible for comfort." It was then she realized that, even though she had read the Bible for many years, she had never truly *studied* it. Captivated by this idea, she embarked upon a self-directed program of reading both the entire Bible and various works of scripture scholarship. That, she says, "was quite the eye-opener." She began to see inconsistencies among the books of the Bible, which, she also discovered, were written at different times to different audiences. She learned that many of the events recorded in scripture could not be confirmed historically. She encountered other epistles and gospels that, for various reasons, had not been incorporated as part of the biblical canon. This was only the beginning. The end result, recalls Cecchini, was at first unthinkable. Then it became unavoidable for her. "After a full year of wondering and thinking logically about what I had been taught and held true for my entire life, I discovered one morning that I simply had ceased to believe any of it," she recounts. "Heaven, hell, Jesus, Noah, angels, prayer, eternal life, everything: it all seemed like a story about Santa Claus and about being good in order to get the best gifts."

Now more than a decade ago, that fateful morning was hardly a welcomed dawning of a newfound atheist identity for Cecchini. She railed against it and experienced herself as being a "reluctant atheist" for very good reason. Fearing he would lose her for eternity, her husband broke down and wept when she informed him of her disbelief. Her father, Bible actually in hand, harangued her about her impending damnation, and her in-laws accused her of corrupting their grandchildren. Keeping all this a secret from people outside of her family, she began to feel distanced from her once-close friends whom she felt would almost certainly condemn her if they knew her true mind. Most of all, she experienced a feeling of acute loss:

> It's been a painful transition, very painful. I lost a source of continual comfort. I had prayed every day, sometimes dozens of times during the day. I had a great fellowship with other church members. I could put up with suffering and pain in life because I knew it was either God testing me or there was some reason for it. All that leaves you when you give up believing that life has a reason for it. All that leaves you when you give up believing that life has a reason, a point, and that some Being has your best wishes at heart and is there to lift you up when you despair. How does one live without that support?

No rhetorical embellishment, Cecchini's question—"How does one live without that support?"—was one she grappled with and, without exaggeration, agonized over for several years. It took a lot of reflection before she could come to terms with this question and, as she put it, was finally able to "drop the 'reluctant' adjective."

One way she did this was to reimagine what it means to be a decent, conscientious person independent of religiously circumscribed understandings of community and goodness. "I discovered that doing things like helping people, providing emotional and financial support, and working to lessen suffering for others doesn't require a Bible, telepathic messaging, weekly worship sessions, or even adherence to a Bronze Age philosophy," she says. "It's its own reward. A person can do all that, and be a kind and gentle human being, and still not believe in God." Another thing she did was work through and ultimately give up her prior, largely unexamined conviction that, as she states twice in the block quotation above, "life has a reason." "I have had many occasions," she remembers, "where I wished I still believed in prayer, particularly in times of emotional stress." Now, she insists, she is able to resist this "wishful, magical thinking." She no longer needs a reason for being. "I don't see anything special about the fact that humans exist on this planet. The earth existed for billions of years before people showed up. And it will continue to exist for billions of years after we manage to poison or blow up ourselves into extinction. The question of why we're here requires a huge amount of ego, does it not? One might as well ask why turtles are here, or bacteria, or kelp." As with our being here, she no longer needs a reason for why, as mortals, we eventually cease to be. "When I'm gone, I'm gone," she now asserts flatly. "I'll return to stardust. Maybe my atoms will make up a part of a redwood tree, a gull on the wind, the person who cures all cancers, or float out into space to spin endlessly in the cosmos. None of these lack appeal to me."

Having reached the other side of her "painful transition" to atheism, Cecchini now feels, using a word with much resonance among atheists, unexpectedly "free, really *free*." Given the judgment she feared from her religious friends and actually experienced from her religious family, it is interesting that she does not also feel any resentment or look askance at believers. "Why should I feel differently toward people who are just like how I used to be?" she asks. As long as people do not "use religion as an excuse to do hurtful things to other people," she sees no reason to hold onto the anger toward organized religion that had welled up inside her during her tough transition. Having moved on, she now feels no bitterness and claims a wider perspective. To illustrate this, she tells about reading a journal account of a seventeenth-century colonist in Maine who was captured by a tribe of Native Americans:

> The colonist wrote that he said to his captor, "You worship a false god; I know the one, true God." The Native American asked him why he thought his god was better. "Because I have his book," he replied. The Native American said that his God's book was better because it was written in the trees, the earth and the stars. He didn't need men to write for him.

The captured colonist said that he realized the Native American's God was just as real to him as his God was, and maybe they were worshipping the same being, just in different ways. But, I thought, "Yes, they're both worshipping the God they've created—the same God, just in different ways." That led me to thinking that all gods are the same—created by people for our own purposes.

Notice that she does not echo Daly's sensitivity to individual and religious difference. The great diversity of individual believers are monolithically encapsulated by her as being "just like the way I used to be," and in the end, all conceptualizations of God, even seemingly disparate ones, "are the same." It is really that basic for her.

Narratives of Atheist Identity Acquisition

With respect to the actual process of their becoming atheists, there are two more differences in Daly's and Cecchini's recollections that are worth highlighting. The first has to do with what I call an acquisition frame, which refers to people's understanding of what initially goaded them to, over time, identify themselves as atheists. Sometimes people describe this in teleological terms, as a natural result of their personal growth and, especially, of their innate propensity for asking questions about the world around them. Daly's experience is a good example of this. As she describes it, the impetus for her becoming an atheist was very much within her. It was her own inborn compulsion to find answers that, played out over many years, made the ultimate acceptance of her lack of belief seem practically inevitable. This is not the case with people like Cecchini. Rather than coming from within, their accounts of becoming atheists begin with stimuli originating from the outside. They speak in situational terms and thus frame their becoming atheists as a consequence of unforeseen experiences and ensuing insights that flow from the context of their everyday lives. One gets the impression from Cecchini that had her situation been different, had she not "turned to the Bible for comfort" in the wake of her family troubles, she may not have turned to atheism at all.

The second difference between these two women's accounts pertains to the level of effort they say was needed to make good on their turns toward atheism. Daly's journey was not an especially onerous one. It took time, but it did not take an enormous amount of work to move from the precocious fourth-grader in Sister Maria's catechism class to the forty-something, self-avowed atheist facing breast cancer straight on. Requiring more by way of simply growing into and coming to accept one's identity as an atheist, I call this a modest level of effort. Other people, in contrast, need to do more than this. Like Cecchini, they expend lots of time and energy in the (sometimes "painful") project of becoming atheists, which they experience as a more thorough transformation of self, and which I classify as a considerable level of effort.

Taken together, these two sets of categories encapsulate four "ideal types" of narratives people use to consolidate—for both themselves and others—what the experience of taking on an atheist identity actually felt like for them. As depicted in figure 2.1, *inquisitives* like Margaret Daly talk about becoming atheists in teleological terms and without having to work too hard at it beyond exercising their natural proclivity for questioning things. Others, whom I call *searchers*, use the same teleological language but describe their coming to their atheist identities as a result of significant exertion on their part. Similarly, *responders* like Joanne Cecchini recount finding themselves presented with situations that caused them to question religious faith, and then truly struggling until finally being able to identify as atheists. Yet others, usually people raised in less religious or nonreligious households, are what I call *consolidators*, insofar as they describe themselves as basically accepting the atheist label—as opposed to other labels or none at all—as an apt signifier of who they, without too much effort, have come to understand themselves to be.

Allow me to elaborate just a bit further on the two sets of categories that constitute these narratives. First, the category of "acquisition frames" denotes the basic fact that being an atheist is an identity these respondents have indeed acquired. This is true of even those who were not particularly religious as youngsters, including the two-thirds of consolidators in this study who were raised in nonreligious households. Even they, at one point or another, had to come to grips with their misgivings about faith in God and, usually after some deliberation, make the conscious decision to call themselves atheists. To repeat, this is what they, and all the respondents in this study, say they became. None of them would classify themselves as "believing without belonging," a

	Teleological (atheism as an outcome of one's growth)	Situational (atheism as a consequences of one's context)
Level of effort required — Modest	Inquisitives	Consolidators
Level of effort required — Considerable	Searchers	Responders

Figure 2.1. The four types of acquisition narratives.

phrase sociologist Grace Davie coined to identify people who maintain some religious beliefs while steering clear of any religious affiliation.[1] No, to a person, they do not believe. Likewise, none of the people in this study would qualify as "apatheists," philosopher John Shook's clever moniker for those who are essentially indifferent to religious concerns and do not much care about the whole God question.[2] No, they show scant evidence of being indifferent. If, as sociologist Steve Bruce puts it, "you have to care too much about religion to be irreligious," then this is especially true of those who, beyond simply being nonreligious, also go the extra mile and identify themselves as atheists.[3]

Turning now to the second set of categories, it should come as no surprise that acquiring an atheist identity would take some measure of effort. I say this because, despite some signs of religious decline in the past few decades, the United States remains, to use the title of historian Jon Butler's book on religion within the original thirteen colonies, "awash in a sea of faith."[4] The majority of Americans continue to believe in God or a "higher power," and as we have seen, even though increasing numbers of people are uncertain about this, nearly two-thirds of them say they believe without any doubt whatsoever.[5] There are also approximately three hundred thousand religious congregations—more, incidentally, than the total number of McDonald's, Wendy's, Subways, Burger Kings, and Pizza Huts combined—that comprise the nation's most ubiquitous form of voluntary association membership.[6] The point is that atheists are generally surrounded by religious people and institutions that reinforce normative expectations of piety. Even their intimates often do this. Nearly one-third of the respondents in this study have partners or spouses who are religiously affiliated. About two in five of them say "most" of their friends are religious, and nearly three-quarters agree with the statement "My family members and I disagree about religious matters." Expectations, disappointment, condescension, subtle pressure, perhaps even rejection: atheists need to expend some degree of effort to push back against all of this as they negotiate the sea of faith in which they are immersed. Even when they find supportive cliques or communities of the ideologically compatible, and even when they come to their atheist identities through a more modest level of effort, at one point or another, all of them had to eschew simply "going with the flow" and exert themselves against sometimes powerful religious currents that could otherwise have carried them along.

As I further delineate the four types of stories they tell about becoming atheists, I should state that my intentions for doing so are quite restrained. Largely because my conversations with respondents were so wide ranging and focused much more on being, rather than becoming, atheists, they merely touched upon other analytical questions— Who? How? Why?—which, of course, are also well worth examining. With respect to the first of these, my conversations indicate little about *who* is more likely to tell one type of narrative or whether articulating a certain narrative influences *who* they become in the years following. It is true that about three-quarters of the people in this study who were brought up in nonreligious households become consolidators. This points to the power of nonreligious socialization for shaping a pathway toward atheism that, when actually taken, requires a relatively modest degree of effort to follow. And turning the causal arrow in the opposite direction, compared to the other three types, being an inquisitive correlates with having a somewhat less favorable view of religious people, which may be a reflection of their irritation with adults for not seeming to be as critical of religion as they themselves were even as children. However, such observations are merely suggestive and would require additional research before coming to anything approximating definitive conclusions.

The case is the same with respect to the equally worthwhile *how* question. My interviewees' reflections offer little by way of illustrating how people might undertake a discernible, step-by-step path on their way toward forming atheist identities. One scholar, for instance, has explicitly addressed this question and argues that the process of atheist identity formation entails the following stages: (1) theism, (2) questioning

theism, (3) rejecting theism, and (4) "coming out" as an atheist.[7] Another scholar, agreeing that this "standard trajectory" seems to be the
path taken by the majority of atheists, nonetheless argues that, because
people experience different degrees of religious socialization and undertake more or less religious seeking before "coming out," there are
actually four additional paths they take toward atheism.[8] Once again,
the narratives I delineate here touch upon this question. Consolidators,
as discussed, generally experienced the least degree of religious socialization. And with respect to the degree of religious seeking, my "level
of effort required" category may provide a helpful reminder that, while
religious seeking (exemplified by searchers) certainly qualifies as effort,
so, too, do the sorts of emotional and interpersonal struggles responders
typically experience. This suggests that a broadening of the "religious-
seeking" category to include other forms of effort may be useful, something that, again, further research could tease out more fully.

Lastly, these narratives do not provide a systematic presentation of
the main reasons *why* people become atheists. This work has already
been done very ably by sociologist Phil Zuckerman who, in his insightful *Faith No More: Why People Reject Religion*, spells out the nine most
regularly mentioned reasons.[9] First, he says, is the influence of one or
both parents who are nonreligious. Second is the eye-opening effect of
education, especially secular postsecondary education. Third is being
exposed to other religions, which can undercut the previously unquestioned truth of any one faith. Fourth is the direct or indirect experience
of some misfortune that may undermine belief in a good or just God.
Fifth is the politically conservative tenor of many churches, which can
prove especially alienating to people of a more politically liberal persua-
sion. Sixth is the repression, guilt, and homophobia often perpetuated
by the sexual teachings of many, especially more conservative, faith traditions. Seventh is the resentment people can feel toward many of the
same faith traditions as a consequence of their fear-inducing teachings
about Satan and hell. Eighth is the influence of having a positive relationship with people who are not religious. And ninth are the negative
experiences with hypocritical and judgmental people whom one knows
to be religious, including malfeasant church leaders. As Zuckerman
himself rightly acknowledges, even this is only a partial listing.[10] Different people have lots of different reasons for rejecting God. Still, it is a

very helpful one, the validity of which is reinforced by the fact that my respondents refer to these, and other, reasons again and again.

So, then, how should we understand these narratives? Rather than providing slam-dunk answers to who, how, or why questions, they actually express *what it felt like* for people to swim against the current of the pervading religious culture, let go of God, and opt for an atheist identity. They convey the rough inner contours of a personal, sometimes emotionally charged experience that marks them as being different from who they once were.

As sociologists studying religious conversion have long observed, the value of these narratives rests not on their spot-on accuracy in recounting past events. Research subjects generally attribute being drawn to and then carefully assessing a new worldview as the impetus for their conversion, thus failing to mention other, often more determinative, factors such as their predisposing personal dispositions, unsettling life circumstances, and access to social networks that facilitate the discovery and embrace of new ideas.[11] The same is true here. These narratives are inevitably selective and oftentimes exaggerative recollections from the past with the aim of emplotting what William James once called the "big blooming buzzing confusion" of people's otherwise chaotic lives such that they cohere and make sense.[12] Hence, as ex post facto constructions, these narratives tell us much less about the details of the past than one might hope. They also, I hasten to add, say nothing about the future. It is true that, compared to other groups within the nation's ever-fluid religious marketplace, the nones are the group with not only the highest number switching *to* it but also the lowest percentage switching *from* it.[13] So, one would expect the decidedly atheist subset of this broader category to be particularly firm in their perspective for the long haul. But one never knows.

The reality is that these narratives primarily organize past events in order to situate people's identities in the present.[14] Their reliability is actually more a matter of feeling than fact in that they denote a truth about the actual felt experience of acquiring an identity that is not authenticated by the surrounding culture. Having a story to tell encapsulates that experience for atheists and signifies to themselves and others that this identity was not acquired willy-nilly. Highlighting the affective, experiential dimension—*what it felt like* to care enough about the

God question and reject religious belief—is the most effective, cultur-ally available way of marking this acquired identity as real. Organized religions, for instance, have initiation rituals, sacraments, professions of faith, membership rolls, distinctive clothing and symbols, and then some. Atheists have something else. They have feelings, organized into stories, that perform an identifying "signal function" in terms of denot-ing who they have become.[15] In other words, they have an experience of swimming, sometimes nearly drowning, in a sea of faith, an experience that marks their new identity as authentic and that they articulate via four narrative types.

Inquisitives

People like Margaret Daly describe themselves as being unsettled about religion even as children. They were generally raised in a faith tradition. But, they recount characteristically, something always seemed amiss. Partly because they were so young at the time, it was initially unclear to them what was going on. For Rick Childress, it was really just a feel-ing—or, better put, a lack of one. Brought up Catholic, he says he "just never really bought into it, even back then." Reminiscing a bit more, he elaborates, "I'd go to church on Sundays with my family and I'd go with my class when we were getting ready for our First Communion, and I never felt it. That's the best way to describe it. I never felt it." The doc-trine that the eucharistic bread and wine are the real body and blood of Christ, the virgin birth, humanity's salvation through Jesus's death and resurrection—none of this made sense to him. He "wasn't feeling it," and there were many occasions when he wondered, "Maybe I was doing something wrong."

Being naturally inquisitive, Childress was not content to simply won-der about this. He wanted answers. So, at about the time he entered mid-dle school, he decided to discuss his religious doubts with the people in his life. Unfortunately, he soon found himself isolated. He tried to share his doubts with his mother, but "it hurt her feelings, and so she didn't want to hear about my lack of faith." Next stop: his father. But this did not go far since "he just wasn't a philosophical guy and wasn't really equipped to think it all through." And his friends? Most were fellow stu-dents at Mater Dei, the Catholic high school he attended (or "survived,"

as he now describes it), and were not especially open to thinking critically about religion. "Almost all of them were brought up Catholic, and
they just wouldn't even consider what I was saying," he complained. "It
made me angry because they never even seemed to think about these
things or even consider the possibility that all these things were just superstition or stories." After a while, Childress got "tired of being angry."
He even began to empathize. If people were unwilling or unable to think
critically about religion, then theirs was surely a "blind faith," but also
one that provided them with clear ethical guidelines, a set of family rituals, and a connection to a long-standing tradition. Not needing these
things for himself, by the time he graduated high school, he realized,
"[Religion] just wasn't for me. . . . You know, it's just not my thing."

This basic story line gets repeated over and over again among inquisitives. Jenna Suptin was raised in a strong Southern Baptist family. Her father was a deacon at their local church, her mother doubled
as both the church secretary and resident pianist, and her two sisters
were both unquestioning in their faith. Given all this, she heard plenty
of religious conversations and "witnessing" throughout her childhood,
but also chiming in—persistently, enticingly—was that "little voice." "I
actually always had a quiet, little voice that doubted the whole thing,"
she explains. "Even as a kid, it all just seemed so improbable to me. I
once asked my mother about dinosaurs, and she said that, since they
weren't mentioned in the Bible, they were a construct of Satan to cause
us to doubt the Lord. I remember thinking she was an idiot." This was
only the beginning. Suptin was baptized at twelve years old, and despite
wanting to believe as did her "sweet," "passionately Christian" sisters
and friends, she just could not. At age seventeen, she actually took the
summer to read the entire Bible "cover to cover" in the hopes of better
appreciating her faith. This backfired though. After all her reading, she
decided it was essentially a book of stories that, like the sacred texts of
other cultures, merely helps to "explain things that are frightening and
confusing" to believers. At age nineteen, she stopped attending church
altogether. And at twenty-two, there was one, memorable evening when,
driving alone in her car, she first "began to allow myself to think about
whether there was really a God or not." This was a truly "frightening" experience for her. Persisting nevertheless, as she continued to think about
this during other drives, on long walks, or just randomly, she eventually

came to the conclusion that she was an atheist. "There was that little voice," she reiterates, "and it just seemed that I kept this private library of collected questions and doubts and inconsistencies in my head—and just added to it all the time."

Omid Rizvi conveys his early discomfort with religion not in terms of having "never felt it" or of giving in to a discomforting "little voice." Instead, he says, it simply reflects how his mind has always worked. His Christian mother and Muslim father each instructed him in their respective faiths. Regardless of his sincere interest in each and the fact that he was actually "a little envious of religious people," he just experienced too much dissonance. "My mind works fairly analytically, and I think the whole God thing just never made sense to me," he explains somewhat wistfully. "Even very young, I felt the mental gymnastics required to believe in a higher power to be exhausting." For instance, he thought hard about the different faiths throughout the world and even within his own household—and he could not understand how there could be a single "right way" to believe. He thought hard about the incredible poverty he encountered during his visits with extended family members in Syria—and he could not understand how a just God could allow such discrepancies in people's living conditions. He even thought hard, while enrolled in a high school physics class, about Einstein's theory of special relativity—and he could not understand, if even time can vary from one context to the next, how one could possibly believe in any absolute, including God. Exhausting indeed, eventually he got tired of doing all these mental exercises. As he began to put his energies elsewhere—school, career, and relationships—he found new things to occupy his mind, and he eventually felt himself moving beyond the religious questions that had once vexed him so thoroughly.

In each case, these inquisitives describe early experiences of discomfort with religious belief followed by a slow, plodding process of acknowledging their nagging feelings, little voices, and analytical musings as being legitimate, as reliable indicators of how they should grow into the adults they ultimately became. This is the typical pattern. The only variations one sees are some people's greater specificity with respect to both the juncture at which they began to pay careful attention to these indicators and then how they eased into their newfound, nearly inevitable identities as atheists.

None of them describe this time as some momentous A-Ha! situation. In fact, because they think of their atheism as a natural outcome of growing into their more authentic, adult selves, they are usually prone to talking about when they started paying attention to their religious qualms in relatively nondramatic terms. Similar to the evening when twenty-two-year-old Suptin took that drive, these are just points in time when they gave themselves permission to take their doubts seriously. Consider Carl Krestman, for example. Common among inquisitives, when he looks back upon his religious upbringing, he notes, "I mostly went through the motions, and I never really connected with it." Having questions about God for as long as he can recall, it was during his college years that he decided he was "on a mission to get to the bottom of it." "I don't remember an A-Ha! moment when, all of a sudden, I stopped believing in God," he says. Still, he does point to the day he read Richard Dawkins's *The God Delusion* and then being able, for the first time, to think of himself as an atheist instead of someone who was just perpetually confused. For Mick Reardon, this occurred when, at the age of twenty-eight, he took an Introduction to Philosophy course from a professor who exhibited the sort of commitment to "facts, logic, and reason" that he soon learned to embrace and, in doing so, let go of God as a consequence. And finally, it was not until her early fifties that Mia Jaynes, who always doubted but "never wanted to truly commit to not having a God," subscribed to Facebook. "Social networking woke me up to see what people actually believed. It was incredible. I realized they [religious people] didn't believe in evolution, they didn't believe in global warming, all that stuff. I think that's what got me started." Once started, she did not look back to her earlier religious prevarications. "It was liberating because, all of a sudden, I realized I had made up my mind and actually that this is what I was thinking the whole time," she says. "It's like I made up my mind, and this is the road I went on."

If inquisitives describe the specific time when they turned toward atheism in a nondramatic manner, the same is true of their accounts of how they experienced actually making this turn. The ease by which they did this is reflected in two framings, which they rely on with great regularity: the awakening frame and, somewhat more clumsily named, the moving-forward-fairly-effortlessly frame. As depicted above, Facebook did not turn Jaynes's life topsy-turvy. It just, she says, "woke me up." Likewise, she did not need to arduously hack away at a thicket of ideological possibilities. Instead, it was much easier in that she eventually found atheism's already established "road," which she then decided to traverse.

Usually inquisitives use one or the other of these framings. But, like Jaynes, some actually rely on both. Thus, Krestman looks back and says, "It was my deep-seeded curiosity that led to a gradual change or awakening as I like to think of it," and elsewhere in his reflections, he talks about his enrolling in college as what "truly started me down the path of introspection" that brought him to atheism. In a similar vein, when Reardon looks back at that Introduction to Philosophy class that had such an impact on him, he likens this to being "reborn." Rather than merging onto atheism's road or stepping onto its well-worn path, his experience, as he put it repeatedly, was that "the gates opened" upon a newly available vista that he could survey and in which he could situate himself. The point is that coming to consciousness ("awakening," being "reborn") does not connote much effort. The same goes for the second framing. Merging onto a road, not working hard to pave it; alighting onto a path, not cutting it; finding gates opening, not needing to push them ajar: these images all suggest that the process of acquiring an atheist identity for inquisitives is, while often lengthy, not an especially difficult one.

Searchers

Searchers are similar to inquisitives in framing the acquisition of their atheist identities in clearly teleological terms. However, where inquisitives talk about growing into and accepting an atheist orientation that was actually theirs all along—"from the get-go," "for as long as I can remember," and so forth—searchers talk about growing into and accepting themselves as people committed to discovering truths about the world. Their atheism is simply an outcome of this proclivity for truth seeking. Unlike inquisitives, then, as youngsters they were generally quite religious, which at the time was their preferred, or most available, means for seeking truth. They also began the process of questioning God's existence later than did most inquisitives—even though there is no age difference between the two groups in terms of when then ultimately came to call themselves atheists. What is more, acquiring their identities as atheists required more of them than an experience of waking up or turning toward a new road, path, or recently opened gate. It required considerable effort, and it frequently caused them much consternation. To be sure, many inquisitives felt alienated at worship services, frustrated at having their resistance to religion written off as a soon-to-be-outgrown "phase" by condescending adults, and worried (often justifiably) that their nonbelief would upset or offend their religious friends or family members. Even all this, though, pales in comparison to what searchers recount.

Michael Nashaat is a good example. Raised in a very pious Coptic Orthodox Christian household, his faith played a "huge role" in his upbringing. He attended weekly (and lengthy) church services, participated in Sunday school classes and Bible study groups, served as one of his church's younger deacons, and was even a consecrated *Ognostos* ("gospel reader"), which he enjoyed immensely. Yet, just as being religious partially defined who he was, so too did his critical thinking. At first these two qualities reinforced one another until, starting at about the age of fifteen, this began to change. He started to have doubts. For the next several years, he set out to seek answers: "I continually asked church elders, priests, bishops, and teachers in the church about my questions, and I discussed my doubts with them." All this to no avail. He was told to have more faith, to avoid reading material that was critical of religion, to stop questioning so much. When he persisted, he was met with hostility. This bothered Nashaat. Far from being dismissive of religion like many inquisitives at this same age, he ran into problems for taking it too seriously, as did many other searchers. "Most people don't take the question of God seriously. I take it extremely seriously. I think it's the most important question in life. I get angered by the lack of truth seeking in others." When his own truth seeking resulted in the "slow and painful" acceptance of atheism at the age of twenty-one, things only got harder:

> After coming out with my atheism, several of my friends cut ties with me, even childhood friends. I even came out to my parents, and I was put down, cursed at, and bullied into thinking I was a diseased, defected, selfish, evil person. I became angry at my former friends, at my parents and at society. I soon logically followed my disbelief in God to

its conclusion in nihilism. I then went into several existential crises during which I contemplated suicide often.

Although he gets cynical at times, and he knows members of his family "still believe I deserve to burn in hell for all eternity because of my views," Nashaat is much happier these days. Now pushing thirty, he looks back and realizes he has come through something quite difficult, something that now distinguishes him as a person concerned with seeking truth.

Another such person, Jared Raymond, is very upfront about this. "My commitment was always to find truth," he recollects. For many years, this commitment was synonymous with his identity as an Evangelical Christian who grew up attending church services three or more times each week. After graduating high school and resolving that, as he headed to college, he wanted to be "the best witness for Christ [he] could be," he decided that becoming more familiar with the Bible would be a good way to solidify his religious convictions. But after reading it through (twice!), he realized that (1) in order for the Bible to make sense to modern people, it needed to be interpreted; (2) there are various interpretive frameworks for understanding the Bible; (3) there is no way to determine which framework is best; and (4) since these different frameworks present people with different conceptions of God, there is no way to truly know God. This marked the outset of a search that Raymond describes as "quite grueling":

> The realization that the foundations of my beliefs may very well be false caused a nearly suicidal depression in me. I became self-destructive, burning my skin with hot knives and other things that seem so crazy now. I felt like all my life I'd been worshipping an *idea* of God, not God himself. I wanted desperately to find God as God, not God as my idea of God. I wanted the actual relationship that I was told I could expect. . . . I would often pray, "Jesus, you said that, 'Blessed are those who believe without seeing.' I will forgo the blessing. I just want to know you. I have to see." I figured ["Doubting"] Thomas got the choice to see, so why shouldn't I? At my lowest point, when I really wanted to do myself in, I had an epiphany. I realized in a sudden burst of insight that I didn't need God to provide my life with meaning; that all the love and connectedness I'd felt in my life were real regardless of where I chose to attribute it; [and] that no one, not God, not anyone, could give my life purpose unless I already believed

> I had it. I started to laugh out loud at how crazy I was behaving. I walked
> outside, and the grass looked greener, the sky bluer. I walked to a local
> ice cream shop and got a cherry malt. It was the best malt I've ever had!

Note that this "epiphany" did not mean the scales immediately fell from Raymond's eyes, and he became, for lack of a better word, converted to atheism. What makes the experience so memorable, he says, is that it initiated a process during which he "was able to ask the questions without fear." It was not until years later that he began to call himself an atheist, and even now, he is less committed to this particular identity than to what he honestly discerns to be true. "Perhaps I'll get new information that'll change my mind," he muses. "Who knows? I doubt it, but I'm more interested in finding what truths are available for me to learn in life than to stick dogmatically to any particular perspective."

The atheist label is not especially important to Linda Reems either. While "leaning toward agnosticism," she calls herself an atheist because, in the South, "if you tell a religious person you're an agnostic, they take it as a license to start trying to get you saved." Paramount for her, as with Nashaat and Raymond, is the quest for answers. "I think my moral and intellectual base is mostly from my father," she reflects, "whose humanistic way of looking at things influenced me more than I think I understood until recently. He taught me to analyze situations and search out the truth of things regardless of what I feel." This is not to say she had a problem with her mother who raised her as a Mormon. Reems enjoyed church as a girl and especially looked forward to attending Bible camp where, one unforgettable summer, she even won a brand-new Bible for her ability to recite scripture passages. "I loved it and the Bible stories, and I still have that Bible today," she remembers. "I also have a Book of Mormon, which I keep because it has my mother's thoughts on various passages written in red ink in the margins. I love reading her thoughts, so I'll keep it forever."

By the time she was seventeen, she decided that too much of the content of these books, as well as certain aspects of Mormon theology, were problematic for her. So much so, in fact, that instead of attempting to delve deeper into her tradition, the route taken initially by both Nashaat and Raymond, she realized she needed to broaden her search. For the next "twenty-odd years," she explored other faiths. First, she looked to Christianity, Judaism, and Islam but found these to be too replete with "all the trappings of racism, homophobia, and misogyny." Then she turned to different New Age and neo-pagan traditions until concluding that "a focus on energy and magic wasn't any more fulfilling than church had been." Then she clung to a kind of "nebulous faith" grounded in personal experience, especially in the feelings of transcendence derived from the innumerable Pentecostal services, meditation sessions, and drum circles in which she participated over the years. "This kept me believing in *something*," she says. It was unsustainable, she admits. A longtime and avid reader in the sciences, she eventually concluded that spiritual experiences are most likely a function of humans' brain chemistry—neurological processes that, at one time, provided some sort of survival advantage. "I don't think people should be content to simply say, 'Oh, well, it's God' when they don't know that to be the case." Not content to say this herself, she finally let go of all "magical thinking," which was the hardest part of her quest:

> The transition from faith was far more painful than I ever imagined it could be. I hadn't prepared myself to be an atheist. I hadn't realized how important it was to me that there was *something* or *someone* out there who cared about us, about our world, and about me in particular, and that there'd be some explanation for all this after we die. . . . I had to claw my way into a new way of thinking a little at a time.

Part of clawing her way has been dealing with a serious, recently diagnosed chronic illness that Reems will likely have for the rest of her life. To her surprise, she has found coping with the disease without a comforting belief in "*something* or *someone*" to be easier than she had feared. She does get just a bit irritated when some of the more devout people in her life assure her of their prayers. "It's really quite offensive," she gripes hesitatingly. "If you think about it, 'I'm praying for you' basically means 'I'm doing absolutely nothing to help you, but it makes me happy to pretend I am.' My atheist friends don't pray for me—they visit, they clean my bathroom, they bring me food. I'd prefer that any day."

Responders

Other people seem to play a much larger role in the narratives responders tell. Other people, in fact, are often cast as being responsible for initiating responders' disquiet about religion and setting them upon the difficult course that ultimately results in the loss of their once-prized religious beliefs. Sometimes it is the religious hypocrites in their midst who cause them to reassess the value of living faithfully. Sometimes it is fellow churchgoers who voice or act upon what they perceive to be hurtful political views. Sometimes it is friends or family members who seem ignorant of their own tradition or who come off as being intolerant toward people with different views. Whatever the case, they unsettle things for responders and precipitate what is usually a trying time for them.

There are many examples of this. One young woman from a very influential Mormon family began to question her faith after an embarrassing episode from her personal life became a subject of intense gossip within her local ward. "I didn't think having oral sex with my own fiancé was the end of the world," she asserted. "But I can tell you this: the way those supposedly morally upright people treated me definitely brought about the end of my connection with Mormonism." As he was learning to accept himself as a gay man, one former Evangelical became increasingly upset about the homophobic remarks he heard on occasion at his church. That gay and bisexual people in the United States are significantly more likely than heterosexuals to be agnostic or atheist suggests that this is not an isolated event.[16] "I quickly realized there wasn't anything wrong with being gay," he explained, "and that allowed me the opportunity to wonder what else the Bible and Christianity were wrong about." A onetime Orthodox Jew recalls reading a book written by a rabbi who lambasted the "Jews for Jesus" movement and, in doing so, expressed a thoughtful and compelling skepticism toward Christianity in general. "So, I was very impressed with that book," he said. "But as soon as I realized I could take that same skeptical mindset and look at Judaism the very same way, well, it all started unraveling." Things started to unravel for Gabe McGrath both early (he was eleven at the time) and quickly. Raised in a very traditionalist Catholic family, he prayed every day, he frequently said the rosary, and he attended mass every Sunday— except for one time when, for a reason he no longer remembers, he did not go. Remorseful, he acknowledged this lapse during his monthly confession, only to be told by his parish priest that this, a mortal sin, meant he would go to hell when he died. This was not easy for him, then a sixth-grader, to hear:

I went back to school with the rest of the class when confession was over. I don't remember the rest of the school day. At night I tried to pray for forgiveness but kept hearing that priest's voice in my head: "You will go to hell when you die." . . . Anyway, over the subsequent years of doubt and self-loathing, I went searching for an answer, some way to get back to God's good graces. I read the Bible from cover to cover looking for an answer or loophole. I read as much as I could about other cultures and religions in antiquity. And I scoured my parent's encyclopedia. And then I just started thinking, thinking about religions and priests and nuns and rabbis and imams and organizations and rituals and churches and synagogues and cultures and the many thousands of years that have passed. I wondered why there were so many gods that people didn't believe in anymore. I wondered why God spoke so often to people back in biblical times but not now. . . . Finally, after four years of research and thinking, I had my answer: there are no gods. It was 1976. I was fifteen years old, a sophomore at the Catholic high school across the street from my home. Just as Christians disbelieve all other gods except their own, I took the next logical step and realized there is actually one less than that. And the Christian God didn't smite me or kill me for my disbelief. Huh! What do you know? So, I decided to test it out loud. Why not? If I'm wrong, I'm going to hell anyway, right? "Fuck you, God!" I said aloud. Nothing. No answer. No lightning or thunder. No picture falling off the wall. No sign at all. I wasn't going to hell because I didn't have an immortal soul to punish for all eternity.

Of course, other people do not just serve to repel responders, ushering them away from religious belief and practice. Just as often, other people—especially good, appealing, morally upstanding people adhering to other faiths or none at all—draw them toward thinking of atheism as a credible option for their lives. Some of my interviewees have been inspired or challenged by nonbelievers whose books they have read, with whom they work or associate, or to whom they are perhaps even married. One strictly observant Jehovah's Witness came across quite a few well-known atheists, "randomly really," when he was searching the Internet for some devotional material he enjoyed reading, and then inadvertently stumbled upon some atheism debate videos. He initially wrote these off as "lies perpetuated by Satan." He was drawn in though. "As I watched debates between Christians and atheists, I found myself nodding at the atheist points and shaking my head with the Christian ones. My faith literally disintegrated in a matter of days." For the next several months, a time during which he was "internally conflicted" and "deeply depressed," he tried to make sense of his inner doubts until, he says, "I took a stand. I shed the shackles of my belief, and ended it once and for all."

Still other responders find themselves pulled toward atheism as a consequence of their exposure to religious difference. Lorraine Petrie is a good example. Brought up in a "conservative Christian" home, as a youngster her parents kept her from secular music and from most television programs. She went to Christian schools and attended church services about three times each week. She even did mission work with her family. So insular was her upbringing that it is hard to imagine her dating someone outside of her small church. But she did. "In my junior year I began dating a boy from a different denomination. And religious debates with him are what first made me think maybe it was *all* bullshit. We couldn't both be right. Yet there were verses in the Bible to support both of our views," she explains. "I was still firmly a Christian at that point, but the divisiveness of denominations was making me believe that all Christians were doing it wrong." This thought stayed with her as she began to question her faith. The centrality of religious difference for spurring this process became evident again when she took a world religions class in college. Covering "everything from the Koran to the Egyptian Book of the Dead," she was bothered when, it being a Christian college, many of her fellow students mocked what they learned about other faiths. "One of the professors made the point that, if we had been born in another country or time period, we would likely believe the religion of that time and place as fervently as we now believe in Christianity. That statement," she concludes, "hit home with me, and I realized that, if any of it is laughable, *all* of it is." Although her process of questioning was "not easy" and she kept on "pretending" to believe until her early thirties, she is at ease with her atheism now and remains extremely grateful to her former boyfriend and to that college professor.

Sometimes it is events, not people, that responders designate as the source of their skepticism. These can be enormously trying. For instance, Beth Richards did not question God when, at sixteen, she got pregnant and then had a miscarriage. When a "D and C" procedure was recommended to remove the dead fetus, she refused and then endured many hours of labor because, as she told her doctor, "only God would decide" the time her pregnancy should be terminated. Her faith also did not waiver when she needed to drop out of high school to care for the first of two children she had by another man who was physically abusive toward her. But it started to more than waiver, she recounts, when, after she became pregnant yet again by a third man, this man assaulted her in front of her children:

> One day he was beating me while my then three-year-old son and mere months-old daughter watched. My son jumped on his back, screaming at him to get off his mommy. I had contemplated abortion before because I didn't think it was fair to have another child experience this. But I thought God wanted me to continue with the pregnancy and mostly because my religious upbringing didn't allow for abortions. But at that moment, seeing my child try to protect me when God seemed too busy to do so, I knew something was wrong. Until this point in my life, I'd never doubted my religion. I didn't even know doubt was an option. So, I did have an abortion. I left that abusive relationship. I put one of my former boyfriends in prison and the other one on the run from the law. I also started to seriously question where my God was. . . . It was very gradual for me. It started out as an emotional thing but turned into a very evidence-based doubt. It was also very difficult for me. During this time of doubt—which was years—I converted to Seventh-day Adventism and also considered Catholicism to try to find what fit. When I realized no religion fit, I understood it was because none of them were true.

Other events critical to responders are far less intense. They can even be joyous. This is how Joe Kaufman describes the birth of his first son. He had been active at his Methodist church since he himself was a child. For as long as he could remember, he considered it "obvious that the message of the Bible was true and would lead to salvation," and he says, "the idea that there might not be a God never even occurred to me." It was not until held his new son in his arms that he began to feel a new kind of responsibility:

> I always assumed that bringing a child up in the Church was the right thing to do. But now that I was faced with that reality, I started questioning what

to teach him. Even though I considered myself a Christian, I was strongly for equal rights for homosexuals—especially marriage equality—and that made me think about what parts of the Bible to teach my son and which parts to omit or contradict. That question naturally led to, Why? Why was the Bible wrong on some teachings and right on some others? I'd always thought it had to be interpreted through the historical context in which it was written, so I started thinking about context. Slowly, over the course of a few years, I realized that the context in which it was written was that of a tribe of desert nomads who had no answers for how and why things came to be—the same as every other dead religion. I remember getting ready for work one day and looking into the mirror and realizing that, in my mind, it was far more likely that God was made in man's image rather than the reverse. It was a tremendously liberating thought.

Finally, some events are just haphazard. Similar to Joanne Cecchini, who turned to the Bible amid some family turmoil, others found themselves being accosted by doubt as they reflected upon a trite eulogy they heard or upon a profound movie they saw, as they witnessed a car crash or received a hard-earned raise at work, or as they married or divorced— all sorts of things. Anne Newton talks about "two major events that I attribute to me becoming an atheist." Her parents raised her in the Lutheran faith, but she describes herself as "surpassing my parents' faithfulness by far," even to the point of going to church on those Sunday mornings when they opted to stay home and sleep in. Her dream was even to become a biblical archeology professor in hopes that one day she would "prove the Bible correct" by excavating key sites mentioned in scripture. Instead, there was that other day—April Fool's Day, believe it or not—when she was stuck in an airport during a blizzard, and she happened upon a discarded issue of *Harper's* magazine featuring an article on certain archeological problems related to the biblical account of the Jews' Exodus from Egypt. "Upon reading that article, I had an epiphany of sorts. I didn't become an atheist," she says, "but I opened my mind to the possibility of there not being a God." This, she continues, "felt like a weight lifted off my shoulders," which, while scary in some respects, freed her to "pursue the concept of atheism" for several months, that is, until that second—far more broadly reverberating—major event. "I woke up that morning as a Christian," she explains, recounting September 11, 2001, "and went to bed that night as an atheist." Not due to a critical, even jaundiced view of Islam, this transition flowed from her critical assessment of a commonplace and, for her, once-held conception of God. Thinking about the now-infamous nineteen hijackers, she reflects:

> If they had been born in the hospital I was born in, they likely would have been Lutheran or some Protestant Christian. The fact that they were drawn to the radical form of Islam that got them to commit suicide and mass murder was also largely due to where they were born. That seemed to me to be a significant hole in the idea that God is just. So, that led to similar thoughts. Is a person born in Africa who is never exposed to Christianity until they are an adult really responsible for not becoming Christian? . . . Yet they are condemned to hell because they know of Jesus Christ and still reject him. This was a huge concept that extended beyond 9/11. From there it really was a house of cards.

Newton says she went to bed that night as an atheist. But as she later mentions, it actually took her about two years of grappling with these and "similar thoughts" before she would be willing to identify herself, both publically and even to herself, as an atheist.

Consolidators

Taking such a long time to identify as an atheist, much less doing a lot of grappling with the issue, is not characteristic of our final atheist narrative. Similar to all of the responders in this study, about one-third of the consolidators had unexpectedly experienced their faith being challenged by certain people or events in their lives. Unlike them, they did not need to work especially hard at coming to terms with rejecting God and religion. For instance, exposure to postsecondary education, particularly at a secular institution, is often a turning point for respondents and consolidators alike. Yet, for consolidators like Sam Dudley, it precipitated neither much hand-wringing nor a prolonged faith crisis. From kindergarten through high school, he attended Catholic schools in his rural Louisiana hometown. Once he began his studies at Louisiana State University, he realized he no longer "bought into" what he had taken for granted during his entire upbringing. For the first time ever, he met people of different faiths ("some of whom had a very negative view of the Roman Catholic Church," he notes), took courses in world history and philosophy, and before long, began to think that his dogmatic parents had "failed" him. "Suddenly, it was like a dam burst and all the doctrines and irrational apologetics that I had unthinkingly accepted just crumbled," he recalls. "Suddenly, I didn't have to struggle with the cognitive dissonance involved in reconciling a loving God with the realities of the world around me. I didn't have to worry about going to hell for having premarital sex or masturbating. As I fell away from religion, I became much more at peace with myself and with human nature, and more accepting of the world as a place where everything is governed by the laws of science."

"Suddenly," "practically overnight," "before I knew it," "without a lot of *Sturm und Drang* ['storm and stress'] really"—these are the sort of phrasings consolidators use to denote the relatively modest degree of effort they extended in acquiring their identities as atheists. In fact, this is the only group from which some people, a small minority, describe coming to atheism as a kind of A-Ha! moment, the fruit of a sudden flash of insight. One person reported that this insight came to her as she sat on a park bench watching a group of children playing soccer and arguing over whose interpretation of the rules was correct. Another, a soldier serving in Iraq, was smoking a cigarette, looking up at the night sky, and thinking about the day's bloody fighting when he realized he inhabited a world that simply could not include God. Doug Simon's account is truly captivating and well worth quoting at some length. He always found going to church (at both his mother's Catholic church and his father's Baptist one) to be boring, no comparison to the wonders he, even as a child, experienced when learning about science, especially astronomy. These wonders, he notes, "didn't seem to conflict with my belief in God" until he purchased several books by Carl Sagan at a used bookstore:

> The next day, a Sunday, I settled into my comfy lawn chair behind the house and began reading my new treasure trove of Sagan books. It was a beautiful fall day. I was amazed at how he could write so poetically about science. The words just seemed to flow off the page. I was spellbound. It was such a beautiful and enjoyable afternoon. At some point, I reached a chapter on evolution. I really didn't know much about evolution at all. I honestly can't remember learning about it in high school. I heard of it as an adult, of

course. I knew it was *only a theory*. I never gave it much credence. Humans from monkeys? Yeah, right. How ridiculous! . . . When I finished reading that chapter on evolution, I was an atheist. Just like that. The way he explained it so gently—it's hard for me to explain how the dawning of it all hit me. But I know for sure, without a doubt, my belief was gone. Gone forever. How strange, right? I was forty-one years old. All that time I had believed what I was taught. During that time, I had spoken to God and Jesus and assumed they'd heard me and were looking out for me. I prayed for help when I needed it, asked for forgiveness when I sinned. Now it was all gone. In the span of thirty minutes or so, a dead author explained evolution to me, and I didn't believe in God anymore. And I was fine with it. Better than fine. I was elated. All this time, I never knew I was related to every living thing, that I was directly descended, in an unbroken chain, from some simple life form that lived billions of years ago. I was more awestruck and inspired than I ever had been in my life, certainly more than I ever felt in any church. I remember going to bed that night and, for the first time, thinking that I was alone in my head, completely alone. No God or savior knowing my deepest secrets, monitoring my thoughts. There was no one else in there. It was just me! I thought that this should terrify me, but it didn't. It was like I was free for the first time in my life. In a way, I guess, I was.

Accounts like Simon's are rare, however. As opposed to a consequence of being challenged by some person or event, for the majority of consolidators—the other two-thirds of the ones in this study—coming to call themselves atheists was actually a consequence of something relatively prosaic. They were raised in nonreligious households, which is true of about 11 percent of American children today.[17] As these children grow to adulthood, many of them become religious in some way—including more than half of those brought up in specifically atheist households.[18] Among those who do not turn toward religion, many still resist identifying as atheists, usually because of either social stigma or their uncertainty about this term's precise meaning, and choose to call themselves agnostics, humanists, or perhaps nothing at all.[19] The "nothing" option is actually the preferred one for some of the atheists in this study, especially for the 13 percent of them who say that the atheist label fits them only "somewhat" well. "I'm just a human being," groused one respondent. "Being called an atheist is as meaningful to me as being called a six-footer or a Sagittarian would be if I lived in a country where most people were obsessed with height or astrology!" Whether meaningful to them or not, this respondent and all the others from this study who grew up in secular homes eventually accepted this label as being an accurate descriptor of who they are—largely because other, usually more nebulous, designations came to seem less satisfying or honest to them.

This was true of Maya Dejung. One might expect an African American woman who has lived her entire life in the South to have had a religious upbringing. Nevertheless, because of her father's premature death and her mother's (unspecified) "personal problems," she was, as she put it, "pretty much left to fend for [herself]," a task that did not include religious instruction of any kind. It was not until high school that, sitting in the library one day, she overheard two other girls talking about someone using a word she had never heard before. "They said it with such anger and hate that, when they left, I went straight over to the dictionary and looked it up. When I did, I just stood there thinking, 'Oh, my gosh, that's me!'" Given the way it was spoken and the fact that she had managed just fine without knowing it anyway, she resolved not to apply this word—atheist—to herself. She preferred nothing, no label at all. By her midtwenties or so, this option became increasingly difficult. By then a single mother of two children, her friends kept trying to set her up with one "good Christian man" after another. Her extended family, especially her two aunts, wondered what church she attended and complained that her kids did not seem to know any Bible verses. It was not until one of those aunts, likely trying to goad her, went on and on one Thanksgiving dinner about atheism being a "white man's religion" that she had enough and snapped back, "Hey, that's me!" That was all it took. Not long after, she remembers, "I finally said it about myself *to myself*. It's me, and I'm definitely cool with it now. In fact, we're an atheist household."

People move from all sorts of other nebulous options to consolidate their identities as atheists. Here are three examples. For years, criminal investigator Larry Dickerson was perfectly satisfied to think of himself as an agnostic or, as he gauzily put it, "I kind of always sort of considered myself, I guess, an agnostic—you know, pretty much okay with 'I don't know.'" That was until he became friends with a couple of guys—an Evangelical and a Mormon—who "talked about religion all the time, and actually seemed to know what they were talking about." Frustrated by this and determined to "weigh the evidence, which is what [he does] on the job everyday anyway," he got online and researched the major religions of the world. Concluding that "there's too many inconsistencies and flat-out fallacies for [him] to believe that any one of them is actually true," he decided that the facts led to atheism. Something like this also happened in Cecilia Leon's life. Not a kinda-sorta-I-guess-agnostic, she was what sociologist David Voas calls a "fuzzy fidelist," someone who is not religious in the traditional sense but nonetheless holds to a variety of supernatural beliefs.[20] Or to use her preferred label, she was a "dabbler." Although never religious, she "loved" mythology, she "looked into" Druidism, and she "did some dabbling in" Wicca and paganism. She was never really serious, and she was unclear about where her convictions were exactly. Then, she says, things got very serious when her three-year-old son was diagnosed with cancer. "That pretty much clarified things for me, and I decided I was an atheist," she recounts. "Because we spent so much time in the hospital, and I saw so many children dying of cancer and all these other illnesses, I decided that, if there was a God or something directing all this, it certainly didn't care about kids. I didn't want anything to do with something like that." For Diana Carey, it was not until her own life was at stake that she began to call herself an atheist. Like the others, she was brought up without religion, but she basically had an easygoing, "Frankly, my dear, I don't give a damn" attitude about the God question. She snickered when one of her high school friends announced that her sister would go to hell for being a lesbian. She scratched her head when one of her college professors tried to explain how ideas and events recounted in the Bible were always compatible with scientific findings. She even got more than a little annoyed when, just recently, she read an article about a divorced woman in New York who, being an atheist, lost custody of her daughter to her abusive ex-husband because he assured the judge he would take the little girl to church.[21] Even in light of all this, her basic attitude was, in a word, "whatever." She avoided thinking hard about her actual viewpoint until the issue became less theoretical for her:

> The defining moment came while I was lying on a gurney in the emergency room. I had just been in a horrible head-on car crash and I was very seriously injured. My femur, collar bone, and ribs were shattered. I suffered a stroke, was blind in one eye, and was having great difficulty breathing. I seriously

considered the idea that I might die of my injuries. I asked myself, "Should I accept Christ?" The absolute truth of that moment was that I didn't believe any of that. I just couldn't pretend just because I was scared. I have fully considered myself an atheist from that moment on. I was thirty-one years old.

Focusing on Feelings

In this chapter, our focus has been on something different from what other sociologists might, quite understandably, want to address. We have not identified strong correlations between narrative types and other variables in order to provide some insight into the *who* question. We also have not explicitly addressed the *how* question, especially concerning the various steps by which one might acquire an atheist identity. And the same is true of the *why* question. These are all important questions. This latter one was particularly tempting because nods to what Phil Zuckerman presents as the nine most frequently mentioned reasons people give for their turning to atheism have appeared throughout this chapter. Of course, as Zuckerman perceptively notes, subjective reasons are not necessarily objective causes. It is always difficult for observers to isolate specific causes for people's actions and convictions, particularly when the very same people being observed have enough difficulty themselves in accounting for what causes them to act and think in the ways they do. As shown in table 2.1, for example, the respondents in this study were united in delineating a mélange of factors—with varying levels of significance to them—which they suspect were instrumental in shaping their attitudes toward God and religion. In addition to dovetailing nicely with Zuckerman's analysis, these data are also interesting on their own. The 11 percent who say their lack of religious upbringing was "very significant" (item a) in shaping their views reflects the reality that the great majority received some degree of religious training as children as well as the aforementioned finding that a minority of Americans (11 percent) have been reared in nonreligious households. The *negative* examples set by the religious (item h) are emphasized by my sample of atheists more than the *positive* examples set by the nonreligious (item b). The equally high proportion (71 percent) of respondents who point to advances in science (item l) and scriptural inconsistencies (item m) as being "very significant" to them suggests a possible connection between these two items in people's minds. There is much to consider.

TABLE 2.1. Influences on one's views on God and religion

People give various reasons for why they are not religious. Among the frequently cited ones below, please indicate how significant you think each was for shaping your current views on God and religion.

	Very significant (%)	Somewhat significant (%)	Not at all significant (%)
a. Lack of religious upbringing	11	18	72
b. Positive examples of people who are not religious	26	40	34
c. The amount of evil and suffering in the world	36	38	26
d. Political influence of religious people and groups	46	33	21
e. The fact that there are many different religions	42	38	20
f. New insights acquired from formal education	42	39	19
g. Religious teachings on hell and damnation	49	33	18
h. Negative examples of people who are religious	47	35	18
i. Religious teachings on sex and sexuality	51	35	14
j. Religious teachings on the role of women	57	30	13
k. Distressing events in the history of religion	53	35	12
l. Advances in science	71	20	8
m. Inconsistencies/problems concerning scripture	71	22	7

Note: Some rows add up to more or less than 100 percent owing to rounding errors.

Here, though, we have considered something else. The stories people tell about their rejecting belief in God are arguably best understood as being answers to the *what* question, as accounts of *what it felt like* for them to acquire an atheist identity. Recollections of these feelings remind them that they have changed. In the absence of such markers as initiation rites, creedal proclamations, and elaborate rituals that function to authenticate believers' religious commitments, the atheists I spoke to have narratives they tell about deeply felt experiences that in turn tell them and signify to them that they have assumed a new identity. This is critical, of course, because the broader society does not recognize "the atheist" as a creditable identity, and at those times when some acknowledgment is made, it is commonly a matter of misunderstanding if not outright stigmatizing.

3

Maintaining Atheist Identities

Stigma, Reason, Feelings

To Be *and* Not to Be: Making Symbolic Boundaries

Disabusing oneself of commonplace presumptions and paying attention to people's accounts of what it felt like for them to become atheists, as we have done in the previous two chapters, are definitely positive steps toward deepening one's understanding of people who identify as atheist today. Another step, which we take in this chapter, is to explore how this identity is maintained through atheists' discursive practices of telling "stigma stories," accentuating the purported irrationality of believers and, once again, deploying feelings as an ongoing means for authenticating this identity to themselves.

As obvious as it may at first seem, it is worth noting that this is in no way an arbitrary identity. It is largely shaped by a *particular* kind of social order within which identifying oneself as an atheist would even be thinkable. Observes, once again, sociologist Steve Bruce, "Self-conscious atheism and agnosticism are features of religious cultures . . . They are postures adopted in a world where people are keenly interested in religion."[1] American culture certainly qualifies. If U.S. currency did not avow that it is "in God" (not in the Federal Reserve) we trust; if the Pledge of Allegiance did not locate our one nation as being "under God" (not, as is more geographically accurate, "under Canada"); and much more to the point, if we did not remain, as innumerable opinion polls continue to reveal, "awash in the sea of faith," then it is quite conceivable that nonbelieving citizens would neither think about nor much bother with identifying themselves on the basis of this single aspect of their lives.

This identity is likewise shaped by the emergence of a *particular*, post-Reformation conceptualization of religion that, as we saw earlier, privileges the objectified, cognitive dimension of faith over other ways of living faithfully. One can only speculate whether it would have occurred to a segment of the nonreligious minority to adopt the atheist label if the religious majority did not so routinely encapsulate their faith in terms of "clear and distinct" propositions about God rather than as practicing "acts of compassion," being accountable to a worshipful community, embracing the inscrutable mystery of life with reverence, honing a heartfelt sense of epistemological humility concerning the sacred, and so forth. Paul Tillich, one of the past century's most renowned and influential Christian theologians, was unequivocal in instructing his broad readership: "God does not exist. He is being itself beyond essence and existence. Therefore to argue that God exists is to deny him."[2] This more analogical posture has largely been drowned out by religious sensibilities that range from creedal fastidiousness to cocksure fundamentalism and that, in any case, frenetically exhibit what the novelist Gustave Flaubert once derided as a simplistic "mania for conclusions."[3] Especially among those inclined to be similarly derisive, such religious sensibilities go a long way in making the atheist identity both a conceivable option and, for the respondents in this study, the preferred one.

Importantly, even the *particular* manner by which one opts for and maintains this identity is far from arbitrary. In the present-day United States, it is more a matter of "role making" than merely "role taking."[4] In other words, one cannot casually take on the identity of "the atheist" as assuredly as one can with such sturdier identities as "the professor," "the grandmother," or "the baseball fan," which are broadly recognized as normative and also impart relatively clear behavioral expectations. When acknowledged at all, this highly stigmatized identity gets framed by the wider culture too pejoratively to be taken on without some elaboration among those who come to embrace it. This is especially the case since clear behavioral expectations are hard to come by because, like the vegans, virgins, and nonsmokers studied by sociologist Jamie Mullaney, atheists are principally defined by what they are *not* doing.[5] What they need to do, then, is engage in a good deal of active role making whereby they constitute themselves as atheists by acknowledging and valorizing the experiences, insights, and feelings that mark them as a distinctive grouping within society.

Sometimes this sort of role making, or what sociologists David Snow and Leon Anderson call "identity work," is conducted through their association with fellow atheists.[6] Opportunities for doing so are certainly possible at what one recent study discovered to be the approximately 3,100 secularist groups of various types within the United States.[7] Added to these are all manner of online forums and chat rooms as well as informal ventures that include small groups ranging from atheist book clubs to parenting workshops, occasional gatherings that run the gamut from field trips to local science museums to "godless drinking" at local pubs, and activities as varied as atheist-sponsored blood drives and skydiving excursions. The sky is truly the limit here. For many people, these sorts of formal, informal, and online groups function as "plausibility structures" that, by facilitating interactions among like-minded others, reinforce the credibility of secular worldviews and the legitimacy of atheist identities.[8] This should hardly be unexpected. After all, critical to the project of consolidating a sense of self are the interactions we have with "significant others" whose perspectives we, over time, internalize and adopt as our own.[9] Less expected, however, is the relatively minor part these groups play in facilitating the identity work of most of the people with whom I spoke. This is especially noteworthy since I initially got in touch with many of my interviewees by publicizing my study on the websites of various atheist and humanist organizations. Thus one would reasonably expect my sample, which is a nonrandom one anyway, to be skewed in the direction of people with closer-than-average affiliations with these and other groups.

Nevertheless, as shown in table 3.1, when asked how influential certain sources of information have been for them in terms of helping to think through and live out their atheist worldviews, respondents indicate that the more community oriented and group based of these sources have actually influenced them the least. They point mostly to their own critical thinking (augmented by their formal educations) and attentiveness to their own intuitions and feelings (items a–c). This emphasis on trusting oneself, thinking for oneself, and going one's own way is very clear. It is absolutely central to atheists' sense of who they are. Looking again at table 3.1, the next most cited clustering of sources (items d–f) all refer to people respondents have never even met. These are the living or deceased atheists who possess certain admirable qualities or who have authored books. Dead last—all with no more than one in five people deeming them "very influential"—are respondents' actual experiences of connecting singularly or collectively with other atheists. This suggests that neither the acquaintances, friends, and family members whom they know personally (items g–i) nor the people whom they may have met or could potentially meet at various groups and conferences (items j–m) are denoted by respondents as being as influential as those atheist authors and notables with whom they have never crossed paths.[10]

One should not consider such data naïvely. Sociologists have long observed that people seldom have a complete grasp of the various factors that influence their thinking (and action) and that they generally minimize the extent to which their own viewpoints and feelings are shaped by the world around them. Yet, while largely suggestive, these data do reflect a reality that can be easily overlooked. That is, despite the increasing emergence and visibility of well-organized conferences, activities, and communities centered upon atheism, only a small minority of American atheists actually participate in them.[11] This is because, for the majority, their lack of religious faith is not truly at the core of who they are. According to a recent Public Opinion Research Institute survey, only 13 percent of American atheists report that being an atheist is "very important" to them.[12] Moreover, since such values as autonomy and nonconformism are so esteemed by most atheists, it makes sense that they generally do not experience themselves as needing the support that affiliating with fellow nonbelievers might provide. In fact, among all the religious groupings in the United States, another study found atheists to be the least likely (22 percent) to say that belonging to a community of people who share their values and beliefs is "very important" to them.[13] Perhaps this is why, in his thoughtful 2012 book *How to Be Secular: A Call to Arms for Religious Freedom*, religion and society scholar Jacques Berlinerblau lamented, "Simply put, secularism has a 'we' problem. Secularists don't do 'we.'"[14]

Albeit both pithy and astute, Berlinerblau's point requires some qualification in terms of the sort of "we" to whom atheists, in particular, actu-

TABLE 3.1. Sources of information pertaining to atheist identity

People sometimes say that it can be difficult to be an atheist in light of the high levels of religiosity in the United States. Thus, they often refer to certain sources of information and motivation that help them to think through and live out their atheist worldviews. Among the frequently mentioned sources listed below, please indicate how influential each has been in your own life.

		Very influential	Somewhat influential	Not at all influential
a.	My own critical thinking	97	3	0
b.	My own intuitions and/or feelings	64	29	7
c.	My formal education	47	39	14
d.	Recently published popular books on atheism	32	42	26
e.	My admiration for one or more contemporary atheist about whom I am knowledgeable	25	49	26
f.	My admiration for one or more atheists from the past	22	44	34
g.	My admiration for one or more atheists with whom I am personally acquainted	20	30	50
h.	One or more close friends who are atheists	20	34	45
i.	One or more family members who are atheists	10	22	68
j.	Online atheist groups	17	37	47
k.	Atheist websites	16	44	40
l.	Conferences, lectures, etc., on atheism I've attended	10	21	68
m.	In-person atheist groups	8	23	69

Note: Some rows add up to more or less than 100 percent owing to rounding errors.

ally imagine themselves being connected. Yes, they may tend not to look to the fellow nonbelieving travelers in their lives when going about the task of role making. And it is true that they usually do not single out any of the various groups and communities they might know of as being associative loci for the identity work they undertake. Yet they actually do "do 'we,'" that is, think of themselves as part of a larger group, by doing something else: they look both *beyond* their ranks to religious believers (for comparative purposes) and *within* themselves (for emotional cues) and, in the process, maintain their identities as atheists by situating themselves less often within in-person or online communities than within an "imagined community" of nonbelievers.[15] Like all communities, this one is constituted by a symbolic boundary distinguishing "us" and "them."[16] Sociologist Anthony Cohen addresses this long-standing sociological notion, the symbolic nature of communal belonging, with exceptional nimbleness. "Community thus seems to imply simultaneously both similarity and difference," he observes. "The word thus expresses a relational idea: the opposition of one community to others or to other social entities. . . . The consciousness of community has to be kept alive through the manipulation of its symbols. The reality and efficacy of the community's boundary—and, therefore, the community itself—depends upon its symbolic construction and embellishment."[17]

Maintaining this imagined community, of course, can be aided through interaction with other atheists. But this is not necessary. As Cohen suggests, a sense of opposition to those on the other side of the community's symbolically constructed boundary is at least as important. American atheists seem to agree. They look to religious people and then represent what they see through what Cohen calls their "manipulation of symbols," which takes two main forms. First, they tell "stigma stories" that convey the religious public's hostility toward them for being atheists. Second, through the processes of categorization and accentuation, they construct the "irrational other" frame to depict believers as being unequipped, unable, or unwilling to use their rational faculties. Finally, in addition to looking beyond their ranks toward the believing out-group, they also look within. As we saw in the last chapter's discussion of what it felt like for people to become atheists, they access and mobilize their feelings as a kind of affective validation of the identities they have carved out for themselves.[18] Such feelings signal to them that the role making they have engaged in is worthwhile, just as the boundary they have constructed and the community they have thus imagined are indeed real. Let us explore each of these three role-making practices in turn.

Telling Stigma Stories

Sociologists have also long observed that conflict, real or imagined, between groups often enhances a collective sense of in-group identity. "Conflict with other groups," writes Lewis Coser in his classic treatment of the topic, "contributes to the establishment and reaffirmation of the identity of the group and maintains its boundaries against the surrounding social world."[19] In the eyes of most American atheists, some level of conflict with the religious majority surrounding them is very real. As one national survey discovered, 41 percent of them report experiencing some form of religion-based discrimination within the previous five years, which is about three times more than what people in the more encompassing "none" category report.[20] Whereas only about one-third of my respondents say they "tend to dislike religious people," the vast preponderance experience themselves as not being particularly accepted or well liked by their believing compatriots—or at least not to the degree they think they would were they not atheists. Nearly nine in ten of them either strongly agree (41 percent) or agree (47 percent) with the statement "People who aren't religious are discriminated against in our society."

They do not settle for merely saying this. They also actually *portray* it by casting their experiences of stigma in narrative form and, in doing so, discursively maintain the symbolic boundary between the imagined community of atheists and the wider, oftentimes antagonistic public. These narratives, or what I call stigma stories, convey experiences, presented in the order of increasing intensity, of out-group hostility. Even beyond portraying these experiences, the tellers of these stories *use* them to assist with the work of role making, the work of constituting "the atheist" as an identity that is both distinctive and legitimate. Lastly, while certainly commonly expressed among atheists throughout the United States, this is the only role-making practice that varies regionally in that these stories, especially those of greater intensity, are more often heard among people living in the South and Midwest than from those living elsewhere.

Suspicions

The mildest type of stigma story is told by people who, in the absence of much clear evidence, are left with suspicions that they are perceived or even treated unfairly by others because of their lack of belief. "I wonder sometimes," "I don't think I'm paranoid, but I sometimes get the feeling," "I have the occasional sneaking suspicion"—phrases like these frequently preface such stories. "People have never been rude or insulting directly to my face," says Amber Binoche, a nurse from Virginia who attributes this partly to the South's trademark genteel culture. "Usually, when people have treated me differently, it's a sense of stiffness or discomfort I get from them. They become cooler, less friendly. It's difficult to pin down because they remain polite. No one's ever said anything overtly rude or confrontational to me, but you know how you can tell when someone is uncomfortable with you."

What Binoche explains in general terms, others convey with specific reference mostly to either the public sphere of the workplace or the private sphere of family relations. Concerning the first of these, social worker and former president of a Des Moines freethinker organization Rich Severs cannot help but wonder whether his being openly atheist has hurt his career. "I have applied for many jobs, for which I feel very qualified, and wonder if my background in nonbelief is a hindrance— particularly in social nonprofits where religion can be an undertone." Musing on this topic a bit more, he concludes, "I don't know for certain if I've been passed over because of my nonbeliefs, but I wouldn't be surprised. Unfortunately, it's always in the back of my mind. It's like the African American who didn't get the job and wonders if it's because of his race, or a woman because of her gender."

Like Severs, Gary Tarrett is also an "out" atheist in a midsized midwestern city. This is a newer development for Tarrett, though, since he has only just begun to identify as an atheist on his Facebook page within the past year or so. As he is a professional chemist, should his current coworkers or potential future employers discover this, it would almost certainly have no effect on his career prospects. Regrettably, the same cannot be said for what happened within his own family. For many years, his wife's grandfather read the Nativity story (preferring the Luke 2:1–20 account) to the extended family gathered together each Christmas Eve. As he advanced in age, he passed on this tradition to Tarrett who, honored to carry it on, was more than happy to read the story every year until the older man's death, and then for some years thereafter, that is, until this past year when he began posting atheism-related material on Facebook. He is not entirely sure about what happened next, but he has his suspicions. "Last Christmas, when it became time for the reading, it was announced that my brother-in-law would read the story," he recounts plaintively. "No warning. No discussion. My wife and kids knew what probably happened, and I have a feeling they're probably right."

Slights

By far, the most commonly told stigma stories are accounts of the ubiquitous slights—in the forms of disrespect, condescension, and affront—people endure for their nonbelief. Taking these three forms in order, consider Linda Rodgers, who left both her home state of Minnesota and her Lutheran faith in her early twenties. Now living in Southern California, she cannot recall a single time when she has been treated poorly or discriminated against because of her atheism, which she seldom hides from friends and family. She often feels disrespected, however. This occurs when she gets informed by certain family members that she has been "prayed for" or when they send her religiously themed birthday and holiday cards. Most recently it happened when, together with her family at a restaurant in her hometown, she was once again expected to join hands and bow her head during the saying of "grace" before mealtime. "It's awkward and embarrassing when it's in public," she explains. "But because it's what *they* believe, everybody must do it—regardless of *my* feelings or beliefs."

Other people talk about their not being taken seriously as atheists. This is especially ironic in Yasser Kibria's case. Raised in Egypt until his midteens, he spent his first few years in the United States as a "deeply religious" Muslim. Before too long, he found himself plagued by doubts. He struggled to live according to the tenets of Islam, he studied the Koran intently, and he even made contact with various imams and other Muslim scholars in order to find answers to his many religious questions. This difficult period lasted about three years until, finally, Kibria acknowledged to himself and eventually to others that he could no longer call himself a Muslim. What most of those others seem completely unable to acknowledge, he rues, is the seriousness of his journey. "I often get an insulting, condescending tone from some about how they will be vindicated when I get older. They tell me they were atheists when they were younger—and presumably less wise—but they grew out of it." He concludes, "I find such interactions to be incredibly offensive."

Whereas Kibria gets angry when he reflects upon interactions like these, this barely compares to the "utter rage" with which Doug Paulsen responded to the effrontery of his stepson. Despite raising him as his own, when his wife's born-again son became a father himself, he asked

Paulsen to sign an actual contract affirming that he would neither drink alcohol around his new grandson nor question the validity of the Bible in his presence, teach him about dinosaurs or evolution, or allow him to watch television programs pertaining to such topics as science, sexuality, and non-Christian worldviews.

Understandably, people often react to these sorts of slights with frustration, exasperation, and anger, and even, as Paulsen admits he did, by "flying off the handle." Just as often, others contend, a bit of humor (accompanying eye roll optional) seems to suffice. For instance, when research biologist Jason Boyer looks back at the time when, during an in-flight conversation, his fellow airline passenger insisted that theories about the Big Bang and evolution were simply lies told by scientists to disprove the existence of God, he just chuckled: "I felt like jumping out of the plane. Instead I just told him my job is already hard enough and I'm just too busy during the day to take God on!" The same is true of the woman whose soon-to-be mother-in-law threatened to skip the couple's "ethical humanist" wedding and then, when she did decide to show up, told others in attendance that the newlyweds were not truly married. "You have to laugh," she says while, true to form, laughing. "Thirty-nine years later, we kinda feel like we *are* married." Laughter, rather than rudeness, is also considered the best medicine by still another person who gets tired of religious people's presumptions that everyone sees things as they do. He gives the example of the times when acquaintances, and even a few strangers, have told him that his children are a blessing from God. "I know they mean well," he acknowledges, "but how would they like it if a Muslim told them that Allah had blessed *them* or if a Scientologist praised *their* kids for having so few thetans?"

Worth noting is that these are not atheists' only responses. Especially among the majority who told stigma stories of lesser intensity—involving suspicions and slights—one also discovers a good deal of forbearance, patience, and in a word, gracefulness. Perhaps no one exhibits this more fully than Leah Busey. Both of her parents died tragically when she was still in kindergarten, and this, along with her overall "questioning nature," has long made her wary of the untowardly "rosy image of a Santa God" to which she is often exposed. Living in the heart of the nation's Bible Belt has meant that she, not one to be bashful about expressing her religious views, has also felt her share of slights over the years:

People pass judgment, don't trust you, scrunch up their faces in disgust. They start arguments, make accusations, treat you as lesser, behave as if you're stupid, assume you're angry and jealous. They assume that you know nothing about religion and couldn't possibly understand their personal relationship with God. They assume you've never read the Bible, assume you have no moral compass and go about your life stealing, microwaving babies, and murdering people—all for kicks. They instantly take a condescending tone and laugh at you because they think you think people come from apes. To be perfectly honest, all this is extremely damaging, frustrating, and hurtful.

In the face of all this, like many respondents, Busey responds in ways that include humor and anger, while also exhibiting something more. As did quite a few other people, she wrote a thank-you note to me after filling out her questionnaire online. It reads, "As you may have noticed, I have grown to have a very negative perception of religion. I know that the person reading this is probably a Christian who is kind, compassionate, and respectful enough to open his mind up to differing views. And I appreciate that. I tried to be very candid, and I only hope I was able to voice my frustrations with religion in a considerate manner." If the dominant stereotype of atheists focuses more on their anger than their humor, then this is even more true of their frequent displays of gracefulness, which is every bit as apparent among them.

Difficulties

Stigma stories depicting the various difficulties associated with being atheists invariably fall into one of three categories. The first, told mainly by the searchers and especially responders described in the previous chapter, recount the often intense struggles they experienced in claiming their atheist identities in the face of other people's misunderstanding, judgment, and disapproval. Within the second category is the wide array of complications and exertions that can come with being nonreligious within a religious culture. A community college instructor was accused by one of her students—who knew she was an atheist—of giving him a poor grade because of her alleged bias against his religious convictions. A school board candidate, right before Election Day, discovered that his opponent took some atheism-related material from his Facebook page, copied it onto a homemade flier, and posted it throughout their small, predominantly Evangelical town. A parent complained to her daughter's public school principal (to no avail) about ongoing Wednesday morning prayer sessions, and another parent requested (to no avail) some accommodation for her son who was uncomfortable with the religious tenor of his Boy Scout troop. A young man looked for romance on various dating websites only to discover his nonbelief to be a "deal breaker" for the women with whom he chatted. A mother preferred that her nine-year-old twins remain clear of religious instruction and, as a result, has experienced a growing tension between herself and her Catholic husband who, she fears, may be contemplating divorce. One hears such stories over and over again.

Whereas these are more commonly told by people living within relatively conservative parts of the country, a third category is heard from seemingly every corner. These are stories about the nuisance of self-censorship, the everyday strain of needing to be on guard when interacting with others. Marilyn Ahern, a thirty-something accountant who works in downtown Chicago, expresses this in the same exasperated tone that many others use. "I see religious words, phrases, poems, and pictures every day. But if I say something atheistic, I'm accused of being intolerant, ignorant, and cruel to those who are religious. I find this absolutely ridiculous and infuriating," she complains. "Politicians are allowed to say that women who have abortions are murderers and that gay people are an abomination. Yet, if I say something about how religion causes people to fly planes into buildings, I'm a horrible person who's exploiting the victims of 9/11." While most of Ahern's friends are "believers of one sort of another," many other atheists address the burden of navigating the waters of giving no offense to religious people by taking a different tack—away from believers of any sort and toward the calmer waters of the like-minded. Deidre Jones, a graduate student living in Memphis, is a good example here. She has some churchgoing friends, she says. At the same time, she finds associating with fellow nonbelievers to be "*sooooo* much easier":

> Around atheist friends, I don't have to "watch myself" [uses finger quotes]. I can freely express any idea about atheism or religion and

not have to fear being falsely accused of something. . . . With religious people, if you merely criticize or critique their beliefs in any way or try to ask them logical questions, they take offense and accuse you of attacking them. This always leads to arguments in which the religious person doesn't want to risk losing their faith by thinking about any logical questions—probably because they know that logic conflicts with their faith—and thus one can't carry on a civilized discussion. So, when I hang out with religious friends, I'm not entirely myself and I feel somewhat on edge because I have to make sure I don't say anything offensive.

Incivilities

Of course, not everybody is as inclined as is Jones to watch themselves and thus refrain from saying anything offensive. Stigma stories featuring unapologetically offensive believers are not at all uncommon. Anthony Marchetti's story is about the time when, as a high schooler, he was invited to participate in the Bible study group on campus. "I declined the invitation. I wasn't rude about it," he insists, "I simply said I didn't believe in it." This, he remembers, brought about a tongue-lashing from his pious classmates and, when he tried to explain his own views, was met with assurances that he was succumbing to "the devil's deception" and that "hell awaits you." A few days later, when returning from physical education class, he discovered that someone had burned a cross onto his backpack.

Bob Marsh's story is a good reminder that this sort of incivility is not limited to high school bullying. Being a "proud and vocal" atheist was never an issue when he lived in Philadelphia. It was only when he opened his own law practice in the small Ohio town where his wife had been raised that he ran into some problems. At first, his car—which sported an atheist bumper sticker with a Darwin fish—was "keyed" by some passerby. This may have been a random act of vandalism, he thought—that is until, passionate about First Amendment issues, he began to write letters to the editor of his local newspaper about topics pertaining to church-state separation. "Despite my phone number and address being unlisted," he says, shaking his head in obvious frustration, "I've gotten a few threatening phone calls and postcards after some of those letters made it into the paper. Hateful e-mails, of course, are always coming in."

As these two examples illustrate, most of these stories depict experiences of religious people's incivility, which take the form of either bullying or disdain. On rare occasions they even verge on the comical. "It's probably best to keep a sense of humor about situations like this," suggests Aaron Epstein, an undergrad at a large midwestern university, when recalling the time someone "literally threw the book at me!" This was one of the Gideon's Bible distributors who seemed to show up on campus just about every fall:

> When we were walking by, he offered me a Bible, which I politely turned down and then explained why. As soon as the word "atheist" left my mouth, the guy's entire demeanor changed toward me and toward my friend who happened to be a pagan. So he proceeded to yell at both of us about how we were going to go to hell and how we needed to repent and maybe Jesus would forgive us. I said—again, politely—that I'd never do such a thing, that I thought he was being very rude and unchristian, and that I hoped he'd have a nice day despite being unable to convert us. As my friend and I went on our way, I felt something hit my foot. When I turned around to see, there was a Gideon's Bible at my feet and there was that guy staring at my friend and me as if we were the worst people on the face of the planet.

Accounts of suspicions, slights, and difficulties abound among the people I interviewed. On the other hand, stigma stories about incivilities like these, which typically involve some mixture of outspoken atheism plus religious conservatism (if not fanaticism), are much rarer. Only about one in twenty told stigma stories of this sort. Regardless, because virtually all of my respondents know of such stories or are at least aware that nonbelievers are occasionally subject to the sort of poor treatment they describe, they still function as important boundary markers for their imagined community.

Rejections

The same is the case with the severest of stigma stories, those that detail experiences of being rejected by others. Some talk about their atheism becoming known in one way or another and, subsequently, their getting the cold shoulder from churchgoing colleagues at the office. Others report that they no longer receive Christmas cards from certain people or find that they have been "de-friended" by people with whom they had been in contact through Facebook. Still others grumble about no longer being asked to chaperone the annual Boy Scouts camping trip or about getting dumped at an early stage of what looked to be a promising romantic relationship.

Hardest of all are the rejections by friends or family members. Just ask Terry Schmidt. He has experienced plenty of rejection because of his atheism. Born into a nonreligious household in mid-1950s Mississippi, his classmates considered him something of an odd duck. This never really bothered him since it just struck him as being "the price of being a hell of a lot smarter than they were." Even later, when he was three-quarters of the way into a twenty-year army career, he had no problem brushing off Vice President George H. W. Bush's purported comment to a reporter about people like him. "I don't know that atheists should be considered as citizens, nor should they be considered patriots," he replied when asked about atheists in the United States. "This is one nation under God."[21] Given his stellar service record, Schmidt confesses to finding this statement "pretty mind-boggling," but not one that had much of an emotional impact on him.

That emotional reaction occurred several years later. It was the weekend he stayed at his longtime friend's house on the occasion of a local motorcycle rally. Not having seen him for a while, he felt uncomfortable at first. "He had been getting more and more religious over the years since his divorce," Schmidt explains. "The room I was staying in had Bibles on the table and religious verses on the walls. He knew I was an atheist, so I thought it was pretty rude, especially since I wouldn't put atheist reading material in his room if he were staying with me. But it was his house, and I didn't mind." Things changed the next morning, to be sure. He and his friend were having breakfast at a nearby restaurant when a Jehovah's Witness entered with the intent of distributing some religious pamphlets. As he placed one on their table and assured them that "Jesus can save you," Schmidt, out of reflex, muttered in reply, "He probably didn't even exist." "I figured that, since I wasn't in my friend's house at the time, then I should be free to speak my mind. So, he asked, 'What did you say?' And when I told him, he stood up, wagged his finger in my face, and said, 'That's it. I want you out of my house.' Then he walked off."

That was nearly fifteen years ago, and Schmidt has not been in contact with his friend since. This, he confides, has been really hard on him. Usually harder still is when the rejection comes from family, which is what Jerry Krause has experienced. Not uncommon for conservative Baptists in North Central Texas, his life "really revolved around church." What was uncommon about him was the intensity of his faith combined with his charisma and leadership abilities. When he was in high school, he was president of his school's Fellowship of Christian Athletes chapter, he helped lead four mission trips to Mexico, he gave devotional talks at a weekly Bible study he organized at his school—with a regular attendance of about five hundred students—and he had every intention of becoming a preacher when he got older. This was his plan when, considering Abilene Christian University to be too religiously liberal, he enrolled in a more rigorously Evangelical small college out of state.

It was there that he was caught sleeping in his fiancée's dorm room—an "unforgiveable transgression" at this particular institution—and, with her, was promptly expelled. This unexpectedly precipitated a lot of soul-searching. Krause began to realize that "my whole Christian life was public" and that he actually lacked a strong, interior sense of religious conviction. "That was the moment when I stopped lying to people and to myself, and I really started to investigate." From there, he discovered that he honestly did not believe in certain foundational Christian doctrines. He began to think that much of the Bible was totally implausible. He realized, especially in light of his increasingly relaxed lifestyle, that he did not respect many of the moral norms of his upbringing—and, before long, he had to admit to himself that he no longer believed in God.

Thus began a series of rejections. He married his fiancée, but complaining that they were "growing apart," she divorced him three years later. From an impressive eight hundred or so friends on Facebook during his college years, he now has about sixty. Of the six groomsmen at his wedding, only two remain in contact with him. And when he told his parents he would not be going back to church, they were absolutely devastated. After no contact for a few months, they at least now have a "very surface-level relationship," although his mother recently told him that "she would have preferred that [he] had told her that [he] was gay rather than an atheist." What hurt most was the reaction from his big brother, to whom he had looked up for most of his life. They were at a Texas Rangers baseball game when his brother kept asking him about "where I was with my faith." Reticent to address the topic, Krause remembers what happened next "like it was yesterday":

> So, I told him that I'm not going back to church, I don't believe in the Christian Bible, and in fact, I think it's bullshit. . . . I remember it was about the third or fourth inning, and he said, "Well, that's not the brother I know. If you believe that way, you're not my brother." So, I came back and asked if we can't just agree to disagree. But then he said, "I'd rather sacrifice my relationship with you on this earth for a relationship with you after death." Those were his words, and that's what he's doing.

That was a 2009 Rangers game. Since then, they have had "separate Christmases and Thanksgivings," he has never met his brother's four-year-old son, and the whole situation has taken quite an emotional toll on Krause. He does have a sense of perspective on things. "I know I had to do what I had to do," he says with more than a hint of sadness, "but I've also gained over fifty pounds and my personality has changed a lot—and a lot of that is just from loneliness, frustration, and depression."

Accentuating the Irrational

Atheists' stigma stories are often compelling and, as Jerry Krause's family situation indicates, sometimes nothing short of wrenching. Like the identity acquisition narratives presented in the last chapter, these narratives are also significant even if one does not take them at face value. This is worth keeping in mind because, frankly, it is hard to know how much exaggeration and selective memory inform their telling. And what of their tellers? Do they all act as "politely" as Aaron Epstein insists he did when dealing with that representative from Gideon International? Are they all as "respectful" as Terry Schmidt says he was as he settled into his friend's guestroom replete with Bibles on the table and scripture verses covering the walls? Have none of them—even on the rarest of occasions—succumbed to a moment of weakness and slighted a pious friend or family member, or even made someone's life just a bit more difficult on account of their religious convictions? These are valid questions, of course. What I want to emphasize here is that much more certain than the true-to-life validity of these stories is the function they perform in terms of situating nonbelievers within an imagined community.

This is equally true of a second practice that contributes to this symbolic boundary maintenance: casting believers as irrational. Along with their telling stigma stories, atheists' use of the "irrational other" frame is another example of what Anthony Cohen describes as the maintenance of a community's boundaries through the "manipulation of its symbols." Once again, this portrayal does not need to be entirely true to be truly effective in helping to reinforce intergroup distinctions. Even though people of faith are typically depicted as unthinking dullards and fundamentalist yahoos in the New Atheist literature and elsewhere, they are typically no less rational in their everyday lives—including, as addressed in chapter 1, their religious lives—than anyone else. That reality notwithstanding, to one degree or another, each and every respondent I spoke with engaged in this practice. As we will see, they do so with a kind of subtlety that is in short supply within the New Atheist canon. Also important to emphasize it that, when they point to believers' irrationality, they assert themselves as not merely passive—albeit polite and respectful—objects of out-group hostility. They do so as active subjects. They do to believers something akin to what believers so often do to them.

What they do is perhaps best described in terms most often used by social psychologists. Michael Hogg and Dominic Abrams, for example, explain how human beings deal with the complex, chaotic world around them by engaging in "categorization" such that they simplify matters for themselves. In other words, imagining a world inhabited by broadly defined categories of people just makes life more manageable. By making comparisons among such categories, people are better able to determine which of these seem most suitable to them and thus could feasibly be internalized to consolidate subjectively meaningful identities for themselves. "Basically," they argue, "the categorization process produces stereotypic perceptions, that is the perception or judgement of all members of a social category or group as sharing some characteristic which distinguishes them from some other social group."[22]

Whereas moral rectitude seems to be the shared characteristic religious people often highlight when distinguishing themselves from atheists, for atheists it is, without doubt, rationality. Nearly all of my respondents say that the term "intellectual" describes them either "very" (67 percent) or "somewhat" (31 percent) well. The same goes for the term "freethinker," which also, they say, fits them "very" (77 percent) or "somewhat" (20 percent) well. And as we will discuss more fully in the next chapter, their respect for scientific method and reasoning is nearly unbounded. About 85 percent of them agree that "science will eventually provide the solutions to most of our problems." As important as such viewpoints are, symbolizing this overall commitment to rationality is not merely a function of saying yes to *this* category of person or yes to *this* imagined community. It is also about saying no to *that* category/community, which is helped along by what Hogg and Abrams call "accentuation." By this they mean the inevitable exaggeration of the characteristic that purportedly differentiates one category of people from the other. As they put it, "The automatic accentuation effect which categorization produces is overlayed by a motivated attempt to amplify *even more* the ingroup/outgroup difference on those dimensions which evaluatively favor the ingroup."[23] Nonbelievers, as Hogg and Abrams suggest, have considerable motivation for accentuating believers' irrationality. Doing so assures them that, when compared to an irrational other, and despite all the stigma directed their way, they are nonetheless the right *kind* of person and that atheists as a social category can rightly be imagined as being synonymous with a "community of reason."

Cultural Sources: Believers as Insufficiently Equipped to Be Rational

Atheists' understanding of themselves as particularly rational becomes clear when, in the face of so much religious practice and devotion, they inevitably account for the resiliency of faith in terms of a disconcerting paucity of reason. Although many of them just throw up their hands in either censorious scorn or dismayed confusion about this, more often than not they, true to form, offer thought-out reasons for why this would be the case. These reasons fall into three sorts, each of which points to a distinct set of sources of the irrationality that purportedly afflicts and largely defines the religious.

The first are cultural sources. Here it is helpful to think of culture, as sociologist Ann Swidler describes it, as a kind of "tool kit" replete with the internalized ideas, habits, and skills that differently tooled people draw upon to both make sense of their lives and determine how best to act in the world.[24] For instance, many people's access to such cultural tools as ideas about the desirability of the American dream, habits of disciplined work, and good "people skills" go a long way toward equipping them for successful careers. But such tools are unevenly distributed, which partly explains why people experience varying levels of success. Although they never explicitly reference Swidler's work, according to the implied logic of many atheists, this sort of unevenness is also key to understanding why so many of their fellow citizens are believers. They, my respondents suggest, frequently lack important cultural tools—namely, critical thinking and religious literacy—which essentially leaves them insufficiently equipped to utilize their rational faculties and thus escape the bonds of religious adherence.

When people bemoan the absence of critical thinking in believers' cultural tool kits, they usually place the blame on public education. Sometimes their focus is more on the public than the educational system itself. They often suggest that students, shaped by a wider cultural milieu, are not receptive to learning critical thinking skills because they are too distracted: "It seems like it's too much to ask anyone to turn off their TVs and iPhones long enough to actually turn on their brains!" Or they are unduly prone to boredom: "Learning to think can be tough sometimes. You know, it's slow, and it takes persistence. It's not going to happen if kids need to be stimulated or entertained to keep them engaged." Or it is because students largely see education in economically instrumental terms: "For a lot of them [students], going to school is what people do in order to buy a Lexus and a McMansion in the suburbs." Most of the time, however, it is how educational institutions go about their work that draws people's ire. Only a few years out of high school in Lexington, Kentucky, himself, Doug Freeley represents this perspective quite well:

> I'm not sure I can speak for the entire American educational system, but from my experience, classes in public schools seem to be much more geared toward teaching students *what* to think instead of *how* to think.

In science class, we learned the different facts, theories, and discoveries that science had already brought us instead of studying the actual process of the scientific method in a way that would teach us to value the kind of thinking that science is really all about. So, we learned more about the knowledge the world has already accumulated instead of learning the tools used to expand that knowledge—such as critical thinking, which just happens to fly in the face of religion.

Like so many of my interviewees, Freeley is convinced that, if religious people were better tooled to think critically, they would be as dubious as he is about what he later derides as, using an occasionally heard phrase, religion's "house of cards." Interestingly, while many people insist that critical thinking could knock this house down rather easily, about as many say the same for religious literacy. Anne Newton, the woman who at once dreamed of becoming a biblical archeology professor, definitely shares this view. "It doesn't help that our public schools aren't allowed to discuss religion," she complains. "Without open dialogue, we'll never grow as a culture. That's what I wish for most—more reasoned and civilized discussion and debate of religious and nonreligious viewpoints." If more people were religiously informed, this line of reasoning implies, then one of two things would likely occur. They would either realize on their own that religious faith is untenable or be apt to discuss religious matters more openly and, in the process, have this demonstrated to them by others. Craig McCloud, a firefighter in San Jose, touches on both of these possibilities. In his estimation, atheism is all about "an embrace of evidence and rationality in how I try to live my life." When he turns his attention to the question of why so many Americans are people of faith, however, he focuses less on a lack of evidence or rationality and much more on their lack of religious literacy:

I think much of the persistence of religious belief in this country boils down to people's ignorance about religion itself. People are raised religious and perceive this as part of their identity and, therefore, questioning one's beliefs is heavily discouraged. People don't read the Bible intellectually. But they're encouraged to read it in a biased manner—to get closer to God or something like that. That is, assuming that they've actually read it; I'll bet 90 percent of them haven't. If they did, they'd see the same serious problems I saw when I was younger. On top of this, it's impolite to question people's religious beliefs, and it's really impolite to challenge them to defend what they believe. Since so few of them actually learn about their faith—and thinking about why they believe what they believe—then any intellectual challenge is perceived as being an attack on their intelligence or on who they are as a person. So, they don't have to take that challenge seriously.

A widespread lack of religious knowledge means that faith tends to get reduced to being essentially a dimension of personhood, and since personal identity is deemed so sacrosanct in contemporary American culture, it is thus impervious to the sorts of challenges that could shake its foundations. The upshot is that, as with a generalized lack of critical thinking, believers' dearth of religious literacy renders them inadequately equipped to be what, by comparison, atheists are quite sure they are—rational.

Social Sources: Believers as Unable to Be Rational

Rather than stressing an absence of cultural tools, other people draw the symbolic boundary between themselves and believers by highlighting the presence of social institutions that naturalize and thus perpetuate religious sensibilities. These institutions are thought of as being, to use a term from social theorist Antonio Gramsci, "hegemonic" in the sense that they operate according to certain taken-for-granted understandings of the world that then come to be accepted by the those who participate within them. This is how arbitrary and sometimes highly problematic ways of behaving and thinking rise to the level of unquestioned "common sense" whereby alternative ways cease even to be imaginable by the majority of people.[25] Instead of saying believers are ill equipped to be rational, atheists who follow this logic conceive of them as being basically unable. They cannot be rational about religion, in other words, because they so buy into commonsensical understandings of the world—in effect mistaking *a* specific, historically contingent way of thinking and behaving for *the* way—that they see no pressing need to exercise their rational faculties when it comes to any ideology, much less to matters of religious belief.

Occasionally, people talk about how economic institutions keep believers from thinking too hard about religion. One way they do this, as mentioned above, is by keeping the public so entertained, so absorbed by their TVs and iPhones, and so determined to buy that Lexus and McMansion that they are simply too distracted to think critically (even if equipped to do so) about what they believe and why. Another, more subtle, way is by shaping patterns of religious thinking and behavior such that they come to emulate the existent patterns within economic institutions. Religious institutions, they suggest, act like economic ones, and consequently, they keep their customers satisfied. "The churches are like big businesses," opined one former Evangelical. "They're all about the bottom line: keeping asses in the pews, not making people too uncomfortable, giving them feelings of being squeaky clean, saved, holy, better than and more important than they really are. Once people have all this, then the churches will have created a strong brand. As we all know, people are loyal to that!" Once they go for Skippy, the argument goes, consumers need not do much more thinking about other brands or even whether they should be eating peanut butter in the first place. Moreover, apart from the behavior of religious institutions, even the way individuals have come to think about what it means to be religious has been distorted by economic rationality. As firefighter Craig McCloud put it, religion is part of people's identity. Others go further by noting that, rather than spend time thinking rationally about religion, believers treat it like yet another commodity they consume to enhance their sense of self. "People buy art so they can say they're sophisticated. They buy clothes to be stylish. They buy 'Black Lives Matter' T-shirts so they can be politically correct," said one interviewee. "That's what faith is for a lot of them. They buy it so they get to say, 'Hey, I'm deep' or 'Look at me, I'm a respectable person.'"

More often, it is the state that gets mentioned as an institution most responsible for religious hegemony. Despite the First Amendment, atheists claim (or just imply) time and again, the state does a much better job at protecting the "free exercise" of religion than it does in helping to avoid a de facto (if not de jure) "establishment" of religious symbolism and morality. She says she is not very politically active, yet Abby Cullen-Smith is still very concerned about the state's role in promoting religious sensibilities:

Because of acts of Congress that have bombarded the country with instances of Christianity, because of what's on our money, because of what's
in our oaths—it creates a lot of groupthink. When Americans are forced
to see these establishments of religion, which are forbidden by the Constitution, or when they hear that our country was founded on Christian
principles—a common misperception—this all contributes to the overwhelming support for Christianity. So, when it appears that a majority
of people believe in something, then people end up going along with the
crowd. We want to be socially accepted. . . . When no person in Congress,
let alone a presidential candidate, has ever come out as an atheist or an
agnostic, then we end up finding *un*-belief to be *un*-acceptable!

If the state has a role in legitimating "groupthink"/"going along with
the crowd" at the expense of rational thought, even this is a relatively
minor one compared to the part played by the family, the most frequently cited institution. Barry Karowitz, a self-described "avid reader,"
talks about two books that were pivotal for opening his eyes and allowing him to see beyond his Jewish upbringing. The first, Plato's *Republic*, made him realize that, like the people depicted in the "allegory of
the cave," he was just staring at shadows and needed to climb out into
the light of day in order to look at reality straight on. The second, religion scholar Huston Smith's classic introduction to the world's major
faiths titled *The Religions of Man* (reissued as *The World's Religions*) was,
Karowitz recalls, "probably a bigger influence on my thinking about religion than anything I ever learned in Hebrew school." Given the topics
of these two books—public philosophy and world religions—one might
imagine that he would highlight Americans' dearth of both critical
thinking and religious literacy as the source of their widespread faithfulness. Instead, like so many others, he looks to the institution of the
family. "Because it's what their parents taught them, most never think to
question their specific beliefs," he explains. "Evidence of this can be seen
in the number of born-again Christians whose newly discovered faith
just happens to be that of their parents. Just as it was no accident that,
when I was younger, I truly revered the Torah." Reese Carlita elaborates
on this view. We all eventually reach the "age of reason," he says, but the
likelihood that we will be able to live rationally as adults is largely shaped
by our primary socialization within the family:

Most American children have been, as a matter of family and cultural tradition, inculcated into the religion of their parents. Early exposure to religion appears to be critical in creating a religious individual. If one can make it to the age of reason without ever having adopted a religious belief, the odds seem stacked against adopting a religion later on as an adult. My wife's family is a great example. She comes from a multigenerational family of atheists. Consequently, neither she nor her siblings have ever felt any need to investigate religion or felt as if something was missing from their lives. They all see religion as just a primitive set of beliefs that are more of a cultural affliction and a political tool than anything else. Now, my family illustrates the flip side to this idea. We all had early childhood exposure to religion, and therefore, one would expect it to be harder to completely break free. And so it was. Out of the five of us, I'm the only one who broke free.

Personal Sources: Believers as Unwilling to Be Rational

People like Karowitz and Carlita, especially the searchers and responders among them, often expend considerable effort in emerging from the depths of illusion to acquire critical thinking skills. Many, like Karowitz, are even willing to take the time to become religiously literate. It is also extremely common to hear accounts of atheists who have struggled, as Carlita puts it, to "break free" from the grip of taken-for-granted verities, from worldviews accepted as commonsensical by others and, of course, from the religious socialization they so typically experienced within their own families. Hence, in light of so many hard-won success stories, even though Karowitz and Carlita lean toward the view that people of faith are essentially unable to be rational, it makes sense that many other atheists would tilt in another direction. The fault, these others contend, actually has less to do with cultural tools or societal influences, and is much more a function of religious people being unwilling to exert themselves by thinking rationally. Reasons for this unwillingness are straightforward enough. For one thing, as evidenced by atheists' stigma stories, it is oftentimes difficult to go against the grain of a religious culture. "If we've learned anything from Socrates," Karowitz mused while discussing *The Republic*, "it's that the 'examined life' isn't for wimps." For another, the incentives for not bothering to climb out of the cave and breaking free are enormous. Terry Schmidt still fumes about being kicked out of his friend's house, "but I get it," he says. "Religion offers rewards and the assurance that those you don't like will be punished after death, although there's no confirmation of either of these ideas," he explains. "Some people take great comfort knowing they'll be rewarded while others will suffer. It's the same reason why people buy lottery tickets—just the hope of a reward gives them comfort. It's a way out of the real world and all its problems."

This is the usual story line. People give a few dollars for a lottery ticket, and they get the hope of winning. People give up a connection to the real world replete with its all-too-confirmable problems, and they get the comfort of living in an imaginary world with its potential, though nonconfirmable, rewards. There is an irony here. People of faith are unwilling to be rational, this account suggests, because they are essentially what sociologists call "rational actors" who, at various levels of self-awareness, weigh costs and benefits before choosing a course of action.[26] They choose to be religious—understood as giving up rationality—because, in a sense, it is rational for them to do so: they get compensated with so much in return.

Just as none of my respondents explicitly referred to culture as a "tool kit" or actually used the term "hegemony," no one articulated a detailed rational actor theory either. Still, one hears this basic story line with great frequency. So, what do believers get? According to onetime Evangelical Angela Harold, "They enjoy the community, the worship, the comforts of a faith community, the networking opportunities, the sense of belonging. They enjoy the rituals and customs. They like what it brings to their families and friendships. They think it's good for their children. They derive satisfaction from high holy days and from sacrifice, and also from the sense of identity that comes with all this." Then what do they give willingly in return? Their rational faculties, she says. "In a life filled with uncertainty, I think people really like tenets they can accept as known and incontrovertible. The mindset is actually captured in Proverbs 3:5: 'Trust in the Lord with all your heart and lean not on your own understanding.'" This same calculus of give (rational faculties, "your own understanding," etc.) and then get (comfort, community, etc.) shows up repeatedly in conversations with interviewees. In a particularly eloquent version, Rich McCutcheon, an ex-Catholic explains:

I think most people believe in religion because of the social aspects. For the price of believing in God, among other various elements depending on the specific religion, you get quite a lot back on that investment. You have a social group of like-minded people, most likely of the same socioeconomic class and ethnicity. These people probably see the world similarly. Around that social group a lot of family-centric activities take place, which is certainly a good thing. The lessons endemic to religion are certainly positive reinforcement for helping to rear young. Didn't someone once say, "It takes a village"? Church communities are that village now. Religion helps provide people's lives with meaning and helps instill a sense that somewhere, somehow *someone* is steering this ship. That is extremely comforting. . . . I think ultimately they gain a lot and are thus willing to stomach some degree of absurdity.

Not unexpectedly, atheists who emphasize believers' underprovisioned cultural tool kits complain bitterly about Americans' poor educations, anti-intellectualism, lack of religious literacy, and the like. It is also of little surprise that those who emphasize the power of social institutions should sometimes quite acerbically lament, to use some regularly heard terms, the broad-based "indoctrination," "conformism," and "herd mentality" they are said to engender. Yet, one of the most interesting things about those who highlight people's unwillingness to be rational is their relative lack of bitterness and acerbity. There are exceptions, of course. One hears sarcasm on occasion: "I just wish people would outgrow their infantile dependence on celestial daddies and mommies and their incessant need to feel connected to some imaginary friend who'll save them!" Some anger, especially directed at people who bring their private convictions into the public's business, also flares up at times: "The phrase 'fuck you' is overused in our culture. But it can be appropriate in a world of head-in-the-sand creationism, holier-than-thou homophobia, and one flat-world fatwa after another!" All this notwithstanding, a sizeable majority of those atheists who talk about others' unwillingness to be rational nevertheless, as Terry Schmidt put it, "get it." Despite their talk about faith as springing, to some extent, from *individual* choice and thus a matter of *personal* responsibility, they generally show less recrimination and far more understanding—and even empathy—toward the religious than one would expect.

"They're scared about dying, about the abyss that awaits them." "People want to know what a good life is; they want to know how to be good, and most of all, they need to know that they *are* good." "It's part of our evolutionary wiring to explain the unexplainable, right?" Instances of my interviewees getting it are plentiful. Many of them were themselves religious at some point in their lives. Certainly most have wrestled with questions related to death, meaning, morality, and other less readily comprehensible facets of their lives. All this is to say that, just as atheists maintain the symbolic boundary between themselves and believers by accentuating the irrational, they also typically have some understanding that irrationality has its reasons, and hence, they often empathize with those "willing to stomach some degree of absurdity." Rich McCutcheon certainly can. "Now that I've thought it through and finally freed myself from the bondage of religion," he says with a heavy sigh, "I'm at the point where I sometimes feel sorry for the people who are still trapped by their religious beliefs."

Feeling One's Way

Many scholars who talk to people like McCutcheon would very likely be more attentive to the first, pre-sigh part of this closing comment than to the second. This would be understandable. That he "thought it through" seems to reflect atheists' frequently observed proclivity for, well, thinking things through. As we have already seen, one indication of this is how often, when faced with religious quandaries (sometimes even as children), people take it upon themselves to dive into all sorts of books pertaining to theological, philosophical, and scientific topics or even search for answers by reading difficult sacred scriptures (usually the Bible) before turning to atheism. Furthermore, as mentioned earlier, nearly all of my respondents are comfortable with using the terms "intellectual" or "freethinker" to describe themselves. Findings from other studies tell a similar tale. One of these points to "intellectualism" as a personality trait broadly esteemed among atheists.[27] This no doubt helps to explain why atheism and higher educational attainment are positively correlated in the United States.[28] Atheism also seems to be correlated with a specific manner of thinking. Concludes another recent study on this very point, atheists are "more likely to employ a cognitive

processing style emphasizing logic and rationality at the expense of intu-
ition."[29] Still another emphasizes their "preference for logic and their
enjoyment of rational reasoning."[30] Finally, as psychologists Bruce Hunsberger and Bob Altemeyer matter-of-factly summarize the consensus
viewpoint in their widely read study, atheists are, generally speaking,
"quite intelligent."[31]

The only problem here is that simply determining McCutcheon to be
quite intelligent, while also quite true, can end up leaving much unsaid.
He himself goes on to say that he sometimes feels empathy toward the
religious ("I sometimes feel sorry . . ."), yet such feelings seldom become
part of the scholarly discussion of atheism. Remedying this means that,
at the same time that we examine how atheists look beyond themselves
both in parlaying out-group hostility into in-group identification and in
accentuating the purported irrationality of the religious other, we must
pay similar attention to how they also look within themselves. Especially when the believers in their lives neither shoot stigmatizing glares
at them nor appear to be entirely opaque to reason's gleaming rays, they
are then apt to look within and enlist their own feelings as a means for
shoring up the symbolic boundary that distinguishes themselves from
their fellow citizens. These feelings, as theorists since Charles Darwin
and Sigmund Freud have claimed about emotions in general, function to
remind people of their own core priorities and attitudes.[32] Atheists rely
on such emotional signals. As we saw in the last chapter, these can be
organized into acquisition narratives that account for the initial impetus
and degree of effort required—in short, what if felt like—to claim their
identities as atheists. They can also be experienced as discrete feelings.
These essentially indicate to them that their project of role making is on
the right track and also provide a kind of affective validation that they
are part of a larger, imagined community of people whose experience is
basically similar to their own. "It is through emotionality, imagination,
sympathy, fellow-feeling, and revealed self-feelings," argues sociologist
Norman Denzin astutely, "that persons come to know themselves and
one another."[33]

So, then, what are these feelings? They vary, certainly. Empowerment,
attunement, awe, excitement, happiness—these feelings all get expressed
now and then. However, as McCutcheon suggests when referencing the
"*bondage* of religion" as well as those still "*trapped* by their religious

beliefs," none comes even close to being mentioned as routinely as the powerful feeling of being free. Brought up Lutheran in a small South Dakota town, Madeline Potts is now a high school English teacher in Chicago. She actually wrote a poem about her atheism—titled "I Am Free"—and this feeling comes out in her everyday speech as well:

> I feel empowered as an atheist. I have no need to grovel before an imaginary being for my salvation. I don't have to do mental gymnastics to try and harmonize irrational religious doctrine with observable realities. I am free to follow the evidence and find truth without fear of supernatural consequences. I also feel that I can be more just. I have given myself permission to let my judgment supersede all other authority. That means I am free to determine right from wrong based on how actions affect sentient beings and not on some arbitrary diction or interpretation of the perceived offense taken by an invisible being. I am hopeful and encouraged that we can make real progress in bettering humanity through the amazing power of science and reason.

Philosophers sometimes make a distinction between positive and negative freedom.[34] The former, which emphasizes taking control of one's life and realizing one's own fundamental convictions through action, is mostly what Potts talks about here. She is "free to follow the evidence and find truth" by her own lights and according to her own authority, not in accordance with the imagined authority wielded by some "invisible being." What is now true of her intellectual life is equally true of her ethical life: she feels "free to determine right from wrong" on her own and in her own way.

Unlike Potts, the majority of people I spoke to lean more in the direction of articulating feelings of freedom in the negative sense, as freedom from the previously experienced religious constraints that kept them from flourishing as human beings. The list of these constraints seems interminable. Some people, like the former Muslim Yasser Kibria, talk about their newfound freedom from *otherworldliness*:

> I had been really depressed because of my religion. But after my conversion to atheism in 2006, I felt incredibly free and immensely joyful. I saw my religion, with its unexplained prohibitions, like a cage that limited my

potential and pleasure as a human being. So, I felt very resentful toward it. Afterward, I was very happy to partake in premarital sex, dancing, music, and the ability to interact socially with homosexuals and believers of different faiths without denouncing them. . . . My atheism has focused my outlook more toward the present. Previously, I drew solace about my depression from the perverse hope that everything would improve once I die. Once I die, I would be furnished with the finest delicacies in heaven and the people who wronged me would suffer hellfire seventy times hotter than anything found in our universe. That belief encouraged me to take pain under the promise that it will all be better only after I succumb to death. Changing that outlook allowed me to focus more on my life on earth rather than ignoring the present in favor of an imaginary future.

Others have come to feel free from *divine judgment*:

I found the Christian idea of God to be quite depressing. I would much rather believe there is no heaven than believe that, if there is a heaven, then there's also a hell where people are eternally tortured simply for believing the wrong things. I don't understand how anyone who is sympathetic to the needs and feelings of others can possibly find comfort in such a belief. I also feel happy because I don't have to worry about disappointing some perfect being or about how my mistakes might be punished some judgmental deity. I can live my life according to my own morals now.

Or they feel free from what was once their own narrow-minded *judgmentalism*:

I get to have awesome gay friends as well as straight friends because I don't care who anyone has sex with. I get to have friends who aren't just Christians, or any one religion, because I don't care what anyone's religion is. Basically, I'm not required to be a bigot or a racist or a sexist because some religion tells me I should be. I just get to be a humanist. Of course, I have bad days when things just go shitty all day long. But mostly, I'm a happy, positive person who loves life. I have an incredible life of a few close friends, a close-knit family, and a husband who knows how to hit my G-spot because his religion doesn't dictate that sex is for procreation only!

Still others feel free from dogmatically prescribed *illusions*:

> The first word I think of to describe being an atheist is free. Free from all
> the negatives of blind faith—free from the suppression of thought, free
> from the constraints of living within the tenets of an ancient dogma, free
> to learn as much as I can possibly squeeze into my brain, free to change
> that knowledge when new evidence presents itself. . . . I think a great
> analogy for my feeling is presented in the movie *The Matrix*. I equate
> those who are strong believers to those stuck in a computer program
> blissfully unaware of the truth of their existence. Whereas I align myself
> with those who have been freed and are able to see the world as it truly is.
> It's such a feeling of freedom to see it that way.

Some feel free from undue *authority*:

> I just came to realize that all these priests I had looked up to and
> sometimes feared knew a lot about how to preside at mass or how to
> do a baptism or give a dying person last rites or whatever. But I real-
> ized, they didn't know any more than I did about any of the important
> things—about life and death, love and loss. I gave them all this author-
> ity they didn't really deserve. I'm liberated from that now. I don't hear
> their voices in my mind any more. I'm free from it all. I'm in charge
> now.

Others feel free from *clannishness*:

> Everything was all about being LDS, *being one of us*. Mormon family,
> Mormon friends, Mormon girlfriend, Mormon coworkers—all so safe
> and socially contained. As I grew older, this really wore on me and, at the
> risk of seeming harsh, my local ward began to feel more like a psychiatric
> ward. I needed to escape. I'm out now though.

And some atheists feel free from *ritualism*:

> I traded "kneel down," "stand up," "genuflect" for *liberté, égalité, fraternité*.
> Maybe that sounds cornball, but it was a pretty damn good trade.

Hopefully, I have made my point. We could actually go on like this for quite some time. Instead, let us focus on time itself. Feeling free has an implied temporality. Freedom in the negative sense references a past marked by certain constraints, whereas its positive analogue points toward an undetermined future that can be shaped as desired. Moreover, after the feeling of being free, the two next most frequently expressed feelings refer very explicitly to these pasts and futures. Many readers may find this unsurprising since feeling differently about the various seasons of one's life is a fairly common human experience. But there is more to it than this. Different feelings directed at different periods of one's life can also signal personal change and provide a sense that one's life is on a discernible trajectory. "In order to have a sense of who we are," asserts philosopher Charles Taylor in his important book on the modern self, "we need to have a notion of how we have become, and of where we are going."[35] So often, it is our feelings that, quite viscerally, provide us with such a notion.

Perhaps even more surprising to readers—as it was to me—are the specific, most regularly mentioned feelings, in addition to freedom, that respondents experience and that signal to them that their identities as atheists are both more authentic than what they knew before and well worth living out in the years ahead. The first of these, which reflects the emotional contours of Taylor's "how we have become" notion, is regret. As mentioned, the ubiquity of this emotion initially startled me. I had expected interviewees to be more inclined toward what the philosopher Friedrich Nietzsche, perhaps Christianity's most sublime rejecter, called *amor fati* (loosely translated: "love of fate"), a deep acceptance of the realities of one's life, both good and bad, that have amounted to who one has become.[36] Instead, the religious pasts that most of them recall are marked, to varying extents, by regret. The intensity of this feeling roughly coincides with the extent of their religious upbringing. For instance, although it only lasted until her Catholic parents divorced when she was still in middle school, one woman regrets all the masses she had been forced to attend. "Growing up going to church was such a waste of my Sundays," she explains. "Now on Sundays, I have breakfast with my beautiful husband and daughter, and we just spend time together. I wish I could have done this in my childhood. I feel I was robbed of precious time in my life by being dragged to church." More than just of time, another person talks about being robbed, even through his college years, of his later-discovered ability to think critically and thus to properly develop as a person:

> I look back on my childhood now and wonder how I could have been so blind to have completely neglected to critically analyze such a big part of my life. It wasn't until after college that I started to look at some of this. If I had been taught to question everything, maybe I could have become a more decent human being a little sooner in my life. A lot of kids go through a "question everything" phase, but I never went through that as a kid or teenager. I wish I had.

Every so often, especially among those with extensive experiences with religion, the level of regret is nearly overwhelming. Listening to Doug Simon, the man we met in chapter 2 who says he became an atheist at the age of forty-one after reading a book by Carl Sagan, is not an easy thing to do. "I was free for the first time in my life," he said, looking back on that fateful day. But when he considers his life before then, he is filled with regret:

> In a way, this really pisses me off! If I had only known this when I was a kid instead of living a sham of a pipe dream for forty-plus years. How much time I wasted not noticing things. Not taking it all in. Not realizing that it will all be over so soon. This is what I absolutely detest about religion. I was duped, conned out of decades of my life. . . . I spent most of my life thinking, "This world sucks; heaven is going to be so much better." This life on earth was just one long wait for heaven. I pretty much just blew through forty years of it, not noticing anything. I haven't taken care of my body. I knew I was taking years off my life due to my bad habits, but I really didn't care—I'd get to heaven that much sooner.

The second feeling, which correlates with Taylor's "where we are going," orients people toward their futures. Over and over, they say that, in the absence of the clear guideposts religious traditions provide their adherents, they experience a tremendous feeling of responsibility to determine for themselves the direction they think their lives should take. My surprise here is likely a result of my own professional socialization. That I had expected respondents to express feelings of anomie undoubtedly reflects my reading of the great sociologist Emile Durkheim, for whom this term referred to the disquieting sort of moral uncertainty that ensues when broadly shared standards of behavior break down for whatever reason.[37] So much for that. Instead of the disquiet and sometimes even the paralysis wrought of anomie, what typically arises for atheists is the experience of accepting their unscripted agency and becoming artisans of their own futures. This pervasive feeling of responsibility for deciding upon and carving out lives worth living gets expressed in ways that range from the exhilarating to the everyday. Exemplifying the first of these poles, former Catholic Neil Rossi seems to gesture in Durkheim's direction by admitting that being an atheist can be "a bit frightening" (i.e., anomic) sometimes. Mostly, though, he revels in a feeling of responsibility:

> We humans, with all our limitations, have to figure out how best to live our lives. No one else will do it for us. We are our own saviors. Yes, we, the criminal species behind the Holocaust and the genius behind Rembrandt's *Lucretia*. We, the builders of atomic weapons as well as the architectural wonders of Gothic cathedrals and the works of Rem Koolhaas. The exhilaration, for me, comes from the awesome responsibility we have to ourselves and future generations to progressively evolve ourselves to a point where we are fully conscious of our freedom to become, as well as to the point of being able to do so.

Toward the opposite pole, consider Garrett Lough, who accepts the fact that his family members—including his wife—rely on faith in times of trouble. "If it makes them feel better and doesn't hurt anyone," he says jokingly, "what's a little delusion between friends?" Yet, when it comes to taking care of his wife, who suffers from a severe psychological disorder, he much prefers assuming his responsibilities to simply feeling better:

> She is the love of my life. As she suffers from psychosis, there are times when I long for a higher power to call out to for help. It kills me to see her suffer, and there is nothing I can do to make it go away. At the same time, in the therapy groups I attend, I've seen people who rely on a higher power and thus don't actually provide any assistance to their loved ones.

> Because I don't believe, I know it falls on me to learn, to research, and to assist. And because of that, I provide the real help that they don't.

That feeling responsible would rouse someone like Lough to do things to provide "real help" to his wife seems basic (and laudable) enough. What can get lost in such accounts, though, is the easily overlooked reality that feelings themselves do things in the world. Primarily, they corroborate that narrative quality of the atheist self or, to use sociologist Eviatar Zerubavel's term, they inscribe an emotionally authenticated sense of "periodization" onto people's lives.[38] By valorizing a past with a feeling of regret, by feeling free in the present, and by assuming a sense of responsibility for the future, people experience their lives as having trajectories, periods of which can be imagined and described largely because they are each marked by distinctive emotions. Their lives, such feelings signal to them, show movement; they are unfolding in an internally coherent and positive manner.

What is more, these feelings also amplify people's experience of participating within an imagined community of fellow atheists by doing two additional things. First, they disconfirm the viewpoints of those among the religious who stigmatize them for being immoral. Feelings of freedom and responsibility tell them that they are indeed living morally and also remind them, should they need it, that they do not deserve the ill treatment depicted in their stigma stories. Imbued with such "awesome responsibility," Rossi knows that it is only his own ethical discernment that will enable him to choose between the criminality and genius that both define our species. And even though it "kills" him to see his wife suffer—and, at times, he would prefer to look away, toward a "higher power"—Lough faces his responsibilities unflinchingly and makes the harder moral decision to provide "real help."

Along with signaling that they live moral lives, feelings also help indicate to atheists that they are living rational ones as well. What feelings do here is reassure them that they have largely steered clear of the cultural, social, and personal hazards capable of undermining reason. Feeling free to do as he pleases and experiencing himself as responsible to his own and future generations, Rossi clings to his rational faculties: he is more than willing to accept this burden and "figure out" how to proceed by his best lights. The same is true of Lough. He could leave his wife's side, look to a higher power, or stick his head in the sand of wishful thinking. Instead he decides to actually *use* his head "to learn, to research, and to assist." Feelings of freedom and responsibility, in other words, present people like Rossi and Lough with the gapingly wide-open question of how best to live, and to which they respond in a morally deliberative and self-consciously rational manner.

Being but Not Necessarily Belonging

Only a small minority, about one in ten, of my interviewees claim any level of meaningful and sustained participation in an atheist community, either online or in person. For the majority, this simply is not important to their identities as atheists. I learned this very early on in my research. In fact, the very first four people I interviewed—from whom I will draw conversational fragments—made it abundantly clear to me that they, as atheists, do not experience any of the typical things one associates with community belonging. They, for instance, are short of feelings of solidarity. (Interviewee 1, Daniel, from the preface: "I don't feel bonded to other people just because they're atheists.") Nor do they experience a sense of commonality. (Interviewee 2: "Atheists come in all shapes, sizes, colors, and viewpoints. We are liberals and conservatives, capitalists and socialists, athletes and couch potatoes.") They generally steer clear of shared ideologies. (Interviewee 3: "I'm not into groupthink or some new orthodoxy. A lot of the better-known atheist writers and bloggers just seem a bit too lock-step to me.") And most lack even the requisite intentionality that normally precipitates affiliation with a group or community. (Interviewee 4: "What I am is a pragmatic, intellectually honest realist to the best of my ability and courage. Atheism is one product of that, not the cause.")

What this all suggests is that scholars, journalists, and pundits of various stripes may be seeing only one segment of a larger universe of nonbelief in the United States. Various, easily noticeable constellations of atheist communities, advocacy groups, well-publicized conferences, and so forth garner lots of attention, which is perfectly understandable. Nevertheless, there also seems to be plenty of—likely far more than we know—atheist "dark matter," people living nonreligious lives on their own, as they see fit and, since they are not part of such constellations, largely imperceptible to observers' detection.

They normally do not coalesce by giving in to the draw of community membership. However, they still demonstrate a considerable degree of what sociologists call "identity convergence" insofar as social context is so instrumental in shaping the parameters by which people organize their sense of self.[39] In other words, in a society where, as we have seen, atheists are persistently stigmatized as an "immoral other," it makes sense that they would be subject to experiences of subtle to outright hostility, and then encapsulate those in narrative form. Similarly, in light of the previously discussed modern conceptualization of God and the objectivization of religion—and, consequently, the putative tensions between faith and reason and, as we will address in the next chapter, between religion and science—it also makes sense that, in rejecting belief, people would accept and even accentuate the supposed irrationality of believers. Finally, in the absence of such objective identity markers as common socioeconomic characteristics in the case of class identity, shared physiological traits vis-à-vis racial identity, and of course, the collective rituals and creedal affirmations that identify one as a participant in a faith tradition, atheists are left with identity markers of a distinctly subjective sort. These are the feelings people experience and that signify to them that, as we saw in chapter 2, they have acquired new identities for themselves and, as discussed in this chapter, these identities are also legitimate and worthwhile.

In sum, that the practices we have explored in this chapter would be broadly imaginable to people and they in turn would converge in terms of engaging in them so regularly are facts reflective of the social context in which atheists find themselves. Given their shared experience of living within a *particular*, faith-"awash" social order in which religion has been generally conceived in a *particularly* objectified, proposition-based manner, the people I talked with become oriented to one another less through group membership and more by dint of their gravitating toward the *particular* project of role making their context makes available to them. They undertake this project by essentially casting themselves as part of an imagined community constituted by a symbolic boundary between themselves and a stigmatizing, irrational wider public that, while not a real boundary per se, engenders the real effect of bringing about feelings that validate it as such.

PART II

Digging a Bit Deeper

Cultivating Atheist Sensibilities

4

The Empirical Root

Science without Scientism

The Science versus Religion "Conflict Myth"

As we have seen, stigma stories and feelings (sometimes organized into acquisition narratives) are important for situating atheists within an imagined community and thus distinguishing them from people of faith. Without doubt, though, it is accentuating the latter's purported irrationality that most stands out as atheists' central role-making practice, especially since it identifies them, in contrast, as rational. Not immoral, not heretical, not sinful, not shallow—rational. They are rational, discerning people, they insist, who look upon the world as it is, consider the facts, weigh the available evidence, and then arrive at whatever conclusions seem most fitting. As such, their primary style of thinking through and expressing their atheism reflects the evidence-based empirical root described in chapter 1, which pits data gathering against superstition, reason against faith, and ultimately, science against religion.

Crucially, the fact that empiricism's challenge to the Athenian religious establishment took place nearly three millennia ago does not mean that the notion of there being an agonistic relationship between science and religion stretches back that far. Classical Greek metaphysics, predicated upon a sharp distinction between appearances and reality, begat a general skepticism about knowing the world too deeply through observation. This, in turn, hampered the practice of science on an appreciable scale. It was really only the emergence of monotheism in the West that, in positing creation as God's handiwork and thus governed by discernible laws, cast the natural world as humanly comprehensible and, consequently, made empirical observation of it seem generative of actual knowledge and thus worthwhile.[1] This frame of mind, of course, was

essential for the centuries-long development that, manifested most notably by the Scientific Revolution (sixteenth to seventeenth century), gave
birth to what we would eventually come to know as modern science.

Even this development did not mark the beginning of the now-
commonplace view that science is necessarily in conflict with religion.
At the outset of the modern age, students of nature—many clergy or
individuals at least motivated by religious convictions and guided by
religiously sanctioned worldviews—generally thought of themselves as
pursuing "natural history" or "natural philosophy," both very much in
conversation with and deemed complementary to the theological scholarship of the day. Only by keeping this in mind can we truly appreciate the title Isaac Newton gave to his most famous work, *Philosophiae
naturalis principia mathematica* ("the mathematical principles of natural philosophy," 1687), as well as the anachronism of calling Newton's
contemporary Robert Boyle the "first modern chemist" when he much
preferred describing his work as the "philosophical worship of God."[2]

Things did not change much until well into the nineteenth century,
for reasons that were considerably more political than epistemological. As investigations into the natural world expanded, investigators
themselves, beginning first in Victorian England, attempted to achieve
independence from ecclesial authority and secure their own status as
producers of distinctly secular varieties of knowledge.[3] This project of
promoting the political fortunes of science (and scientists) was abet-
ted by the publication of highly polemical and historically inaccurate
works that portrayed heroically indefatigable scientists as struggling to
defend truth against a relentlessly repressive Catholic Church. By far
the most widely read and influential of these were John Draper's *History of the Conflict between Religion and Science* (1874) and Andrew
White's *A History of the Warfare of Science with Theology in Christendom*
(1896).[4] Almost uniformly disregarded by scholars today, these books
were nonetheless instrumental in establishing the popular stereotype of
a long-standing and intractable conflict between science and religion,
which persists to the present.[5]

Looking back at these books, more remarkable than their denigration
of religion is their unalloyed exaltation of science itself. Such exuberance
does not appear among more serious scholars, even among that time's

most vociferous challengers to religion, who also bequeathed to us important insights underwriting the critique of reason. As we have seen, Karl Marx (1818–83) confidently denounced religion as the "opium of the people," but he was far less confident in the Enlightenment's promise of a universal Reason that could reliably discern truth. Rather, he argued ceaselessly, powerful social and economic factors structure people's lives and thus shape perspectives in ways they, scientists included, seldom fully recognize. Something similar can be said of Sigmund Freud (1856–1939), another of the West's great "masters of suspicion," to use philosopher Paul Ricoeur's adroit phrasing.[6] His succinct, easy debunking of religion as an "infantile illusion" did not make trusting reason any less difficult. His work in psychoanalysis has made people aware that, despite pretensions to rationality, human thoughts and actions are very frequently driven by emotions and repressions that operate on an unconscious level. Even the work of Charles Darwin (1809–82), the intellectual darling of the New Atheists today, provides much reason to question Reason. At least, in his more ruminative moments, he thought so. "With me, the horrid doubt always arises," he once confided to an academic colleague, "whether the convictions of man's mind, which has been developed from the mind of the lower animals, are of any value or at all trustworthy."[7]

Despite such warrants for epistemological humility, the conflict myth remains alive and well. Nowhere is this more obvious than in the pages, written very much in the Draper and White tradition, of the New Atheist best sellers. One could flip through these quite randomly to find childish religious superstition counterposed with mature scientific rationality. Why nuance the matter when it is obvious enough to state plainly, as Christopher Hitchens does in *God Is Not Great*?

Religion comes from the period of human prehistory where nobody—not even the mighty Democritus who concluded that all matter was made from atoms—had the smallest idea what was going on. It comes from the bawling and fearful infancy of our species, and is a babyish attempt to meet our inescapable demand for knowledge. . . . All attempts to reconcile faith with science and reason are consigned to failure and ridicule for precisely these reasons.[8]

We see the same polarity in Richard Dawkins's *The God Delusion*. Like Hitchens, he presumes all religious people to be scriptural literalists and all religions to be both synonymous with one another and essentially flailing exercises in scientific ineptitude. God is imagined by him only in terms of the so-called God of the gaps, an intellectual placeholder bound to shrink to extinction as the explanatory prowess of science inexorably expands:

> Creationists eagerly seek a gap in present-day knowledge or understanding. If an apparent gap is found, it is assumed that God, by default, must fill it. What worries thoughtful theologians . . . is that gaps shrink as sciences advances, and God is threatened with eventually having nothing to do and nowhere to hide.[9]

Statements like these, which perpetuate the conflict myth, litter the New Atheist literature. They come with little elaboration because they are based on three suppositions that are equally ubiquitous: (1) human reason is a trustworthy source of truth about the world; (2) as the best instantiation of human reason, science will eventually replace the irrationality of religion; and (3) this process will inevitably make the world better.

What is most astonishing about these suppositions is that they have been roundly problematized for some time now. As examples of this, consider again the "old" atheist thinkers mentioned earlier. Concerning the first supposition listed above, Darwinian theory should cause us to seriously doubt what we now take to be rational when this changes so radically over time and when, according to many scientists, dynamics related to natural selection have produced such false concepts in the human mind as the notion of a free will and theism itself. "Natural selection does not care about truth," notes philosopher Stephen Stich, addressing the often unrecognized limits of human reason; "it cares only about reproductive success."[10] Then there is the second supposition concerning the inevitable triumph of science. Here the Freudian insight about the often irrational tenor of human drives and aspirations is important. If, as the New Atheists contend, religion is both a human creation and thoroughly irrational, does that not imply that irrationality is actually a constitutive dimension of human beings and thus a pronounced feature of any era, including the present, scientifically ascendant one? Two world wars, multiple genocides, the proliferation of nuclear weapons, persistent global poverty, and the looming specter of climate change—to take only an off-the-cuff accounting of the past century or so—suggest that this may indeed be the case. Such realities, all conspicuously exacerbated by scientific developments that mark our "advanced" societies, also put into question the third supposition concerning the inevitability of progress. Not to see this, Marx reminds us, is itself an indication of the perspectival quality of human knowing. It is hard not to think of his frequently quoted line "The ideas of the ruling class are in every epoch the ruling ideas" when one realizes that the New Atheist writers who see the world getting better and better all the time are primarily white, well-educated, economically privileged men.[11] "If ever there was a pious myth and piece of credulous superstition," writes Marxist literary critic Terry Eagleton ironically, "it is the liberal-rationalist belief that, a few hiccups apart, we are all steadily en route to a finer world."[12]

Beyond all these shaky suppositions, more recent scholars who have turned their attention to the conflict myth and have interrogated it more explicitly have found it devastatingly short on complexity. It is easy to cherry-pick historical episodes, simplify these, and then hold them up as evidence of the inescapable and ongoing battle between science and religion. The classic example is the Galileo-versus-Inquisition narrative typically told without mention of the fact that this episode was driven less by resistance to scientific inquiry, which the Catholic Church had long supported, than by ecclesiastical politics. The same is true of depictions of the landmark 1925 Scopes Trial. Seldom does one hear that, while certain Christian fundamentalists found Darwin's theory of evolution to be inappropriate for biology classrooms, this was not (and certainly is not) at all true among Christians of other theological persuasions. The reality is that at different times, within different local and national contexts, with respect to different scientific fields and findings, and among representatives or adherents of different faiths, the relationship between science and religion can actually be quite different—ranging from conflict to harmony, mutual encouragement to independence, and just about everywhere in between. Demonstrating this and, in the process, dismantling the conflict myth in his monumental survey *Science and Religion:*

Some Historical Perspectives, historian of science John Hedley Brooke proposes that we adopt a "complexity thesis" to better capture the varied and protean nature of the science-religion relationship.[13]

As Brooke and many other scholars have noted, the overwhelming complexity of this relationship reflects the usually underappreciated complexity of the terms employed. In other words, the conflict myth is predicated upon the clumsy essentializing of "science" and "religion" as if these were meaningful in a universal sense. As noted in the first chapter, though, there is no one thing called "religion." Instead, this constructed category functions to encapsulate a great variety of faith traditions and a great variety of ways—beyond the objectively propositional—in which people engage with and quite often adapt these traditions. So, too, with "science." Meaningless in the general sense, this similarly constructed category includes a variety of sciences, each with its own object of study, history, empirical methods, guiding (often unproven) assumptions, and relationships with religious actors and institutions. That many church leaders and other citizens of Dayton, Tennessee, were resistant to evolutionary theory back in 1925 was really no more predictable than have been the contemporary Christian (and other) theologians who are excited about the scientific work being done in quantum mechanics and cosmology today.

Complicating things still further is the reality that, despite modernity's differentiation of science and religion—and the accompanying, but simplistic, distinction between reason and faith—the barrier between them is not entirely impermeable. Most Americans who think of themselves as religious also marvel at the discoveries and practical achievements wrought of the natural sciences. And as we also saw in the first chapter, believers are likewise prone to marshaling their rational faculties in questioning aspects of their faith, critiquing the religious institutions with which they affiliate, and to varying extents, thinking through the religious pluralism around them. As, once again, philosopher Charles Taylor notes, coming to religious faith is itself very often the product of a kind of data gathering. Rather than slavishly adhering to some stereotypical "blind faith," he sees many people seriously examining the "felt flatness" of their everyday lives and arriving at the conclusion that secular worldviews fail to account for a key, transcendent dimension of human experience.[14] The porousness of this barrier is also evident when looking more closely at science. If nothing else, philosopher Thomas Kuhn's *The Structure of Scientific Revolutions*, which explores the maintenance and transmission of highly institutionalized scientific paradigms, shows that belief systems, and even dogmatisms, are not the province of the overtly religious alone.[15] Writes philosopher of science Paul Feyerabend on this very point, "Science is much closer to myth than a scientific philosophy is prepared to admit."[16]

Of course, Feyerabend is not using the word "myth" to denote, as in common usage, merely a false belief. He is rather using it in the more anthropological sense, as a nonliteral, community-based construal of a not-yet-fully-grasped reality, which then coordinates individual thought and action. Whether or not the term, in this nonliteral sense, helpfully describes theoretical frameworks within the sciences has been hotly debated for some time now. It does, however, apply quite well to the matter of the conflict myth. In other words, scholars like John Hedley Brooke use the term "myth" solely in the first, more common, sense—as a belief in the inherent, universal, and enduring conflict between science and religion, which one historical and sociological study after another have shown to be false. Generally overlooked, though, is its helpfulness in this second, nonliteral sense. While empirically invalid, the conflict myth is itself a cultural construct that gets enlisted by atheists to signify that they, in rejecting religion, possess or at least aspire to the sorts of qualities that they see as defining science. It is in this second usage that the conflict myth proves itself to be a useful, and thus persistent, imagined community-based construal for those aiming to live full, conscientious lives as nonbelievers.

Living the Myth: Leaning toward Scientism

Indicative of the pervasiveness of this myth is the predominance of a particular kind of atheism among my interviewees. They run the gamut from "closeted" atheists to the "loud and proud" sort—and everywhere in between. In about equal numbers, they espouse what is sometimes called "negative atheism," which is simply a *lack of belief* in God, and "positive atheism," the more assertive *disbelief* in the existence of God. Despite these and other differences, most of them clearly skew considerably away from humanistic grounds for their atheism and much more toward science-related ones. Only a minority of them, in other words, are what some observers call "humanistic atheists" who generally see religion as an epiphenomenon, as the byproduct of social and psychological maladies that then precipitate the need for the ultimately dehumanizing "opiates" (Marx) and "illusions" (Freud) that religion is thought to provide. Address modern society's sources of injustice, ignorance, and repression, this camp argues, and religion will become unnecessary and, in time, a thing of the past. Notice that, while this position primarily targets the shortcomings of modernity, "scientific atheists" direct their critique at religion itself as the chief inhibitor of scientific advance and thus of the full flowering of modernity's promise. In short, scientific atheism casts religious superstition as the very antithesis of science and, as such, views it as the main obstacle to human enlightenment and progress.[17]

As mentioned, like American atheists in general, the people in this study are very well educated. When asked about sources of information that undergird their atheist identities, nearly half of them say their formal educations have been very influential, and an astounding 97 percent of them say this about their own critical thinking. Whereas formal education and critical thinking can steer people in various directions, the most heavily trodden path for my sample leads to scientific atheism. There is no question that they respect science. The great majority either strongly agrees (46 percent) or agrees (39 percent) with the statement "Science will eventually provide solutions to most of our problems." Even more telling is their pronounced tendency to see science and religion as being at loggerheads with one another. Most strongly agree (52 percent) or agree (34 percent) that "Science and religion are incompatible," and more than nine in ten of them cite "advances in science" as being either very significant (71 percent) or somewhat significant (20 percent) for their deciding to turn away from religion. These data, incidentally, corroborate the findings of recent national-level studies. According to one of these, while atheists are much more likely than religiously affiliated Americans to agree both that science will solve our problems and that it is incompatible with religion, their agreement on these two items is also significantly higher than that expressed by such other secular Americans as self-identified agnostics, nonaffiliated believers, and the nonpracticing "culturally" religious.[18]

Of course, convictions like these do not necessarily constitute scientific atheism. One could have them and come to a more accommodationist position. Probably the best known of these is evolutionary biologist Stephen Jay Gould's argument that, instead of being in conflict, the realms of science and religion represent "non-overlapping magisteria" (NOMA) in that they address different questions and hence attend to different aspects of existence.[19] Alternatively, given that they actually do overlap on occasion and square off in sometimes cantankerous public debates, one could declare a stalemate between science and religion and leave the matter there. So suggests geneticist Steve Jones, who compares the intermittent conflicts between science and religion with a battle between a shark and a tiger. On its home terrain, each is victorious, but put one within the terrain of the other, and it will be resoundingly defeated.[20]

These are not the preferred images among my respondents, clearly. Instead of being engaged in different, "non-overlapping" pursuits, they tend to see science and religion addressing the very same questions. This, as discussed, is partly a function of Western religion (particularly Christianity) emulating the propositional, rationalized tenor of the Enlightenment. Or to use the seventeenth-century philosopher and mathematician Blaise Pascal's brooding formulation, it represents a privileging of the highly intellectualized God of the philosophers over the experiential, utterly mysterious God of faith ("God of Abraham, God of Isaac, God of Jacob").[21] The end result is that, rather than agreeing with Gould about there being no conflict or with Jones about intermittent, indecisive conflicts, the people I interviewed have deeply internalized the conflict myth, thus imagining science and religion as hypostasized entities in unavoidable contention. Instead of a comparably matched shark and tiger, they see one species of knowing as being eminently superior. In fact, they lean perilously close to what is often termed scientism, which, as philosopher Jürgen Habermas explains it, means that "we no longer understand science as *one* form of possible knowledge, but rather identify knowledge with science."[22] No nonoverlapping pursuits and no comparably matched antagonists, science is imagined to be in a binary relationship with religion and, as such, is deemed to be demonstrably superior in the epistemological, attitudinal, and consequentialist senses described below.

Epistemologies—Religion : Science :: Comfort : Integrity

Epistemologically speaking, my respondents routinely contrast what they take to be the satisfying comforts of religious faith with the rigorous search for empirical evidence and, concomitantly, the greater integrity that presumably defines science. (Hence they naturalize the "religion is to science as comfort is to integrity" analogy.) One respondent, a community college history teacher in Atlanta, sums up this first sense quite well. Like Richard Dawkins, he refers to a "God of the gaps," an entity projected onto the world as an overarching, but inadequate answer to complicated questions about the natural world and, consequently, inhabiting a cognitive space that is ever diminishing with the advances of science:

> We have been filling in these wide gaps in our knowledge for tens of thousands of years. Every day, every minute, we are able to explain a little more. . . . Thanks to scientists, we have a pretty good idea of how the universe started and when, how life began on this planet, and how we evolved from single-celled organisms into what we are today. Religion has done literally nothing to help explain the hows and whens and whys. Instead it teaches us to be satisfied with not knowing any of these things: "God did it." "Just take it on faith." "No, there's no evidence of that, but shut your mouth and just trust that God did it." Religion is the opposite of knowledge. It's the active suppression of it.

Also presuming science and religion to be about the very same "hows and whens and whys," another respondent makes a similar point by getting a bit more specific, weighing the scientist against the believer. "It makes no sense to believe someone who has no proof and turn away the person handing you the facts," he declares. "Scientists may not have all the answers, but as time goes on, they are able to answer more and more. I would much rather learn from someone who is willing to admit ignorance—but who makes an effort to discover the truth—than someone who has no real answers and tells you to believe it 'just because.'"

Like the other two binaries I will address momentarily, this one, adeptly expressed by these two respondents, is quite simple. Religion (simplified as one thing) and religious people (simplified as bossy ideologues with no real answers) are all about learning "to be satisfied," taking things "on faith," and feeling comfortable in believing with "no proof." And should religion's "just because" ilk of assertion fail to satisfy, then there is always the authoritarian rejoinder "shut your mouth." On the other hand, science (presumably not phrenology) and scientists (Josef Mengele excepted, one imagines) are about admitting ignorance and expending enormous effort in getting to the bottom of things. In a word, they are about integrity. Having integrity is persistently framed as the opposite of the comforts and ease of "making up" things. No one expresses this better than Greg Stoppach, a nurse living in upstate New York. He has no problem equating the Greek and Egyptian myths that fascinated him as a child with Aesop's fables and even with the fairy tales he now reads to his three-year-old daughter some nights. Since his early college days, he has included the world's major religions in this fable/fairy tale category as well. "I fail to see the value of making up answers to questions" about such things as the origins of life, why bad things happen to good people, and what happens when we die. Elaborating, he explains:

> The hill people of Palestine said, "God did it." That is not an answer; it is not an explanation. It's just making up stuff, believers refusing to really look. . . . When atheists don't know the answer, they say, "We don't know; let's look at the world around us and try to figure it out." Every atheist I know is also completely open to the possibility that everything they know may be incorrect and, if some new piece of information comes along, will say, "Wow, that's really fascinating. I guess I was wrong." If I'm going to have answers to life's questions, I want them to be correct answers.

Attitudes—Religion : Science :: Closed-Mindedness : Open-Mindedness

Notice how Stoppach shifts from competing epistemologies to a more person-centered distinction. Contented, then and now, to simply say "God did it" and "refusing to really look" at the world around them, religious people are unswervingly portrayed by Stoppach and many others as the very opposite of the "completely open" atheist who looks around, looks deeply and honestly, and not infrequently says, "Wow."

Such portrayals are never accompanied by explanations of whether these contrasting attitudes toward the world are chickens or eggs. In other words, does closed-mindedness lead to religious conviction, or is it instead an unfortunate result of being immersed in a faith tradition? How about open-mindedness? Does it come first, or is it born of one's prior awareness of scientific method and discoveries? One hears very little about this. In place of analysis, interestingly, one hears steadfast conviction in the veracity of this particular binary. Jennifer LaRosa, a graduate student studying nonprofit management at a midsized New England college, spells out this conviction especially well:

> Believing in one answer, regardless of the lack of evidence, keeps a person from asking questions about life. It's almost insulting to all the wonderful things the world and life can offer us. The universe is an amazing place. We should be doing our best to discover the answers for ourselves about how we got here and what the meaning of it all is, not closing our minds with one religious explanation. Science tells us that there's billions upon billions of planets out there, and the universe is expanding still. To think of how much there is to potentially discover about it all just completely blows my mind. . . . Life and the universe are amazing enough, so why would you want to belittle it with mythology about a god creating it all with magic?

LaRosa does not just look at the world around her. She finds it to be "amazing." In excess of just being open-minded, what she has learned from science, she says, "blows my mind." In short, if scientific method is superior to faith because it valorizes integrity over mere comfort, then open-mindedness seems to her to be the better posture toward the world because expressions of belief pale in comparison to experiences of awe. Such experiences provide yet another kind of affective valida-tion, evidence that one is on the right track in venturing beyond the familiar fleshpots of belief, mythology, and magic. "Religion chooses to ignore the world that is and instead clings to books written by ancient goat herders," insists former Southern Baptist Aaron Clemente. "There is nothing in the Christian Bible that is outside the knowledge base of the people who wrote it. To limit your understanding like that is a hei-nous act of willful ignorance." Clemente, in contrast, chooses to neither ignore the world nor limit his level of understanding. As good as that is, he experiences something even better: a sustaining feeling of awe that validates his choices. "I do have a strong sense of awe and wonder about the physical universe, its sheer size and complexity, its beauty, and the unlikeliness of some of its features," he muses. "I don't need to believe in a higher power to marvel at the Milky Way stretching across a dark sky, or revel in the presence of a deer making its way through a forest." Ben Zeller, a copyeditor who had been raised as a Jehovah's Witness in Maryland, knows very well what Clemente is talking about. He was once so slack-jawed by an IMAX film about the Hubble space telescope that he actually broke into tears. Years later, he still gets a bit emotional, not to mention giddily effusive, when he recounts that afternoon in his local movie theater:

> I love how our solar system came to be, with atoms forming molecules, forming dust, forming clumps, forming rocks, forming asteroids, forming planets, forming mass, forming gravity, forming orbits, forming atmospheres, forming water, forming life. It sounds so impossible . . . every decade brings us closer to the very beginning. But eventually you have to accept that you'll reach a wall that you can't pass. Beyond that wall is left to the imagination. Is our universe part of a multiverse? Is our universe just a cosmic yo-yo that will return to its starting point to be shot in another direction and create a completely new universe? Are we an ant farm in a child's bedroom in some other universe? The possibilities are endless!

Consequences—Religion : Science :: Regression : Progress

When atheists widen their focus from personal attitudes to considering societal consequences, the chicken or egg problem disappears entirely. Religion indeed comes first, they say. It is a feature of, to repeat an earlier-quoted phrase from Christopher Hitchens, "the bawling and fearful infancy of our species." Science, on the other hand, represents progress with respect to both supplanting religious worldviews with a truer understanding of reality and, ultimately, helping to bring about a better society.

"Humanity has outgrown religion." "Religion helped us the way squinting helps to see small things, but science is the electron microscope." "We've moved beyond talking snakes, parting water, and strange, fantastic stories: now it's all about logic and things that can be proved." This is what one hears when atheists talk about science and religion, or more accurately, about how science has progressed beyond religious perspectives. Retired Sacramento attorney Gary Byrnes lends some more detail:

> I think of religion as a creative tool that has promoted our biological aims of survival and proliferation. This tool has taken on many forms over the millennia. Science is a relatively new form of this tool and, in my opinion, it's substantially superior in terms of our species' needs. I think science is able to provide models and theories of cosmology, geology, and living systems that are supported by evidence—unlike the subjective projections and fantasies rooted in the mythologies of theological belief systems. I also think the scientific worldview, for those who adopt it, can be as emotionally rewarding, even having its own transcendental moments, as any religious experience.

Science progresses beyond religion, Byrnes argues, because they are essentially better and worse "tools" for doing the same things. Religion is simply a less sophisticated attempt to do what is consistently understood as being the province of science ("provide models and theories of cosmology, geology, and living systems"), and as a matter of fact, science can reliably deliver the kinds of "emotionally rewarding" and "transcendental" moments—including feelings of awe—that have long been associated with uniquely religious experience.

Critically, since science is widely taken to "overlap" with and be an improvement upon religion, its ascendency is almost uniformly described as being synonymous with social progress. If there is an atheist dogma, it is that religion is, on balance, a retrograde force within society. Pauline Martinez, a homemaker living just outside of El Paso, acknowledges what many other nonbelievers say is true about religion. It brings people "peace of mind in times of trouble," she says. It provides access to "close, sometimes loving communities." It conveys "some basic moral lessons." She basically hits the same high notes as do most others, including her concluding one: "Overall, though, it's terrible to believe in something that just isn't true." When asked to say more about this, she is happy to oblige:

A poor family's faith that one day they will win the lottery and their whole lives will improve. A mother's faith that, if she prays hard enough, God will save her son who lies gasping at her feet dying of an asthma attack. A man's faith that, as long as he confesses his sins and truly repents, his murders and rapes will be forgiven and he can enter heaven. A Muslim's faith that, if he plants a bomb in a Christian church, he will be rewarded in the afterlife with a lineup of virgins. . . . See, faith is detrimental to human development, both personal development and as a species. Science, not faith, saves babies, feeds mouths, builds houses that can withstand hurricanes. Science develops the vaccines, heals the sick, grows the corn, explains the workings of the universe. Faith keeps people uneducated and dependent on others. It causes death, oppression, war, unhappiness, and hatred.

Gaps of the Godless: Backing Away from Scientism

The polarity could not be clearer. Whereas science "saves," "feeds," "builds," "develops," "heals," "grows," and "explains," Martinez tells us, religion's bestowal is a legacy of "death, oppression, war, unhappiness, and hatred." It is easy to see why atheists in the United States are so often thought of in terms of scientism. First off, the majority of them have bought into the science versus religion conflict myth. Perhaps not always with the acclamatory verbs Martinez uses, but certainly most of the people I spoke with have internalized the three binaries discussed above and, as we will see, thus associate their own life projects with the integrity, openness, and tilt toward the side of progress that science exemplifies for them. Second, they tend to mirror many religious adherents' stigmatizing presuppositions about them by trucking in stereotypes of their own. Even as it is not uncommon for them to have an appreciative soft spot for their churchgoing loved ones, whom they often think of as specific exceptions to the general rule, this can still be a real blind spot for many atheists today. It would be difficult to imagine religious believers, movements, traditions, and institutions surviving for so many millennia if they, in ways subtle and profound, did not also have at least something to do with representing integrity, encouraging open-mindedness, and contributing to cultural and social betterment. Few atheists, however, seem willing to seriously consider such possibilities.

Finally, and most of all, the vast majority of them talk about science in ways that suggest that its edifice is built on a firmer foundation than thinkers like Kuhn and Feyerabend are willing to concede. Understandings of what constitutes integrity, what is and is not an instance of openness, and what (and for whom) one calls progress are all context-specific and usually highly contested categories. Typically presumed by people, scientists included, such understandings reflect evaluative claims that cannot be *proven* per se. And what of all the big-ticket questions of our time? If religious traditions have no credible answers to these, then does science really fare much better? If nature, as Alfred Tennyson famously put it, is "red in tooth and claw" and humans are most assuredly part of nature, why do we insist on trying to be moral, and how do we know when we are succeeding? What exactly is consciousness, and how does it emerge from human physiology? What is the purpose of life, and how can one justify one value-laden take on this over any other? How, as working scientists need to simply assume, do we know that the universe is comprehensible and that what we know about it is actually true rather than, given the nature of our ever-evolving brains, simply appearing to be true? Lastly, what of perhaps the biggest of big questions, the one so niggling that the philosopher Martin Heidegger once lamented that each of us is "grazed by its hidden power"? This is the seventeenth-century philosopher Gottfried Wilhelm Leibniz's query "Why is there something rather than nothing?"[23] That's a tough one.

As is the case of religious faith, science actually offers no definitive answers to any of these questions, and what is more, scientism scraps them, insofar as they cannot be addressed through scientific method, as being of little importance. Scientism's logical result is a relatively stark view of the world, one that, in a book on Darwinian theory, Richard Dawkins conveys to his readers quite candidly. "In a universe of blind physical forces and genetic replication," he explains, "some people are going to get hurt, other people are going to get luck, and you won't find any rhyme or reason in it, nor any justice. The universe we observe has precisely the properties we should expect if there is, at bottom, no design, no purpose, no evil and no good, nothing but blind, pitiless indifference."[24] Along with its candor, what is particularly arresting about this depiction is how rarely one hears versions of it among rank-and-file atheists themselves. They may lean toward scientism, but they generally back away from its logical, starker conclusions, as spelled out by Dawkins and others. Seldom is this important nuance acknowledged. There is a tendency among scholars and pundits to place American atheists, about whom they usually know quite little, into the same basket as the New Atheist writers, whose work they know quite well. As a result, they tend to assume that the degree of scientism that one clearly finds in these works is also consistently manifested among the larger population of atheists themselves, which is patently untrue.

Actually, in much the same way as churchgoers' "lived religion" departs in many respects from the orthodoxy typically upheld by religious authorities, everyday atheists' viewpoints frequently differ from the "official" versions one gets from best-selling atheist authors. They instead have much more in common with a growing number of more scholarly and much less polemically inclined nonreligious voices who reject scientism and, at the same time, question whether the regnant scientific paradigm fully captures the fullness of what it means to be human. For example, in his appropriately titled essay "An Awareness of What Is Missing" (2010), the aforementioned German philosopher Jürgen Habermas, long admired as a champion of Enlightenment rationality, expresses dismay at a "naturalism founded on a naïve faith in science" and points to the importance of religion for preserving those "collectively binding ideals" that reflect undeniable features of human experience.[25] Another example is the American philosopher Thomas Nagel. In his recent *Mind and Cosmos* (2012), he argues that the neo-Darwinian and current scientifically orthodox explanation for the evolution of life, consciousness, and moral values is "almost certainly false" and will likely "come to be seen as laughable in a generation or two." "I conclude that something is missing from Darwinism," he writes, and speculates that there is some sort of "cosmic predisposition" toward life and consciousness that is "biased toward the marvelous" in ways that humans can fleetingly glimpse but as yet never fully comprehend.[26] The French philosopher André Comte-Sponville is our final example. What he finds missing within the modern world, and what is especially difficult for atheists like himself to address, is a sense of spirituality, which he defines as a commitment to community and a fidelity to such values as truth and love. "Not believing in God is no reason to amputate a part of our humanity," he insists, "especially not *that* part!"[27]

Something is missing, these scholars contend in unison. All unabashedly nonreligious thinkers, they nonetheless chide scientism for offering a description of—and, in some respects, a template for—contemporary life that fails to account for essential facets of human personhood. Whether or not they have read these works, the atheists I interviewed clearly share this sensibility, this *Zeitgeist*, this experience of something missing from the standard scientific account. In other words, while well-known atheists like Richard Dawkins talk about the inexorably diminishing "God of the gaps," the considerably lesser known atheists with whom I spoke, even as they applaud the scientific enterprise, detect therein gaps of its own. This is generally a tacit awareness, and these gaps are filled in ways underwritten not by scientific findings but rather through people's attempts to live decent and full lives. "Life cannot wait until the sciences have explained the universe scientifically," the Spanish philosopher José Ortega y Gasset once quipped, "We cannot put off living until we are ready."[28] So, too, with this study's more than five hundred atheists. They lionize science, but they, again usually quite tacitly, fill scientism's gaps with affirmations of personal meaning and, for many, even of spirituality.

Meaning . . . "In the More Personal Sense"

Further evidence of a pervasive feeling that there is indeed something missing from the prevailing techno-scientific worldview can be found at the local library. There one finds, since about the turn of the new millennium, an expanding array of books that attempt to fill in the gaps by specifically addressing a somewhat brash topic: the meaning of life. Even a partial listing gives a sense of just how summoning this topic seems to have become: Luc Ferry, *Man Made God: The Meaning of Life* (2002); John Cottingham, *On the Meaning of Life* (2003); Julian Bggini, *What's It All About? Philosophy and the Meaning of Life* (2004); Richard Holloway, *Looking in the Distance: The Human Search for Meaning* (2004); Roy F. Baumeister, *The Cultural Animal: Human Nature, Meaning and Social Life* (2005); John F. Haught, *Is Nature Enough? Meaning and Truth in the Age of Science* (2006); Terry Eagleton, *The Meaning of Life* (2007); Owen J. Flanagan, *The Really Hard Problem: Meaning in a Material World* (2007); Claire Colebrook, *Deleuze and the Meaning of*

Life (2010); Susan Wolf, *Meaning in Life and Why It Matters* (2012); and Edward O. Wilson, *The Meaning of Human Existence* (2014).[29] This is only a partial listing made up of works by relatively acclaimed scholars. I mention them because, though certainly a perennial concern, the question of life's meaning seems to have become a particularly ripe one within the contemporary public discourse. Why this would be the case is not totally clear. Perhaps it has something to do with the complexity and pace of American society. After all, compared to developing countries, this is a question that tends to be more consternating to significantly more people in wealthier, postindustrial nations like the United States.[30] What is abundantly clear is that this is a question wholly inaccessible to science, a fact readily acknowledged by the Nobel Prize–winning physicist Steven Weinberg. "The more the universe seems comprehensible," he opined, "the more it also seems pointless."[31]

Even as he is a favorite source of provocative quotations among American atheists, the preponderance of them would entirely disagree with this one. They have tremendous regard for science, and at the very same time, they blunt the fine point of Weinberg's experience of pointlessness by talking unreservedly about what is meaningful for them. Rather than in some ultimate, universal understanding, atheists, as one respondent clarifies, find meaning "in the more personal sense." Three-quarters of them agree with the statement "I do *not* believe there is any ultimate meaning in life." They are, however, quick to trade "ultimate" meaning for a more modest, individuated notion of what they find to be meaningful. More than eight in ten of them agree that their lives have "real purpose."

The overall attitude of the minority who think otherwise can be summed up by one Wisconsin bank teller who describes human beings as "elaborately developed, mobile protective suits for genes to pass themselves onto the next generation." Science, as indicated by his reference to genes, has drawn a picture of the world for this young man that does not include any assertion of meaning. While he is actually rather nonplussed by this, others feel differently about living in a world that they also see as being devoid of some larger, overarching meaning. Some, not surprisingly, emphasize the feeling of being free. "Sports is meaningless, too, but we still play," said one graduate student. "So, I say, 'Game on!' I'm going to play the way I decide to play." For others, living in a world without meaning is melancholic. Although also using a gaming metaphor, Mike Barnes, an architect from San Diego, does not have the same "Game on!" attitude:

> Unfortunately, we live in a vast, mainly inorganic, indifferent universe. Random things happen without purpose or intent. We must do our best to cope. In some ways, the greatest tragedy of mankind is being aware of our own mortality. There might be other intelligent species scattered throughout the universe sharing our same fate. I reflect on this from time to time. It sucks. The old joke about the physics of the universe is actually true: you can't win, you can't break even, and you can't even quit the game. So, here we are.

Most people in this group fall somewhere between "Game on!" and "It sucks." They are the ones who face the meaninglessness of the universe with an equanimity they unfailingly associate with being an adult. Understanding that children want to feel special and are prone to accepting easy answers, Jamie Routledge wants something else:

> I don't want to be told I'm chosen or saved. I just want the most logical and verifiable explanations. I want explanations that are more than the hand waving, magic, and claims of self-importance that I get with religion. I want fossil evidence. I want DNA tests. I want re-creations of early earth amino acids. I need more than someone telling me, "The man in the sky says we're special." I think it's foolish for people to claim the world needs to have some special meaning. Why does anything need to have meaning? To me, this view is very simplistic and childish. When I was young, I thought I was the center of the universe. Well, I grew up and learned I'm not so important. It's tragic that people insist that their lives have to have special meaning. That's just a security blanket they're clinging to.

People like these are few and far between, though. The great majority of atheists have had their worldviews shaped by science and—whether or not they are also feeling free, melancholic, or adult—still think of life as meaningful "in the more personal sense." They fall into two additional groups, with nearly half of all interviewees in each. For people in the first of these groups, what is meaningful for them is rather implicit. Their attitude is perhaps best captured by a music teacher living in Connecticut. "What I learned from science totally changed what I thought I knew," he acknowledges, "but it didn't have a speck of influence on what I actually do with my life." People like him cannot and do not, as Ortega y Gasset states, "put off living." They live according to what feels right to them. "My purpose in life is to do what I'm doing," says a scuba instructor in Rhode Island. "I don't fear God, I'm not afraid of the afterlife because I don't believe in it anymore. So, what I'm all about right now is to raise my daughter, enjoy my work, have a whole lot of fun—and then skid in sideways when it's all over!" All the way across the country in Seattle, one can hear echoes of all this from a social worker: "I get that I'm not part of some big, divine plan," she starts out. "Still, I have lots that's motivating me. Right now, my purpose is to help raise my two boys, be a good wife and a good daughter. Obviously, that project I mentioned [on replenishing fishing areas in the Pacific Northwest] is important because I think we need to care for our planet for future generations."

Notice that there is plenty that is meaningful to these two even if, as they each mention, it is merely meaningful "right now" and thus might change in the years ahead. They care about their families. Their jobs reflect their desires to enjoy nature (scuba diving) and help others (as a social worker). They value the environment, future generations, and in their spare time, having "a whole lot of fun." In short, they accept that they live in a universe that, as Dawkins describes, includes "no design, no purpose, no evil and no good," but they shore things up for themselves by filling in those gaps with meaning.

The next group of people also fills in gaps pertaining to design, purpose, and moral conviction, but they do so in a more intentional manner. The son of an Orthodox rabbi provides an animated summation here. "There's so much stuff that gives life meaning: music, poetry, hacking computers, love of nature, the world of ideas!" he exclaims. "Pick any of it. Pick all of it. It's not like you're an actor in someone else's play— *you're* writing the script!" So, what do playwrights of their own lives look like? They look like Sue Stanton, a Houston schoolteacher who left the Methodist church in her early twenties. "I believe meaning has to be found in each person individually," she says, and then continues:

Because meaning has such different definitions for people, it's difficult to have one, cohesive definition that applies to all people. When children are allowed to see that moral goodness can come from one human caring about another without religion, they will come to rely on and believe that meaning in the world can come from their own place in that world and from the connections they develop with other people. . . . When a parent claims the only way to raise a decent child is through God, then that is both wrong and an act of disrespect to nonbelievers, and I won't tolerate that in my home. All humans have the capability of being good people, moral people who value life and want to develop our potential for the greater good and for the success of our species.

They also look like another Texas woman, Yolanda Williams, who was a longtime member of a Pentecostal church in Dallas before she had a second "born-again experience"—this time to secular humanism. "I don't believe we're here for a divine purpose," she explains:

The meaning of my life is derived from the people in my life and from the activities I engage in. I know my time on earth will be relatively short. So, I intend to live my life well, to enjoy my loved ones, to be happy, to learn and grow through learning, art and music. . . . I can't imagine looking to God for comfort and meaning. If your life isn't happy you should evaluate why you're unhappy and do something about it. If you stay on your knees and wait for God to show you the path, then you're essentially refusing to take responsibility for your own decisions and choices.

No hint of scientism here. These women have plenty of convictions that far exceed the bounds of scientific reasoning. They "believe" and they "don't believe." They believe in developing connections with other people, valuing life and the greater good, enjoying loved ones, being happy, and learning and growing, and most of all, they believe in taking personal responsibility for finding one's own meaning in the world. On the flip side, they do not believe in living life "on your knees," being disrespectful, or expecting everyone to abide by a single, cohesive definition of what comprises a purposive life. This is because, for them, there is no cohering, ultimate meaning that comes to them from above. There is only personal meaning that, either implicitly or more explicitly, people cobble together by appropriating notions from the wider culture in which, despite their simultaneous embrace of scientific reasoning, they believe with great conviction.

Spirituality . . . "If This, Then Yes"

André Comte-Sponville's *The Little Book of Atheist Spirituality*, which I quoted above, is hardly in a class by itself. Seemingly an oxymoron, "atheist spirituality" has now become a topic of interest for a growing number of authors aiming to supplement a denial of God, dismissal of faith, and denunciation of organized religion with something more affirmative, highlighting what can be embraced by atheists as truly sublime features of this-worldly human experience.[32] And as with the topic of life's meaning, atheist spirituality is not just a concern limited to ivory-towered academics and other authors.

Relying solely on survey data could tempt us into thinking that spirituality's salience may actually be limited to such people. As we saw earlier, when asked what terms accurately describe them, almost all the atheists in my study say the labels "intellectual" and "freethinker"—each at 97 percent—describe them either very or somewhat well. Given their overall educational attainment and emphasis on critical thinking, there is nothing especially earth shattering about that. Also unsurprising are the 95 percent who say this about the term "humanist," a label that in some ways reflects a filling of scientism's gaps by denoting a sense of personal meaning, things atheists "believe" and "don't believe" about what is central to real human flourishing. But what about spirituality? At first take, it seems that the language of spirituality has very little resonance for them. Only about 16 percent of those surveyed say the term "spiritual" describes them very or somewhat well, and in response to a national-level poll, only 19 percent of atheists called themselves "spiritual but not religious."[33]

This overall impression gets reinforced when first engaging atheists in conversation about spirituality. Most respondents are fast to debunk it by claiming that those who take spirituality seriously typically fail to do any one of three things. This first is a failure to understand brain science. Such assertions as "I think people's spiritual experiences are neurological in nature, and we've yet to find their scientific explanations" and "I prefer to call spirituality simply the operations of the prefrontal cortex" get to the crux of this viewpoint. The second is people's failure to face reality. The reality, these respondents explain, is that people who call themselves spiritual no longer believe in God but, for a variety of reasons, are loath to admit it. Some, they say, refuse to admit it to themselves: "It's a vague moniker for people who don't really believe in religion, but they're afraid to let go of some higher power and actually accept responsibility for their lives." And some refuse to admit it to others: "A lot of people who claim to be spiritual are really leaning toward atheism, but they don't want to go that far since it's a real no-no in the black community." Finally, many respondents basically shrug and contend that some people just fail to sniff out even the most noxious of intellectual excrement. "It's a bunch of crap." "Seems like replacing Bronze Age bullshit with New Age bullshit." "Spirituality is bullshit, the bastard child of emotional neediness and intellectual vacuity." The language gets pretty vivid sometimes.

Of course, various distinctions also appear among the accounts rendered by the nearly one in six respondents who call themselves spiritual. They inevitably frame what this means in terms of what we have already discovered to be important concepts for atheists—openness, awe, and contributing to societal progress. Introduced in the previous chapter, Doug Freeley graduated from his high school in Lexington, Kentucky, and is currently attending college part time. He says he feels more spiritual and has a far greater sense of awe now than he ever did growing up in the fundamentalist Baptist church of his youth:

> Now I can see the universe for all of the vastness it is, instead of having it be bogged down by a petty God who cares that some people shouldn't eat pork. Also, because I don't see life as eternal, that means every second of my life is so much more valuable because this is the one life I get to live. Even from a biological perspective, we're incredibly lucky to even be born because, out of all the thousands of different genetic combinations that could've been possible, it was us, the living, who actually became reality. . . . Even the existence of our species, the fact that stars would have exploded and spilled their element-rich guts across the universe to form out stars and planets, upon which ours had the proper conditions to support the formation of life, which started out as simple bacteria until it evolved

to the point where we now have brains advanced enough to understand the processes of how all this happened! *That* is the true miracle! As you can see, I'm spiritual in that naturalist sort of way.

Others talk about being spiritual in a more pro-social sort of way. A good instance of this is a former Catholic, now a yoga instructor, from Portland, Oregon. When asked if she considers herself to be a spiritual person, she responds, "Yes, I feel that I have respect and compassion toward other human beings. I help people through volunteer work. In my yoga practice, I teach kids with special needs as well as the deaf, seniors, and people with disabilities. I believe in doing good: That makes me a spiritual person. Universal goodness: That's what I feel is bigger than me." Another former Catholic, from a "very, very Filipino Catholic family" in Los Angeles, emphasizes this pro-social sensibility this way: "I consider myself very spiritual. And by that, I mean I understand that the subjective experience of life is critically important. Compassion, love, art, interpersonal connection, self-improvement, self-awareness. It's especially about the ability to change oneself, and those around you, for the better."

That some atheists consider themselves to be spiritual whereas the majority does not is not exactly front-page news. More unexpected, however, is that about another one in six of them find the term "spiritual" to be ambiguous, yet if given the opportunity to clarify it, they are more than eager to apply it to themselves. These people adhere to the "if this, then yes" pattern with remarkable consistency. Here are some examples:

> Armando: *If* we define spirituality as the feeling of deep connection we have toward one another and with the universe in general, *then* yes, I am a spiritual person. But if the term is defined in some wishy-washy way that involves actual spirits and other supernatural beliefs, then no, I would not be.

> Sucheng: What does spiritual mean? *If* it means I love beautiful music, beautiful poetry and literature, beautiful nature scenes, the beauty of love and interdependence—all that—*then* yes. If it means spirits and some notion about a soul or something different from what our brains do and acquire, then no.

Gregory: If you define spiritual as believing and connecting with the supernatural or metaphysical, then I'm not spiritual at all. *If* you mean a sense of connectedness with your surroundings, *then* I am very spiritual. Whenever I see the California sunset or the sunrise in Arizona, whenever I'm rocked back and forth by the crashing waves of the ocean, whenever I look up at the night sky in the desert, whenever I share a laugh, kiss a girl, or hold a meaningful conversation with another human being, I'm filled with wonder and awe.

Kate: I experience deep emotion: crushing grief when my mother died; soaring joy when I fell in love; the rising delight of creative inspiration; the wonder of seeing something in a new way; piercing compassion for a friend or loved one in pain. . . . I meditate sometimes, as a paying-attention practice, and experience, when I get to the calm, a deep and profound sense of love and compassion. Sometimes I wonder if love is like breathing—whether it's always there, but most of the time I don't notice it because I'm paying attention to other things. But I don't think the love comes from something that isn't me. Anyway, *if* these things make me spiritual, *then* that's what I am.

Interestingly, when asked how well the term "spiritual" describes them, all four of these people checked the "not very well" box on their survey. When engaging them in conversation, though, we can see that conceptualizations of spirituality—attempts to grasp and live in accordance with such nonmaterial realities as love, beauty, awe, interdependence, and so forth—are extremely salient for yet another one-sixth (for a total of one-third) of the atheists in the study. Such conceptualizations, like those denoting personal meaning, enable these people to subscribe to a scientific worldview while filling in its gaps with convictions that, although not provable in a strictly empirical sense, enable them to attend to aspects of life unaccounted for by science alone.

Looking Ahead

The simplistic, yet persistent myth of conflict between science and religion does not need to be true in order to be functional. Like any widely resonant myth, it has what anthropologist Clifford Geertz terms a "double aspect" in that it is both a "model of" and a "model for" the reality to which it pertains.[34] In its more commonly understood representational aspect, this myth is a "model of" a conflictual relationship between science and religion that, as we have seen, does not accurately depict what is actually a far more complicated reality. That said, it remains enormously functional in its nonliteral, dispositional aspect. Broadly accepted as a true accounting of the objective world, it functions to shape atheists on a more subjective level insofar as it equates rejecting God with valorizing certain inner dispositions. This myth, in other words, serves as a cultural template, a "model for" thinking and acting in a world in which rejecting religious faith is envisioned as tantamount to living in accordance with integrity, openness, and an abiding concern for human betterment.

Particularly fascinating is that, while largely espousing a specifically scientific atheism, the people I interviewed are engaged in life projects that cannot be underwritten scientifically. There is no empirical verification for the choices that define even the best of human lives. To evaluate some choices as being better or worse than others is to rely on convictions, premises, first principles, and so forth that are themselves neither universalizeable nor provable in the strictly scientific sense. To varying extents, my respondents seemed to acknowledge this. Sensing that there is something missing, some dimensions of human personhood unaddressed by the dominant scientific worldview, they enlist culturally available notions of personal meaning and, for some, even spirituality in order to imagine and hence to live lives that exceed the starkly defined bounds of scientism.

Not that these people are somehow inadequate as atheists. I am not making the misleadingly snarky point that a colleague of William James once made about an ardent atheist with whom he was acquainted: "He believes in No-God, and he worships him."[35] No, these people are generally not shallow, unthinking, or prone to replacing one form of dogmatism for another. It is simply that, even as they value science, they cannot "put off living" in accordance with values that are, in the end, unjustifiable by science. They draw upon—and maintain a level of belief in—categories denoting what they consider to be meaningful (in a personal sense) and even spiritual (in a conditional sense) culled from the broader cultural repertoires to which they have access.

Note that atheists appropriate cultural categories both broadly and, important to add, quite deeply. As they go about the business of living decent, worthwhile lives without God, they, like other Americans, rely upon widely shared understandings of what it means to be a respectable citizen, an industrious worker, a loving spouse, an attentive parent, and so on. They also tap into strands of atheist thinking and identity that have, as we saw in chapter 1, impressively deep roots. At the same time as the science versus religion conflict myth—a clear outgrowth of atheism's *empirical* root—serves as a "model for" living with an eye toward integrity, openness, and progress, atheism's other roots are available to abet this project and thus be appropriated as needed. "The past is never dead," observed author William Faulkner wryly. "It's not even past."[36] So, too, is it the case with the cultural categories for thinking about and legitimating secular lives sustained by each of these roots. I introduced these not out of some antiquarian interest or scholarly respect for the dead but because they remain demonstrably vital to present-day atheists as they, while awash in a sea of faith, nevertheless attempt to navigate how best to think, feel, and act as nonbelievers.

When conversing with them about being atheists, they rely on the sets of binaries encoded in the conflict myth to distinguish themselves from the out-group of believers surrounding them and to commend their take on the world over those expressed through religious traditions. These conversations, understandably, wander into all sorts of related topics. In doing so, respondents regularly augment the binaries consolidated through the conflict myth by also drawing upon nonreligious styles of thinking nurtured by the three other cultural roots.

For instance, conversations about atheism inevitably—usually before I even ask about it—veer off in the direction of religion. At such moments, respondents typically speak in a disapproving tone reflective of the "religion : science :: comfort : integrity" relation modeled for them by the conflict myth. They also draw upon atheism's *critical* root to give a more fulsome and nimbler account for their eschewal of religion's comforts in exchange for what they see as lives of greater integrity. We will address this topic, in all its nuance, in the next chapter.

A similar dynamic occurs when they specifically address what it means to have faith. Here one finds them switching to a posture endorsed by the *agnostic* root in order to go a bit deeper into the conflict myth's "religion : science :: closed-mindedness : open-mindedness" bi-nary. As we will see in chapter 6, acknowledging one's lack of knowledge indicates for them honesty in the face of difficult questions, just as their acknowledgment of unknowing signals for them an attitude of openness that is not, they claim, evidenced in the ways most religious people seem to live out their faiths.

Finally, as we will discuss in chapter 7, they tap into the *immanent* root when conversations turn to the practical consequences of belief and nonbelief. When this happens, they go beyond the "religion : science :: regression : progress" relation encoded in the conflict myth. Likely at least somewhat a reaction to the "immoral other" stereotype, they share the details of trying to live morally to the best of their abilities, which in their unwavering opinion, is more precipitous of both everyday good-ness and societal progress than subscribing to a religious worldview. In each of these instances, they rely upon other atheist roots, or styles of thinking and discourse, to provide greater detail, to express in a more elaborated, intuitively appealing way, what is modeled for them in the most general of terms by the conflict myth. Paying attention to these details is the aim of the next few chapters.

5

The Critical Root

Living with Integrity by Saying No

Tending to the Critical Root's Other Offshoot

Fewer than one-half of all religiously affiliated Americans today think of themselves as being "critical." In contrast, a full two-thirds of all atheists in the United States claim this as a personality trait that describes them quite well.[1] Moreover, as we have already heard from respondents in previous chapters, they are not especially bashful about aiming their critical sensibilities in the direction of religion, which suggests that atheism's age-old critical root is still yielding much by way of equipping people to think through and remain steadfast in their decisions to reject religious faith, doctrines, and institutions. Then, given that they have so much to say, why do we hear so very little about what your average atheists think about such things? Why are their criticisms of religion, in all their variety and with all their nuances, never really heard within the public square?

One reason, touched upon in the last chapter, is the widespread habit of conflating atheists in general with the particular subset of better-known, best-selling atheist authors who evince disconcertedly little nuance when addressing religion. The *source* of religious commitment, they tell readers, is merely mass "delusion" (Richard Dawkins) or a kind of primordial and still lingering "spell" (Daniel C. Dennett) cast upon a not-yet-awoken populace. Furthermore, they continue ominously, religion's inevitable *end* is that it ultimately "poisons everything" (Christopher Hitchens) and leads inexorably to "a future of ignorance and slaughter" (Sam Harris).[2] Not much hairsplitting there. Such thinkers represent an influential offshoot of atheism's critical root, and without question, many of their more keenly targeted criticisms of religious intolerance, hypocrisy, patriarchy, dogmatism, and the like are entirely valid. Yet, religion scholar Karen Armstrong undoubtedly speaks for many—both academic peers and people with a more robust understanding and experience of faith—when she finds the New Atheist authors' broad-brush theorizing and unduly indiscriminate conclusions to be, in the end, "disappointingly shallow."[3] When this is presumed to be true of this root's other burgeoning offshoot, the views of everyday atheists, then their criticisms of religion, unfortunately, can be all too easily dismissed as a consequence.

This is compounded by a second problem: the stereotyping of atheists themselves. If their message is widely found "guilty by association" with atheist writers' lack of nuance, the messenger fares little better in the eyes of the general public. Its perception of atheists is as dependably unflattering as it is false. It is worth repeating that, even though they are consistently stigmatized as immoral, there is just no empirical support for this. Whatever else they might suggest, the conversations captured in this book unambiguously reflect people's often considerable efforts to carve out intellectually honest and ethically discerning lives for themselves. The same should be said for the pervasive notion that atheists live meaningless, superficial lives. As mentioned, the preponderance of my interviewees agree that their lives have "real purpose," and according to a recent national study, the proportion (roughly one-half) who report feeling a "deep sense of wonder" at least once every month is about the same as it is for their actively religious counterparts.[4] So, what about the stereotypical "unhappy" or "angry" atheists? Turns out they are hard to find as well. The approximately nine in ten atheists who say they consider themselves to be either "very" or "pretty" happy almost exactly mirrors what actively religious people report. The same proportion of nonreligious and religious Americans (again, about nine in ten) tell pollsters that they are "very" or "somewhat" satisfied with their personal lives.[5] And rather than being angry with them, most atheists have close friends, family members, and for about half of those who are married, even spouses who are believers. Little wonder, then, that only about one-third of the people I queried say they "tend to dislike religious people" despite their purported inclination toward the wrong side of the binaries described in the last chapter. So, what about the religiously ignorant atheists? They, too, are more imagined than real. The majority of American atheists were socialized into religious adherence as children; according to the General Social Survey, 43 percent of them attended church services at least once every week at the age of twelve.[6] Nearly two-thirds of those I spoke with say they enjoy reading books about religion, and according to a recent Pew study, atheists (along with agnostics) are on average the nation's most religiously knowledgeable citizens.[7] Despite this, there is still the repeatedly heard claim that nonbelievers are simply duped by the New Atheism fad. But there is no evidence here either. As mentioned earlier, nearly all (97 percent) of the respondents in my study say their own critical thinking has been "very influential" in terms of thinking through and living out their worldviews, whereas far fewer say this about popular books on atheism (32 percent), their friends who are atheists (20 percent), atheist websites (16 percent), or atheist groups in their area (8 percent).

The cautionary note here is that, if what atheists have to say is presumed to lack nuance and if atheists themselves are habitually thought to be immoral, superficial, unhappy, angry, ignorant, and duped, then there is scant incentive to pay attention to their criticisms of religion. This situation is only exacerbated by yet another reason that atheists' perspectives are so often not heard—they just as often go unspoken. Experiences of stigma and the persistence of stereotypes, even easily debunked ones, likely go a long way toward creating a hushing effect among nonbelievers. According to Pew's 2014 Religious Landscape Study, about two-thirds of all atheists in the United States say they seldom or never discuss their views on religion with people of faith.[8] Most religiously affiliated Americans are not even close to being this tight-lipped.

Fortunately, things loosen up a bit when one takes the time to truly listen. In doing so, we discover some subtleties that can get lost when attending solely to the "official," more polemical offshoot of atheism's critical root.

Unlike the New Atheist authors, my interviewees generally refrain from ungainly black-and-white verities and offer reflections that, as the great G. F. W. Hegel once noted of philosophy, are painted "grey in grey."[9] Not polemicists and not blinkered by scientism's own mythical spell, these people know there is something missing from the story that science, on its own, can tell about the human person. They know they do not reside on some epistemological Mount Olympus, able to see all unimpeded, able to understand and definitively explain all. So, they paint in greyer hues. They accept the basic "religion : science :: comfort : integrity" binary outlined by the conflict myth, but they also, through the contouring and shading wrought of their lived experience and discernment, add important details with an unexpectedly light touch.

They draw upon atheism's critical root with respect to their pointing out and saying no to the personal comforts and intellectual vacuity that, they contend, so often accompanies religious belief and practice. As they critique key dimensions of religion in the manner they do, they come to identify and, importantly, actually experience themselves as people who, as nonbelievers, aspire to live with greater integrity. Yet, because they acknowledge the limits of their own understanding and essentially accept that, like anyone, people of faith are simply trying to make sense of their lives to the best of their abilities, atheists generally exhibit real nimbleness in offering their criticisms. There are grey areas because some aspects of religion are more or less objectionable to them than others, something one discovers when one does not lump them in with polemicists, perpetuate trite stereotypes about them, or appear resistant to actually paying attention to what they have to say.

From General to Particular:
Less about Belief in God than Belief in *That* God

Other people's belief in God is in itself relatively—and, perhaps for many readers, surprisingly—unobjectionable to most atheists. In fact, they sometimes see good things coming from faith. Even though she left the Church more than two decades ago, Barbara Randall lives in the same rural Louisiana town where she grew up, and she has remained close to several of her childhood friends who continue to be practicing Catholics. When she talks about these people, now all in their midforties like her, she comes to the not-especially-grudging conclusion that "belief in God is often a good thing." She ponders a bit: "God is generally presented as the one who gives things to people. Belief in God is a way to express appreciation for the fact that we're alive and for the experiences that we get to have while we're alive. Gratitude is never a bad thing." After talking about her friends, her focus then expands to the religious convictions evident within the broader population. "I really see the appeal!" she announces, raising her voice just a little. "It must be nice to have unwavering faith in something—to be able to completely relinquish control to some force that you trust to have your best interests in mind. It's not a coincidence that people find God when they're at their lowest. And the social implications of faith can't be underestimated because the feeling of belonging is powerful and heady stuff. People like fitting into a structure where they know what's expected of them and expected of the people around them." Then, at last, she focuses inward, sharing some of her own experience. "I actually love the idea of religion. I loved how it made me feel when I went [to mass] with my grandmother as a child, and when I attended later as an adult, usually coinciding with the births of my children or when moving to a new location." In spite of all this, she concludes by highlighting a fundamental distinction. Shaking her head, she explains, "I always run into the same wall [pause]: wanting to believe is not the same thing as believing."

This is the wall many run into. Like Barbara Randall, lots of atheists understand that belief in God can express something as positive as gratitude, surely a "good thing." They, again like her, definitely "see the appeal." They refrain from disparaging their friends or family members or whomever for wanting feelings of being cared for, of belonging, and of intimacy. It is just that they equate scaling the wall that divides *wanting* from actually *believing* with an unacceptable lowering of their own integrity. So, they prefer to remain critical.

This is also why and how Rick Courier, a former Methodist living in Tacoma, Washington, stays on the wall's nonbelieving side. Rather than using the word "wanting," he uses "settling" and "comforting," words that convey the same sort of appeal; and his preferred synonyms for "critical" are "honest" and "evidence":

> Believing in things without sufficient evidence isn't a very noble human attribute. It seems more like settling for some tidy and comforting answer rather than living with the unknown. Also, trying to put a human face upon the entirety of the universe involves making some pretty generous assumptions on our part. If we are honest with ourselves, we would all admit that there is simply no evidence, whether empirical or deductive, that would concretely confirm the existence of supernatural beings.

Even after coming to this conclusion, his perspective on faith is not at all disparaging. "Life can be hard for some folks," he notes, "and some have it easier than others, and some are trapped in a life I could never endure. If faith in God makes life more bearable for some, I would rather they have it than suffer and live in anguish all of their days. I have always liked what John Lennon said on the topic: 'God is a concept by which we measure our pain.'"

People like Randall and Courier "see the appeal" of religious faith. Even as they seldom tire of critiquing the irrationality of believers, they, with some exceptions, mostly keep from personally denigrating those who, rather than hitting the wall, have traversed it, entering the realm of belief. "No harm done," most seem to suggest—unless, of course, belief redounds into the doing of actual harm. So, instead of belief in God per se, the central issue for most atheists is the kind of behavior that faith inspires or justifies among the faithful.

Two men, both New Yorkers, illustrate this distinction quite well. One is a white, seventy-something former Christian Scientist who lives in the Bronx, votes Republican, and is an avid Yankees fan. The other, a thirtyish African American ex- (or, as he put it, "recently emancipated") Jehovah's Witness who lives in Queens, identifies as a lifelong Democrat and, as fate would have it, is a "fourth-generation" Mets fan. What unites these seeming opposites—besides being the only two respondents in this study to mention their favorite professional baseball teams—is their privileging of behavior over belief when it comes to the God question. "Belief in God is not a good or bad thing. It's a personal issue as far as I'm concerned," insists the Yankees fan. "Belief in God as a way to feel part of a community or fulfill a spiritual need is healthy, and while I don't really encourage it, I understand it and support this in my friends. It's when it's used as a justification to perform horrible and unjust acts that I have a problem with it." That is precisely when the Mets fan has a problem too. Although these two men may have divergent backgrounds and opinions, this is a point of convergence for them and for many other nonbelievers. "I'm indifferent," explains the Mets fan. "A person's beliefs seem to affect each one differently, so I try to handle it on a case-by-case basis. In some cases, religion turns people into bigoted hate-machines, while in others it creates beautiful people who would give their last possession to help a complete stranger."

How do different cases turn out differently? If the majority of atheists are essentially, as it were, on the same team with respect to being more concerned about faith's practical fruits than faith itself, then why in some cases does religious conviction blossom into something beautiful and in others become something rotten to the core? The answers people give to these questions often focus on individual believers. Some, they say, mistake a religious faith that is personally meaningful to them for actual knowledge in accordance with which others should lead their lives. Some believers are said to have what psychologists call "authoritarian personalities" and think that, for the sake of order, others should also conform to the dictates of religious (and other) leaders. Some, still other respondents contend, are simply bad people and use religion as a cover for being, to use our Mets fan's expression, the "bigoted hate-machines" they were hardwired into becoming all along. People say lots of things about this, and in saying it, they sound a lot like what one hears from the critical root's more polemical offshoot.

Perhaps most interesting, and where they sound quite different from this, is when they attempt to answer these questions by turning from the believing subject to the object of belief, which occurs frequently. Belief in God, they generally agree, is far less problematic than faith in particular conceptualizations of God they flag as being associated with various modes of irrationality that in turn lead to harmful behaviors.

Notice an interesting twist here. Atheists, as we have seen, think of *believers*, in the most general terms, as the "irrational other." As conversations deepen and they add touches of grey to this black-and-white, us-versus-them framing, one sees them disaggregate with respect to the cultural, social, and personal sources of faith's irrationality. Yet, when thinking about undesirable *behaviors* among the religious, here they once again disaggregate—this time, according to three widely diffused images of God that, in their view, sanction the sorts of irrationality that then lead to objectionable outcomes. Irrationality, then, is essentially the cause of religious belief and the behavioral effect of certain commonplace understandings of God.

The first of these is the widespread and oftentimes fear-inducing image of God as judge. Everywhere one looks, atheists sneer at this image for defying what they take to be commonsense notions of decency. Calling this God the "all-powerful judge, jury, and executioner of souls," Nicholas Saroglou concludes that "a place of eternal torture isn't what one would expect from a loving, merciful God." Expounding somewhat, he reasons, "It is unjust and unfair to hold imperfect beings to standards of perfection that are impossible to meet and then assign them an eternal fate based on what took place within a finite period of time. It's asinine to require people to believe in a specific thing without being guaranteed that they will ever be presented with it in a way that is convincing to them." Equally offended is Ken McFarland. "I finally realized," he recalls, "that any all-powerful deity who could forgive and reward a mass murderer because he believed but condemn and torture for eternity a person who never harmed anyone but did not believe—or perhaps could not believe, like me—was in no way great and, in fact, would instead have to be insane, narcissistic, and cruel."

As alternately unjust, unfair, asinine, insane, narcissistic, and cruel, Saroglou and McFarland write off this God for failing to meet even the most basic human standards of morality. What is more, this image of God, they both agree, also steers humans in this same immoral direction. God as judge functions as a kind of template for the believer as judgmental, a species of irrationality based on the chimera of possessing clear-cut standards for evaluating human lives as well as on the presumption of knowing much more about others than one actually does. "If people use, like my family does, their beliefs to help others and ease suffering, then I think belief in God is a good thing," continues McFarland, referencing the previously mentioned belief-behavior distinction. "But, if they use their beliefs to decide that they know better than a gay couple or an atheist or a Muslim or Hindu family what would truly make them happy, then I consider their belief to be a bad thing." Others do, too, and they are also quick to connect divine image with human action. "What God does in the next life, his believers do in this one." "If the apple doesn't fall far from the tree, why wouldn't you expect Christians to damn those who don't agree with them?" "So many believers pray to a God who is more than happy to throw people away; that sort of explains how they treat people who think and pray differently from them." Comments like these express this basic view reasonably well.

The second image atheists single out as problematic is God as sovereign. This seems irrational to them because it posits an omnipotent deity who, all appearances aside, actually bestows order onto the universe and governs it in an ultimately beneficent manner. The harmful result here is less a type of behavior (as we saw with judgmentalism) than a dearth of behavior. It leads to a degree of complacency that, they argue, is plainly unjustifiable given the enormity of human suffering and injustice in the world.

Joe Kaufman is one of the responders we met in chapter 2. He recalls the birth of his first child as the event that initially spurred him to rethink his religious convictions and decide which, if any, he wanted to teach his son. As he came to terms with his ensuing atheism, it became clear that the notion of a sovereign God was most irksome to him:

> I understand that some people take comfort with the platitude "God works in mysterious ways." But I don't understand why they never follow that thought deeper and ask why. To think that there's an omnipotent, omnipresent being watching over us who allows tsunamis to kill thousands, who allows earthquakes to devour cities, who allows childhood diseases to rob the innocent of life—how terrible! What kind of a murderous tyrant would that make him? . . . Either a creator made human beings as flawed creatures and then punishes us for the flaw he built in or it's all just random. I take solace in the fact that the terrible things that happen in the world are not the result of some insane dictator. They are the result of a chaotic environment filled with billions of people who have often competing self-interests and occasional mental health issues. . . . To say otherwise is to give people a false sense of dependence. Instead of rolling up their sleeves and getting things done on their own, they clasp their hands and pray for divine intervention. A good example of this was when Texas governor Rick Perry gathered thirty thousand Christians at Reliant Stadium in 2011 to pray for an end to America's national decline. Now, imagine what could have been done if, instead of gathering Christians, he gathered elected officials with the expressed purpose of thinking of ways to improve the nation.

Compare this to what Veronica Barro, an ex-Catholic living in Mississippi, thinks about the same God concept:

> Christians and others claim that their God is a good and loving God. But when the immense suffering of the world is brought up, then all one hears

is that God works in mysterious ways or there must be some ethereal purpose for it. Well, if there's a God, it appears that it works in mysteriously evil ways. When I was in the Catholic Church, God's cold indifference to suffering was horrifying to me. Being mysterious is a shitty excuse for allowing people to starve to death, die in floods or hurricanes, or freeze to death. . . . If your God cannot be considered good by its own moral commands, then how can it be anything but evil and how could this possibly be comforting? A good king is not above his own laws. . . . As an atheist, I don't need to come to terms with suffering and death. Natural events like floods or earthquakes are random things that cause suffering. I don't have to justify why my God doesn't lift an ethereal finger to help. Instead, I just accept that the world is a mindless thing where suffering happens. Suffering can make me very sad. But it also motivates me to actually get up and do something to help rather than pray and pretend that I've helped.

Notice that the same three themes emerge for these respondents as well as for nearly everyone who explicitly rejects this image. First, however it gets labeled ("tyrant," "dictator," or "king"), divine sovereignty should no longer be propped up by the legitimating platitude that God works in mysterious ways and, thus, despite the abundance of contrary and deeply painful evidence, the universe is nevertheless ruled and ordered by God. Next is the insistence that the evidence one sees with respect to earthquakes, childhood diseases, people starving and freezing to death, and so on should all be understood as reflecting a reality that, all platitudes aside, is thoroughly "random" and "chaotic." The world, they insist, does not operate according to a divine mind and will. Rather, it is "a mindless thing." Finally, the consequence of looking to platitudes and not facing up to reality is to be plagued by an enervating complacency, which atheists closely associate with this conception of deity. Kaufman's looking outward and contrasting "rolling up their sleeves and getting things done" with Christians' tendency to merely "clasp their hands and pray for divine intervention" relies on the same either/or logic as does Barro when she, looking inward, elevates her motivation to "actually get up and do something" over a temptation to simply "pray and pretend that I've helped."

The third image is in some ways quite similar to God as sovereign. Where atheists think of divine sovereignty as encouraging people to irrationally project agency onto a world where there actually is none, they talk about God as father as steering people, again quite irrationally, toward disavowing the agency that is truly theirs as persons. The result is not mere complacency, a tendency to disengage from meaningful action in a world marked by suffering and injustice. Rather, it is the sorts of inconsequential actions that are not befitting of people's status as rational agents with the opportunity (and, as we have seen, the responsibility) to cut their own life paths and stride these with integrity and purpose. Such actions include engaging in time-consuming religious rituals. Prayer, religious socialization, church activities and involvements, learning and talking about religious teachings, and feeling dismayed about instances of not measuring up to the standards outlined by those religious teachings—all these things belong on this list as well. Most of all, atheists mention the enormous mental energy believers expend in monitoring and disciplining their thoughts and actions in ways they hope will prove pleasing to God. If the watchwords for the previous two images are judgmentalism and complacency, here the harmful behaviors that derive from seeing God as father can be summed up as infantile. It is striking how often atheists counterpoise faith in this God—either once held by them or, more often, exhibited by others—with "being a grown-up" or with such adult-associated tasks as "taking the reins," "accepting full responsibility," "getting behind the wheel and steering my life my way," "putting my big girl underpants on," and "no longer looking over my shoulder for permission or approval." Another former Catholic, Kristy Probasco, seems to have done just about all of these things, and she captures this perspective with singular precision:

> You know, it's odd. Before I threw it [her faith] all away, it was like I wasn't even starring in the drama of my own life. It was like God had the only starring role and I was just part of a very large supporting cast. It was all about this loving, caring, sometimes angry parent, and my role was to be a good little girl—even into my forties—who tried to please Sky Daddy and, in that way, remain in his good favor. The Church talks about a time when people used to "pray, pay, and obey," but, honestly, it's still like that. I'm talking about Catholics and just about every believer I know. You see this in people's constant pleading. "Please help grandma to keep on living." "Please help me to find a halfway decent job." It's really kind of

obsequious, you know? . . . It's other stuff too. All the rituals, memorizing all the prayers, thinking about the bad things you've done and probably feeling guilty or inadequate somehow. Thinking about how upset God is and how to make things better. It's not just that it's infantile. I know a lot of atheists who aren't the most mature people in the world either. It also takes the focus off your own life, makes it seem less important, like it's not something you should take charge of and take seriously. When that happens, then believing in God isn't neutral anymore. It's not like cutting your hair or being into romance novels or something like that—pretty neutral. That's when, in my opinion, it becomes a really negative thing.

Whereas judgmentalism can engender behaviors detrimental to others and complacency can lead to an effectual indifference to others, infantilism primarily harms oneself. As Probasco describes so compellingly, the image of God the father often depreciates one's integrity as a full, mature person as well as one's own sense of agency in the world. When this occurs, and when judgmentalism and complacency occur, belief in God goes from being as neutral as, say, getting a new haircut or reading a romance novel to becoming for most atheists a "really negative thing."

From Subjective to Objective: Less about Religiosity than Religion

Atheists' propensity for painting in shades of grey when it comes to belief in God is also evident in their attitudes toward religion itself. On one hand, for example, about four in five of them contend that "religion causes more conflict than peace" whereas, on the other, nearly two-thirds claim there to be "basic truth in many religions." Are nonbelievers sending a mixed message here? Not exactly. Such data are puzzling until one realizes that they paint with an especially fine brush when distinguishing between religiosity and religion. Although they almost never explicitly use this word, by religiosity, I refer to the subjectively satisfying experiences of comfort, community, meaning, transcendence, and so on that believers seek or acquire through their various types and levels of commitment to their faith traditions. Once again, atheists generally "see the appeal" of such things, and given that they often come from religious backgrounds themselves, many speak from firsthand experience.

In contrast, when these beliefs about God and devotional practices get organized—or, to use a sociological term, get rationalized—into coherent systems replete with authority structures, prescribed rituals, and expressions of orthodoxy, then they become distinctive, objectified religions. At that point they are said to cause nothing but trouble and hence draw the ire of the people in this study.

This religiosity-religion distinction is subtle but extremely pervasive. Eric Stroope, a former Episcopalian still living and working (as an architect) in his hometown of Nashua, New Hampshire, exemplifies it nicely. He talks about believers in terms of their "seeking answers to some of life's biggest questions"—no problem. He then mentions people who "seek individual paths toward spirituality"—ditto. Later on, he focuses his attention on "people taking solace in the thought that a lost loved one has gone to a better life"—"I would never try to dissuade them of this," he asserts convincingly. As nonproblematic as these highly subjectivized intellectual, spiritual, and emotional dimensions of everyday religiosity are to him, things look different when he turns to religion in the more objectivized sense. "My biggest problem with religion," he states baldly, "is that it's a fixed body of knowledge that allows no change. Then it's not so helpful. Then it serves as a refuge for narrow thinking and resistance to change. The basis for quite a number of things held to be immutable are sketchy at best, extrapolated from writings that were passed down from an oral tradition and underwent numerous revisions and translations." While Stroope suggests that personal religiosity can be actually helpful to people, another New Englander, Bostonian and former Christian Scientist Scott Tsang, sees it as merely harmless. Still, he is just as adamant in preferring it to the dogmatism he sees as inherent within religion. "If someone's religion keeps them from accepting the true origins of humanity, the vastness of the universe, and possibility of other life within it, and most importantly, if it makes them hate their neighbors because of ancient scripture, then I would definitely say it's a bad thing," he reasons. "But that's dogma. That's completely different. A belief in a personal God that's more like a genie people occasionally take out of a bottle to comfort themselves, bounce questions off of, and make promises to. That's as harmless as reading one's horoscope!"

As these two men suggest, expressions of religiosity are usually thought of by atheists as being harmless or even somewhat helpful, whereas religion, to quote Kristy Probasco, is uniformly considered to be a "really negative thing." Where people usually differ is in their estimation of whether religion typically becomes a negative thing or always is negative.

People in both of these two camps tend to think either in broadly historical terms or with a focus on the present day. In what we can call the "typically becomes" camp, Wade Thedford is an excellent example of someone convinced of the positive role religion once played in the evolution of humans' moral sensibilities. Looking back to time immemorial and echoing the philosopher Thomas Hobbes's brutish, "all against all" understanding of individuals in a state of nature,[10] he reflects:

> In my view, the beginning state of humanity is the selfish nihilist. But we actually overcame that with religion, which helped us to grow together as a species and as cooperating communities around the world. So, religion has done a lot for our species in the sense that it gave people a crutch when they were not yet capable of judging right and wrong. Because we're animals, we started out fixating on our own goals and needs. But it was religion that eventually told us that there's more to it than that, which in turn helped develop our capacity to think in bigger, more complex ways.

Just as certain as he is of religion's contributions to the development of human consciousness, Thedford is similarly clear about what it has since become and why. "I think religion is pretty tired now," he says. "It's been abused by religious authorities to a point—in the 1500s, 1600s, and 1700s—that was just tragic. They started abusing power and killing people who didn't agree with orthodox teachings and rigid categories. Since religion hasn't changed that much since then, I think, right now, it's obvious that it's outlived its usefulness."

"Right now," the present day, is essentially the timeframe Cristina Gómez has in mind. She has no difficulty listing faith's personal and societal benefits—that is, until they become overshadowed by what Thedford calls religion's "orthodox teachings and rigid categories." As for benefits, she says, "My father is a good example of someone for whom it's really not the doctrines that are important. It's a feeling of meaningfulness; it's the sense of community and sense of belonging; and it's a pathway for doing good. I think there are lots of groups out there that do amazing things. Right? They organize food banks. They start domestic violence shelters. They offer counseling for kids in abusive situations. That's the upside." As for the downside, in Gómez's view, it has everything to do with the objectivization of "orthodox teachings and rigid categories": "The problem is when people say, 'You can't have this food or counseling or whatever unless you tell me you believe in the Trinity.' Or when people are all gung ho about loving thy neighbor until they find out one of those neighbors happen to be a homosexual. That's when religion is bad—when it becomes about doctrines and about compartmentalizing people, which is pretty often!"

"Pretty often" does not quite cut it for the "always is" camp. For these people, religion is *always* about the imposition of definitions and categories onto the world. It is, therefore, *always* a negative thing, and rather than something it typically becomes, this is what religion has *always* been. As with the previous camp, people in this one frame their viewpoints in terms of either the *longue durée* of history or the present moment. Especially distinctive here is their lack of equivocation. This is absolutely true of eighty-something Lee Jelen, who began to question his strict Methodist upbringing as a fifteen-year-old but did not finally call himself an atheist until reaching the age of about forty:

> There is absolutely no verifiable evidence that any ancient holy book on this planet speaks truth. It's all words set to scrolls by ancient people who did not know the earth was not the center of the universe or even our solar system; they thought the earth was flat; they thought disease was caused by demons that could be cast out by spells. What they had to say does not convince me of anything except that they wanted to manipulate the masses. . . . Religion has set mankind back thousands of years with its ignorant views of the universe. Hypatia was the last curator of the great library of Alexandria, and the flesh was flayed from her bones by a crowd led by Cyril, who was later made bishop of Alexandria for confronting paganism. Then we experienced the Dark Ages with the Church in charge of society. Finally, Copernicus was a brave soul to challenge the ignorance of his day, and Galileo was under house arrest until the end of his life only to be pardoned by a pope three hundred years later. This kind of ignorant tyranny put upon humanity by ignorant myths is not a service to mankind. It's a plague.

As Jelen looks back in time, Ari Katzmann's observations seem ripped from the pages of today's *New York Times*. He was raised in a nonreligious household and is Jelen's junior by, I would guess, nearly a half century. Nevertheless, Katzmann mirrors his unequivocal stance:

> I think, if we look at the geopolitical climate of our world and consider root causes of nearly all the hotspots, religion is at the root of it. India and Pakistan are in a Hindu versus Muslim standoff over a little strip of land they both believe to be divinely bequeathed to them. The Israeli-Palestinian conflict is the same. The menacing nature of Iran is due to the fundamentalist theocracy that exists in that country. The 9/11 attacks as well as the ensuing wars in Iraq and Afghanistan are fueled by religious difference. Consider the partisanship that the Religious Right has caused in this country and how they use their religiosity to mask sexism and hatred and for the purpose of rolling back civil rights for minorities and women. . . . These are the facts, and anyone who denies them is either ignorant, deluded, or both. Organized religion is toxic.

Like a plague (Jelen) or a toxin (Katzmann), religion is always a negative thing for people in this camp. The disparate combinations of metaphysical speculations, spiritual practices, and feelings of transcendence that comprise people's individual religiosities may be somewhat helpful or at least relatively harmless to them. But this, they say, is not true of the plague/toxin of religion. When religiosity's subjectively meaningful ideas, practices, and emotions become codified and objectivized as "orthodox teachings and rigid categories," then those *teachings* inevitably tamp down learning and free inquiry, just as those *categories* come to define people in opposition to one another and, inevitably, precipitate animosities, hatred, and violence.

From Personal to Institutional: Less about Religious People than Religious Institutions

Katzmann's mention of "organized religion" brings us to yet another evaluative nuance drawn by atheists. To use a bit more sociological language, they consistently differentiate among levels of analysis to distinguish religious individuals from the larger institutions (churches, denominations, etc.) in which many, but certainly not all, believers participate to one degree or another. Their assessment of both levels is actually quite Janus-faced since they are quick to see both the good and bad in each. The difference is that, although their ambivalence about religious people ultimately leans in the direction of understanding and even empathy, their ambivalence about religious institutions comes down rather heavily on the side of disparagement.

People's criticisms of believers are strewn throughout this book. As we saw in chapter 2, dissatisfying interactions and fervent disagreements with religious acquaintances, friends, and family members are what often led many to identify as atheists in the first place. Religious people, as discussed in chapter 3, are described by atheists as all too ready to stigmatize. They are also seen as being ill-equipped, unable, and even unwilling to deploy their rational faculties. Especially compared to atheists' own powerful experiences of being free, believers are largely looked upon as being unenviably restricted by their faith convictions. Finally, in the previous chapter we saw that implied in atheists' opting for lives of integrity, open-mindedness, and commitment to progress are believers' corresponding inclinations to be comforted, closed-minded, and resistant to assuming their responsibilities for improving the world around them.

Even in the face of all this, on balance, atheists are actually quite generous in their overall assessment of individual believers, especially those closest to them. Not infrequently, one hears very appreciative comments. They appreciate what, from their perspective, people are actually attempting to do through their piety. For one former Catholic, his grandmother is expressing love. "My grandmother says a little prayer every time we talk on the phone. I like it," he admits. "I think it's her way of saying she loves me and thinks about me. Even though I don't believe, every time I have a test or an important interview, I tell her and she lights a votive candle for me. It's a family thing. Some of my fellow atheists would chastise me, but I think it's a harmless way to show love." Another former Catholic (and, after that, a former Baptist as well) appreciates the singular dedication of a friar who happens to live in her Philadelphia neighborhood. "I think about his life every so often, and to be honest, I'm jealous of that experience of being so dedicated to an overarching principle that gives him a sense of depth and meaning," she says. "It's admirable. I'd actually love to be part of something intense like that, but the fact that I don't buy the bottom line—about the supernatural—means I can't be a participant."

Along with appreciation, one hears a tremendous amount of empathy from atheists. They say no to belief in God because they choose to walk what they consider to be the harder path of personal integrity instead of careening off into the direction of faith's comforts. All the while, they understand how difficult life can be and are thus reticent to look too frowningly upon those who need to be comforted. Sean Regan, for instance, refers to religion as a "source of comfort," a "crutch," and a "drug," but rather than with contempt, he talks about people who need such things with real sensitivity. "I have a friend whose thirty-one-year-old son dropped dead of a heart attack right in front of her, another friend whose son was in a coma for eleven years before he died, another friend who just lost her husband and now imagines him in heaven. To these wonderful friends, their religion is a solace. It gives them peace. I would never interfere with anyone's choice for their own lives," he concludes. "Life is difficult." Just as Regan imagines how his friends likely feel amid their misfortunes, another respondent imagines how he might feel if his own life were more difficult than it currently is. "I think if I lived in different times, I would have believed in God," he confides. Elaborating further, he says,

How could you not? If you're an untouchable in India or a serf in feudal Europe, you have to believe that something better awaits you. If I were a refugee in Syria, I would certainly believe in God. Otherwise, I'd give up hope. Being an atheist is a privilege, and it largely means I live a privileged life. As I meet other young atheists, I strive to give them that perspective in hopes of helping them to be more patient with people who still need to believe. I think we, as a species, needed God early on when belief in a supreme being was the only way of exerting control over a world where humans controlled nothing. But I'm not a serf, or in a foxhole, or living in endemic poverty. . . . So, I try to help the people who drew the short economic straw. My wife and I donate considerable amounts of money toward that end. That's the moral thing to do.

Still another person—Ben Zeller, the former Jehovah's Witness who wept while watching the IMAX film about the Hubble telescope—does not need to imagine his friends' experiences or those of other, less fortunate people. He simply needs to recall his own experience as a believer. "I despise organized religion," he says unequivocally. Similarly cocksure, he declares, "Let's face it, religion is so damn easy to ridicule." He keeps his derision from getting the better of him, though, especially with respect to his many religious friends whom he would never allow himself to ridicule. "Sometimes I think to myself, 'Why are they so stupid?'" Zeller says. "When I look down on them like that, it really bothers me because, as I constantly try to remind myself, I was just like them not too long ago. They live their lives believing in fairy tales. It's pathetic. I want to shake them and tell them to wake up. But I tell myself to be more compassionate because I was one of them for so long."

Yet, erring on the side of compassion and empathy is not at all the custom when atheists move from the individual to institutional level of analysis. This is not to say they, as the rampant stereotype suggests, uniformly and instinctively echo Zeller's "I despise organized religion," full stop. Here, too, they are actually more ambivalent than is typically acknowledged. For instance, one recent study finds that fully three-quarters of all atheists in the United States agree that churches and other religious organizations "bring people together and strengthen community bonds." Nearly that many (71 percent) say that these organizations "play an important role in helping the poor and needy."[11] About one-third of American atheists even attend religious services, at least occasionally.[12]

Nevertheless, religious institutions (and frequently leaders) are rarely afforded the same benefit of the doubt atheists give to believers themselves.[13] For one thing, institutions are viewed as the primary transmitters of the "orthodox teachings and rigid categories" that, as we saw, are thought to be far more problematic than individual religiosity. Understandably, then, nearly four-fifths of all atheists agree that religious institutions "focus too much on rules."[14] Second, and closely related, is the broadly held view that they also focus too much on distinguishing their adherents from other people, especially from people in religious groups with which they are in competition for members, resources, and influence. "These organizations draw firm lines between themselves and everyone else and encourage contention," notes a longtime Wyoming atheist, "while, at the same time, claiming they're somehow inclusive. So, I think organized religion is worse than personal belief about the same way organized crime is worse than random crime." Third, as the three-quarters of all American atheists agreeing that religious institutions are "too concerned with money and power" attest, many talk about them as being more focused on mammon than on God.[15] "I consider organized religion not only bad but borderline evil," argues one interviewee, who represents this viewpoint well. "How can someone stand up and preach the word of the God they claim to worship—who ordered his followers to feed the poor and give up all their worldly possessions—and then climb down from the pulpit, collect millions of dollars from an eager congregation in order to build a giant church with a top-of-the-line sound system, a café, a gym, a childcare facility, and funds to advertise itself on TV? How many hungry people could have been fed with that money?" Fourth, religious institutions incite more disdain than do everyday believers because of their engagement within the political realm, especially in terms of their often conservative positions on various "culture wars" issues.[16] Eighty-three percent of atheists in the United States agree that churches and religious organizations are "too involved with politics."[17] Many of them sound quite a bit like David Hahn, a former Mormon who had once been a leader in his local ward. "The power being wielded by organized religion today is disturbing," he reflects. "Political candidates have to pander to them if they want to get elected. Pastors violate the law by endorsing candidates from the pulpit, and the IRS refuses to enforce the laws forbidding it. Government at all levels wastes time and money dealing with religious issues pushed by religious groups—prayer in school, tax exemptions for churches, abortion, gay marriage, stem cell research, school vouchers, prayer breakfasts, the Year of the Bible. It seems endless!"

Easily the most regularly heard criticism of religious institutions is that they make the people participating within them worse than they would otherwise be. Belief in God and personal religiosity are taken to be relatively innocuous overall—that is, until they are steered toward belief in problematic images of God and toward objectively organized religious systems, which is what religious institutions are understood to be doing. Most of the atheists I spoke with, who generally have a relatively positive view of human nature, thus think of religious institutions as a deeply corrupting influence. In fact, no other quote is bandied about as ubiquitously by them as another one attributed to physicist Steven Weinberg: "With or without religion, good people can behave well and bad people can do evil," he opined and atheists repeat or post on their Facebook pages approvingly, "but for good people to do evil, that takes religion." For the atheists in this study, that mostly takes the form of "organized religion." Some, like Dora Oman-Nerina, a pharmacist in Athens, Georgia, address this theme in rather general terms:

> Even as I think an individual's belief in a higher power can be ennobling and a wonderful experience for them, on the whole I think religion has done more harm than good. I can't say I think people's belief in God or religion is good when that very belief has acted as a catalyst for so many wars and so much death, persecution, and violence. I can't say I'm happy we have organized religion when it so often lobbies against the rights of women, homosexuals, transsexuals, and other groups. . . . It goes to show that even decent people can lose a sense of their own goodness when indoctrinated with supposedly sacred doctrines. Ideas of absolute truth, by their very nature, function to discourage free and analytical thinking.

Others make the same point about the corrupting influence of religious institutions by giving more specific examples. Jim Testoni, a Denver restaurateur, does this easily because he reads a good deal about religion and also has lots of friends and family members who are churchgoers. Like Oman-Nerina, he touches upon the bright side of faith but then expresses concern:

> Efforts to clothe and feed the needy are a good thing. Counseling those in need can be good. However, there's a lot of bad that comes from following an organized religion. At its most basic level, it allows people to stop thinking critically about what they feel is truly right and wrong, and then place the burden on an outside source. For example, from interviews I've seen, I can tell you that the members of the Westboro Baptist Church seem to be generally nice people. Yet they see no problem with standing outside of funerals with those terrible "God Hates Fags" signs. In their minds, they're doing good because their religion tells them so. My step-

sister, who is generally also a very nice person, told her young children that their grandmother—while on her deathbed—was going to hell when she died because she wasn't a Christian.

Notice that the logic is basically the same. Religion can be a "good" and even "ennobling" thing and the religious are themselves often naturally "decent" and "nice" people. The problem comes when these very same people get connected with religious institutions, which invariably disconnect them from their own innate capacity for critical thinking. When this occurs, the sorts of things good people, if left uncorrupted, would never think of doing then become thinkable, doable, and ultimately part of the litany of evil things actually done by believers both past and present.

The Irony of Saying No—Presumption Five Again

In the last chapter, we saw that Americans who identify as atheists tend toward a specifically "scientific atheism," the foundations of which are shored up by their broad-based acceptance of the science-versus-religion conflict myth. Sensing that there is something missing here, that the extreme version of this position, often dubbed "scientism," fails to account for important facets of human experience, they draw upon culturally available notions of personal meaning and even spirituality to fill in the gaps inherent in this empiricism-based approach to disbelief. Ironically, this move toward holding unverifiable convictions concerning meaningfulness, purpose, transcendence, and the like brings these atheists closer to faith-based positions and to religious adherents than they almost ever seem to realize.

Here I want to point out another irony. As was noted in chapter 1, just as atheists' viewpoints are not entirely empirical, those of believers are not wholly uncritical. To think otherwise is to blithely or presumptuously (or, in any case, uncritically!) buy into the fifth presumption discussed in chapter 1 concerning atheists as being the "rational other." We should question this presumption. It is true that atheists are adept at elaborating upon the conflict myth's simple "religion : science :: comfort : integrity" framing by tapping into Western atheism's critical root in order to situate and even experience themselves as people who deny themselves the

166 | THE CRITICAL ROOT

various comforts they associate with religious belief and, in doing so, assume the burden of living with what they see as greater integrity. Moreover, unlike better-known "official" atheists, they are more discerning in their criticisms of religion than many observers, sociologists among them, seem to recognize.[18] As we have seen in this chapter, they quite deftly sift the wheat of the general, subjective, and personal aspects of religious faith from the chaff of its more particular, objective, and institutional aspects. For the most part, however, they are far less able (or perhaps sometimes less willing) to acknowledge that many people of faith, especially those leaning more toward the liberal side of America's cultural divide, are engaged in a similar kind of sifting.

Looking back at the discussion of the fifth presumption in chapter 1, it should be clear that more and more believers engage in the same sort of reflexivity and questioning that atheists also exhibit. The criticisms atheists launch against God as judge, sovereign, and father are really not so different from those one might hear expressed by educated believers who understand that images of God are distinct from the reality to which they are believed to point and that the faithful have some agency with respect to selecting images that are conducive to both reverence and human flourishing. They, in short, frequently endeavor to discern what the theologian H. Richard Niebuhr once described as the God behind the "little faiths in little gods" of undue certainty.[19] The same is true about atheists' wariness of the "orthodox teachings and rigid categories" that constitute objectivized religions. Believers very often share this wariness, this nagging sense that, as St. Paul put it, "the letter kills, but the Spirit gives life" (2 Corinthians 3:6). And while bias toward such groups as Muslims and atheists certainly exists in some quarters, more and more religious people have embraced America's religious pluralism to the extent that they are increasingly circumspect about dogmatic, particularist, "my way or the highway" approaches to faith. One important recent study found that 84 percent of Americans agree that "religious diversity has been good for America," and an amazing 89 percent say that a good person of a faith different from one's own can go to heaven.[20] These numbers change very little when one compares the least religious citizens with those who identify as highly religious. Finally, the fact that believers share atheists' criticisms of religious institutions is perhaps best captured in the thirty-year decline in the proportion of the citizenry who have "a great deal" of trust in them—from roughly one-third of all Americans to only one in five today.[21]

Atheists construct a symbolic boundary between themselves and people of faith that is considerably punier than they usually acknowledge. They assert their own integrity by saying no most loudly to the very same features of religion that believers—again, especially more liberal ones—tend also to criticize. Nevertheless, along with saying no, they also maintain atheist identities by saying "I don't know" as well. This, too, is not unique to atheists. But they valorize their unknowing as something especially positive in ways that are well worth considering, which is the focus of the next chapter.

6

The Agnostic Root

Being Open by Saying "I Don't Know"

The Travails and Persistence of Religious Unknowing

"Know thyself" (*Gnothi seauton*), commands the ancient Greek inscription that was purportedly located at the entryway into the ancient Temple of Apollo at Delphi. "Knowledge is power" (*Ipsa scientia potestas est*), Sir Francis Bacon, the philosopher who has come also to be known as the father of scientific method, informs us. "Dare to know!" (*Sapere aude!*), implores Immanuel Kant, perhaps the most pivotal figure in modern philosophy, at the outset of his famous essay titled "What Is Enlightenment?" You get the idea. Suffice it to say that an abiding discourse about knowledge and about what can actually be known have been central to the development of Western consciousness and culture. So much so that we can easily come to neglect the place of unknowing in this development. As suggested by the aphorisms above, this tends to be true in the case of philosophy. That is unfortunate. Upon just a modicum of reflection, one realizes that it is primarily acute experiences of unknowing, made manifest and rendered somehow problematic, that typically spur advances in self-understanding, in our grasp of the natural world, and in the overall project of enlightenment.

Unknowing has gotten similarly short shrift with respect to religion as well. This has not always been the case. To take the example of Christianity, emphasis on the utter inscrutability and otherness of the divine was rife among theological scholarship and homiletics in the patristic and medieval periods. God, according to some of the Church's most influential theologians and teachers, is "at once known and unknown" (Tertullian, second century); "other, completely other" (St. Augustine, fourth century); "beyond all being and knowledge" (Pseudo-Dionysius, sixth century); "transcendentally unknowable" (St. Maximus the Confessor, seventh century); and "indescribable, ineffable, incomprehensible, unfathomable" (St. Francis of Assisi, thirteenth century).[1] More than merely conveyed in catchy phrases, this appreciation of the unknowability of God was also expected of church leaders. "For we explain not what God is but candidly confess that we have not exact knowledge concerning Him," instructs St. Cyril of Jerusalem in his mid-fourth-century *Catechetical Homilies*, "for, in what concerns God, to confess our ignorance is the best knowledge."[2] And most especially, this appreciation was deemed essential for the masses as well. "Man's utmost knowledge," asserts St. Thomas Aquinas, the thirteenth-century theological luminary who, it is safe to say, knew quite a lot, "is to know that we do not know Him."[3]

As difficult as it may be for us to imagine today, this emphasis on unknowing—or what is sometimes termed the more "apophatic" (from the Greek for "to deny") approach to God—was the privileged, even orthodox, approach for many centuries. No wonder, then, that most theologians could readily accept the definition of their discipline, influentially formulated by St. Anselm in the eleventh century, as "faith *seeking* understanding," not possessing it. Similarly unremarkable is that the fourteenth-century spiritual guide titled *The Cloud of Unknowing* and the sixteenth-century poem "The Dark Night of the Soul" ("dark" referring to the mysteriousness of God), penned by the sixteenth-century mystic St. John of the Cross, would find such estimable places within the larger tradition. This is because, along with reflecting sometimes powerful moments of the human experience, such categories as seeking, unknowing, and darkness have long been important ones for Christianity. "Religion is embodied truth, not known truth," writes sociologist Robert Bellah of faith traditions more generally, "and it has in fact been transmitted far more through narrative, image, and enactment than through definitions and logical demonstrations."[4]

This notwithstanding, as we have addressed, definitions and logic have gained a certain preeminence since the dawning of the modern era. The consolidation of religious traditions into coherent, objectified systems means that narrative, image, and enactment have become subordinated to what, in the last chapter, Wade Thedford snubbed as "orthodox teachings and rigid categories." If not entirely known, God certainly came to be thought of as increasingly knowable through one's assent to intellectualized propositions concerning the divine nature and intentions. Centuries ago, for instance, Church leaders made a clear distinction between the kerygma of the Church—that is, its more rudimentary public teaching to the masses—and its dogma. The latter term referred to the profounder, thoroughly mysterious meaning of the kerygma, which defied being put into words precisely, which could only be partially grasped through participating in sacred rituals and prayer, and the understanding of which was thought to change and deepen from one generation to the next. Now, by contrast, the word "dogma" is used to refer to religious beliefs confidently upheld as being *definitively*—not analogically, not partially, not provisionally—known to be true.[5]

None of this is to suggest that unknowing has been totally eclipsed. Thinking of God as knowable and of certain religious beliefs as definitively true runs into difficulty upon the arrival of new, sometimes disconfirming knowledge and insights, which unsettle venerable certitudes and, not infrequently, can result in newfound experiences of unknowing. Something like this occurred in Western nations during the nineteenth century. In her fascinating history of doubt, Jennifer Michael Hecht describes this period as "easily the best-documented moment of widespread doubt in human history."[6] Perhaps the keenest explanation for why this would be the case comes from another historian, Owen Chadwick, whose classic *The Secularization of the European Mind in the Nineteenth Century* describes the combined effect of two kinds of unsettlement. The first, "unsettlement in minds," encompasses the intellectual challenges to faith wrought by advances in the sciences (especially Darwinism), in comparative studies of religion, and in the historical-critical (or "higher") interpretation of the Bible. At the same time, he argues, an "unsettlement in society" came as a result of tremendous technological advance, the growth of big cities, and the increasing size and heterogeneity of populations—all problematic for time-honored patterns of social interaction as well as for the maintenance of communally held belief systems.[7]

Unsettlement has a way of throwing once taken-for-granted outlooks into doubt, which is why the nineteenth century also saw articulate and compelling expressions of religious unknowing come to assume a more prominent place within public discourse. In Britain, as alluded to in chapter 1, the biologist Thomas Huxley, known as "Darwin's bulldog" for his tireless advocacy of evolutionary theory, coined the term "agnosticism" in 1869 and thereafter became well known for promoting this stance vis-à-vis religious conviction. Far from being some new creed, this viewpoint was tantamount to "the vigorous application of a single principle," which, in Huxley's mind, had both positive and negative dimensions. "Positively," he wrote, "the principle may be expressed: In matters of intellect, follow your reason as far as it will take you, without regard to any other consideration." Then, negatively speaking, "do not pretend that conclusions are certain which are not demonstrated or demonstrable."[8] Huxley's directives about wielding unknowing as an analytical principle did not go unheeded. In the United States, for instance, the attorney and orator Robert Ingersoll, aptly nicknamed "the Great Agnostic," also gained fame (and no small measure of infamy) for promoting it. In his provocative 1896 speech "Why I Am an Agnostic," he lost no time in getting to what he considered to be the crux of the matter. "We can be as honest as we are ignorant," he enjoined his listeners, "If we are, when asked what is beyond the horizon of the known, we must say that we do not know."[9]

As these excerpts imply, Huxley's and Ingersoll's assertions of unknowing were principally responsive to what Chadwick called the "unsettlement in minds." Other intellectuals of the era were more sensitive to societal disruption. Though he cheekily preferred "religiously unmusical" to agnostic as a descriptor of his own position, the German sociologist Max Weber is an instructive case. He repeatedly highlighted the reality that increasing knowledge and cultural complexity, as well as people's growing awareness of myriad ways of life with no sure way of adjudicating the superiority of any one over another, all functioned to destabilize what they thought they knew. "Abraham, or some peasant of the past," he mused wistfully within the pages of one of his most noteworthy public lectures, "died 'old and satiated with life' because he stood in the organic cycle of life; because his life, in terms of its meaning and on the eve of his days, had given to him what life had to offer; because for him there remained no puzzles he might wish to solve." That was the premodern past, however. Abraham may have mastered his world, but that possibility, Weber rued, is now gone. More knowledge, more diversity, more cultural styles and frameworks, and more possibilities for how to actually be in the world ultimately mean less and less confidence in the validity of any one set of beliefs or in the worth of any one particular life project. The modern person, Weber continued, "placed in the midst of the continuous enrichment of culture by ideas, knowledge, and problems, may become 'tired of life' but not 'satiated with life.' He catches only the most minute part of what the life of the spirit brings forth ever anew, and what he seizes is always something provisional and not definitive."[10]

That this period gave rise to voices of piercing intellectual honesty, even profundity, seems clear enough. Not nearly as clear is what ever happened to things "provisional and not definitive." Why, after its nineteenth-century heyday, we today hear so little about religious and other forms of unknowing is really anyone's guess. Perhaps it is due to our postindustrial society's relentless expansion of "knowledge workers" whose careers, statuses, and even identities are all too inextricably enmeshed in knowing to admit its perceived opposite. Perhaps it is because knowing delivers too much of the good life—from iPhones to the Internet, from easy air travel to the miracles of modern medicine—to question its ascendance. Or perhaps, as one philosopher contends in a short book on the subject, the "contemporary proliferation of bullshit" in our everyday discourse (and, alas, our politics) depreciates fact-based truth claims and thus makes admissions of unknowing increasingly, if not gauche, then certainly unnecessary.[11] Who knows?

What we do know is that, even though one now needs to strain a bit to hear them, articulations of unknowing persist among Americans when it comes to religious concerns. This is obviously true of the 6 percent of the population who identify themselves to pollsters as agnostics.[12] Less expectedly, one also hears it among people of faith. Even among religiously affiliated Americans, only about seven in ten say they are "absolutely certain" about God's existence.[13] This comingling of faith and unknowing reflects what sociologist Robert Wuthnow sees as the post-1960s emergence of a "seeker-orientated spirituality" in accordance with which an increasing proportion of American believers value doubt and questioning for being actually facilitative of religious growth.[14] It also helps us to make sense of the newly ubiquitous mantra, "I'm spiritual but not religious," as an indicator of many (especially younger) Americans' overall stance of believing in God or a "higher power" while, at the same time, integrating this belief with both a sense of unknowing and a wariness toward dogmatism and, quite often, toward religious institutions.[15]

Least expected of all, expressions of unknowing can even be heard from those who explicitly identify as atheists. Unlike the New Atheist authors who my interviewees repeatedly blast for being "too all-knowing," "way, way, way too dogmatic in their convictions," "Enlightenment fundamentalists," and so on, everyday atheists are generally not allergic to unknowing. Presuming the conflict myth's "religion : science :: closed-mindedness : open-mindedness" binary and elaborating on this further by drawing upon what I have called atheism's agnostic root, they are actually quite forthcoming about it. As such, they valorize their unknowing as indicative of their openness to the world around them as well as of the distinction between them and the ranks of the supposedly closed-minded believers in their midst. The great modern philosopher Ludwig Wittgenstein, himself profoundly influenced by the agnostic root, famously instructed his readers, "Whereof one cannot speak, thereof one must be silent."[16] Well, so much for that! Very few of the people I interviewed take this to heart. There are quite a number of things about which they cannot speak definitively, but their "I don't know" is not at all silent. More often than not, it is voiced with great regularity and always as something unambiguously positive, as a sign that they possess, along with integrity, a level of open-mindedness they generally consider hard to come by within American society.

Sheryl Manahan: Consolidating Her Atheism, Embracing the Unknown

A good example of someone who rarely keeps her "I don't knows" to herself is Sheryl Manahan, a professional painter and illustrator living with her husband in western Massachusetts. An only child who was raised by a "completely nonreligious" father and a mother who "just dabbled" in New Age practices of various sorts, she fits the mold of what, in chapter 2, I called a consolidator. She was always interested in religion and in important questions about life and its meaning, but as "a Daddy's girl from the get-go," she never felt personally religious in any way. When during a period in her late teens, her Evangelical-leaning aunt spent some time taking her to church with the hopes of getting her saved, she remembers "mostly just playing along." A short time later, after looking into some of her mother's books on tarot cards and goddess-centered spirituality, she finally decided to face the fact that, regardless of her intellectual curiosity, religion was just not for her. "I'm a very open-minded person," she explains, "so I'm very tolerant and often super interested in what other people believe—you know, from an outsider's perspective. So, as I paid more attention, I realized I didn't believe this or that or the other thing. Pretty soon, I came to the conclusion that I didn't need to keep sitting on the fence, that I didn't believe in anything at all. I never really did, to be perfectly honest. It was just a process of becoming more grounded in my nonbelief, I guess." After she got off the fence, she was initially tempted to call herself an agnostic until deciding the term sounded "a little too wishy-washy." Now "atheist" is her term of choice even as she is quick to blunt what she describes as atheism's "smarter-than-thou" edge by insisting, "At the end of the day, one really doesn't know all the answers. You can't possibly know, and you just need to accept, even relish, that reality somehow."

How she accepts it is consonant with how she does her artwork. "I do stuff that's more about realist depictions," she explains. "I work a lot from photographs of real life. I don't deal in abstraction. You know, if you really look at something, you can see exactly what it is. You can never capture the whole thing. That's for sure. But I definitely like to look at the world straight on and depict it as well as I can." In short, Manahan brings her artistic sensibilities—marked by both an insistence upon viewing things "straight on" and the realization that one "can never capture the whole thing"—to her stance as an atheist. Just as she studies the parts of the world she wants to illustrate, she claims that coming to the conclusion she is an atheist has unleashed her natural curiosity about religion and allowed her to be more open to the religious believers in her life. She has more empathy for her mother now. She has also had "fascinating" conversations with one of her best friends who, for nearly a decade, lived as a devout, plain-dressed Quaker. She recently read the Koran as well as a number of books on Islam—this along with her reading in the areas of philosophy and history of religions. The fact is that consolidating and feeling secure in her identity as an atheist has opened Manahan up to "really serious and grand questions about life." There is a caveat for her, though: "Some of these questions are about things that are unknown. You can adopt some sort of ideology or even magical thinking that soothes your soul. Or as I try to do, you can acknowledge the discomfort of not knowing and then move on."

Moving on for Manahan has meant understanding that a lack of definitive answers to life's questions gives one the license to live as one sees fit. "I really don't feel there's a meaning to life with a capital *M* written in neon," she says. Asked to clarify, she goes on:

> I think we make our lives meaningful. That's our main task. I know plenty of people, beginning with my grandmother, who got immense joy from baking every day. If that's the meaning of her life, if that's what she gets joy out of and she's not hurting anybody in the process—other than putting on an extra couple of pounds from all that baking—then so be it. For myself, I don't see any reason to have a defining mission statement for my life. I'm really cool with taking it day by day or even year by year. I work on my art a lot, and obviously it would be great to leave a legacy of some sort behind. I would love to be meaningful to enough people that maybe they're happy for knowing me. I think those are really good goals to have, and they're pretty hard to screw up. I'm going to stick with that.

Other people seem less willing to stick with something like this, she notes. The reason they are so often un-"cool" with living similarly open-ended lives is that they fear the unknown. Most people shield themselves from this fear, she goes on, by engaging in normalized life projects and routines—"buying a house, having kids, getting a manicure, going shopping"—that are broadly pursued, collectively legitimated, and thus personally comforting. Anything that disrupts such matters is an annoyance. And it is fear of the ultimate disruptor, death, that she considers to be at the core of all religious convictions.

Because people are so "terrified of death," she says, they need religious assurances of an afterlife in order to close themselves off from actually thinking about it too much. But Manahan does think about it. Rather than her lack of fear leading to atheism, she is convinced that finally accepting the reality of her atheism led to her seeing death in a new way:

> When I think about death, I always think about a person in a hospice bed, and outside the window there are birds chirping and flowers bloom-

ing and cars driving by. At the beginning of a five-minute period, that person's alive whereas, at the end of that period, that person is gone— and nothing has changed on the other side of that window. That's how I've learned to confront this big, scary question. All I can deal with is what's happening. If I'm around to be part of it: fantastic! Then I'll control what I can and live the best way I know how.

I think I see, but why do you think you're drawn to that image of the window with the birds chirping and the cars going by?

I think it's because I find comfort in factualism. Although I may not be perceiving the spiritual angle of what's happening or that perhaps the person's soul is ascending into heaven or becoming part of another sentient being or whatever—I can't truly know about all that. All I can say is that I see this thing happening. And I can see life continuing to go on; people are living and breathing and being born, and I get to be part of it for a while. You know, I'm super grateful. That's really good enough for me.

Asked if she thinks this will continue to be good enough as she ages and perhaps finds her way to a hospice bed of her own one day, she pauses and, like the pensive person she is, takes her time mulling. "I honestly do think it will," she says and then, smiling, offers the puckish addendum, "but frankly, how the hell could I really know for sure?"

There seems to be a lot that Manahan does not know for sure. Significantly, however, her "I don't know" should not be taken to be synonymous with "I'm not smart" or "I don't care." Far from it. Just as people draw upon atheism's critical root and say no to various features of religion in order to, in their estimation, deny themselves believers' easy comforts in exchange for lives of greater integrity, they do something similar with their "I don't know." Whereas many people turn to faith when faced with life's more complicated matters, atheists are prone to assuming a more indefinite, suppler attitude that is reflected within what I have identified as atheism's agnostic root. When doing so, they define themselves as nimbler thinkers who, unwilling to close themselves off to the complexity and sometimes inscrutability of the world around them, are truly open to aspects of life that do not avail themselves to readymade answers. This attitude both entails and yet goes beyond the conflict myth's "religion : science :: closed-mindedness : open-mindedness" commendation of open-*mindedness*. As

Manahan exemplifies so well, and as interviews with other atheists also illustrate, it is also especially evident in their openness to (1) mystery in general; (2) a specific manner of living; and (3) the reality of death.

Openness to Mystery: Knowing about Oneself

If there is a better encapsulation of what it means to have an openness to life's mysteries than Manahan's looking at the world "straight on" while, at the same time, acknowledging that one "can never capture the whole thing," then I have certainly not heard it. The commonest shorthand for this fundamental attitude is, of course, the phrase "I don't know." This I heard with incredible frequency during my lengthy and wide-ranging exchanges with interview subjects. These semi- (emphasis on *semi*) structured conversations included all kinds of questions about family and friends, belief and doubt, life and death, science and religion, and culture and ethics—they moved in many directions. More striking than respondents answering many such queries with "I don't know" or some equivalent phrasing is the fact that they did so without a whiff of self-recrimination. Instead of being a function of their own simple-mindedness—a possibility few would entertain—their expressions of unknowing largely aim to denote their awareness of the yawning and unrelenting complexity of the world around them.

Consider the following sampling of topics about which atheists say they do not know. Note that I did not actually pose the questions that follow as such. Rather, they are either abbreviated versions of questions I asked or, more often, just labels given to the expressions of unknowing that emerged organically from the flow of our conversations. I encourage readers to take some time perusing these excerpts because they nicely epitomize atheism's agnostic root, and while each of these are exceptionally well stated, they are without question representative of sentiments I heard over and over again from people:

Who Are We?

> Peter: People like to talk about a soul even though the human body is basically just an electrochemical machine. What happens to this energy? Science says matter is not created or destroyed; it only changes

form. We're reabsorbed over time. So there's definitely a connection among people, and between them and the rest of the world. You may want to call it spiritual, but because of the social habit of linking spiritual with religious, I'm not really comfortable with that. I don't have another word for it either. The force? Anyway, there's just something about the core of who we are that we really don't know. We don't understand it, which is a disappointment. . . . Throughout history people, sometimes great scholars, have reached the point where they couldn't find an answer and said, "Oh, well, it must be God or a soul or what have you." And I want so ask, "Why the hell can't you just say, *'I don't know'*?" That's the *honest* truth. There are just some things we don't understand. The amazing thing is that most people can't say that. They've got to fill the void in what they know. They resolve their cognitive dissonance by going, "Oh, yeah, it's God," and leave it at that.

Why Do We Suffer?

Adrianna: The issue of human suffering is probably the thing that most makes me identify with being an atheist. No religious answers seem to make sense. You know: The suffering person deserves it; suffering is a test of your faith; or it makes you stronger or is part of God's plan somehow. Actually, now that I think of it, the problem is that these explanations make *too much* sense in that they take something that's truly problematic and unfathomable and then just say, "Here's the reason for it." See, that's just an easy way to separate ourselves from the very hard reality. It's a form of intellectual *cowardice*. . . . When you experience suffering and really take other people's suffering seriously, there's no answer. *I don't know* why people suffer. I've suffered in my lifetime, and I've also been happy. I never felt more deserving of one or the other. One didn't feel more like God's plan. When I think about the things I value most—health, a sense of security, family and friends, opportunities of all kinds—I know there are many, many people who have none of those things. Why? I think it'd be avoiding the issue and an insult to those people if I said I knew the answer to that question.

Why Are We Here?

Arturo: *I don't need to know* why I'm here. I don't think there is a why. I think it just is, and I don't believe things happen for a reason. I think things happen because things happen, and how you deal with it is who you are. . . . I think the world is so amazing, just the way that it is. It's so *awe-inspiring*. Why would we possibly need more than this? . . . I was actually just reading a Brian Greene book about how we could be a tiny particle in a multiverse and there are an infinite number of universes. That just blows my mind. I mean there is literally every conceivable possibility of our being in the world. You know, if you think about it, in one multiverse, I'm sitting here eating a banana when Lady Gaga walks in. It's all so amazing and glorious. There's absolutely no need to make things up to appreciate it more.

Why Is the Universe Here?

Jesse: What happened before the Big Bang? We don't know. We aren't even sure if the question makes sense because time could have come into being the same instant as the Big Bang. Many people are uncomfortable with this notion, but I don't think there's anything wrong with saying, "*I don't know.*" It's the first step to finding an answer. . . . People call atheists arrogant for believing that our accomplishments have been achieved without some higher guidance. If there's no God or gods, then all our accomplishments are our own. Why should we feel ashamed of this? I feel it's more arrogant to think that such a powerful being would create a universe for such an insignificant little cluster of organisms floating in space. Or that such an insignificant little cluster could even begin to understand what that Being's intentions were. . . . Many find the complexity of life and the universe as marks of a creator. I find just the opposite. No description of any god strikes me as having a mind capable of the creativity, complexity, and patience necessary to create a system as intricate as our universe. Of course, my answer isn't very satisfying to many people because, even though "we don't know" is actually a *humbler* answer than what one usually hears, it doesn't lend itself to a good marketing campaign.

What Can We Know?

> Frank: In my opinion, it's much more preferable to honestly say "*I don't know*" than to make something up or believe in something that's not true. Science currently provides the best explanation of how things came to be, but it's a partial, incomplete explanation. That's all we've got though. We know the universe is roughly 13.7 billion years old. We know our planet is about 4.5 billion years old. We know that life has evolved on earth. But how exactly all this started? We're not sure. We have theories, and we test and refine them. But in the end, there will always be unknowns. That's not an issue for me. Science may one day explain these unknowns—and reveal hundreds of others in the process—but it may not. And that's just fine with me. An honest "I don't know" is better than a million fabricated stories. I think we need to resist all those. I think it's wrong to domesticate reality, to keep it caged in and within the confines of our mental categories and our bedtime stories about some made-up guy in the sky. I say we should *keep it wild*! Keep it wild and be satisfied with tracking it the best we can.

Essential to understand is that these quotations, typical of many responses I heard, are not simply admissions of unknowing in the face of mystery. Similar to how Manahan came to "accept, even relish" not knowing all the answers, they actually reflect people's real openness to life's complexities. Moreover, never voiced as a diminishment, their unknowing is inevitably understood by them as productive, as generative of admirable personal dispositions, which are likewise worthy of being relished. As urged, these interview excerpts deserve to be read with care. Yet for the sake of ease, I have paired italicized assertions of unknowing with the correlative disposition that unknowing seems to help engender for each respondent. Thus, Peter's acknowledgment of his unknowing about the core of human personhood assists in his honing a sense of honesty. Adrianna's "I don't know" with respect to suffering makes her intellectual courage (as opposed to others' "cowardice") manifest. Arturo asserts his capacity for awe. Jesse's unknowing evinces his humility. And Frank's insistence that we "keep it wild" and remain open to the inscrutable in our midst rather than domesticating it is suggestive of all these other qualities—honesty, courage, awe, humility, Manahan's open-mindedness, and curiosity—as well as his disdain for reductionism. In sum, their "I don't know" about the wider world also functions as an "I do know" something about themselves. It helps them to both acknowledge and then craft certain dispositions that in turn equip them to lead lives that in their view are marked by less certainty than what people of faith seem to claim for themselves.

Openness to a New Way of Living: Responsibility and Gratitude

Closely related to atheists' openness to mystery is their openness to a kind of life that better reflects their appreciation for things unknown. As we saw in chapter 2, on their way to acquiring their atheist identities, most people's lives felt relatively unsettled; thus they inquired, they searched, they responded, and they consolidated. To varying extents, it seemed that, at every step, they were trudging uphill. After settling on atheism, on the other hand, they almost always felt much more at peace, more even-keeled. Recall that, once she got "off the fence" and accepted her nonbelief, Sheryl Manahan found that she was actually "really cool with taking it day by day or even year by year." Most others make a similar discovery. For instance, David Friedman was a typical inquisitive whose questions about God, the Torah, comments from his parents and rabbi, what he was learning at synagogue—seemingly everything—went unanswered to his satisfaction. Then, as the years passed and he matured, those questions just went away. Now he shakes his head bemusedly at all these questions, and especially at questions pertaining to the meaning of life, which had baffled him for so long. "The bottom line for me is I don't feel a need to have an answer to the why question," he explains, still shaking his head.

> I feel like we just are. I don't need a reason for being here anymore. I think that's part of why I enjoy things—because I feel like I have one life, and this is it. To me, it's not a depressing thought to think it's meaningless or that there's no greater reason for why I'm here. I just am. I don't need to understand it. I get one chance to ride on the merry-go-round and that's it. So, why not take it upon yourself to make the most of it, experience it fully and enjoy as much of it as you can?

This transition from earnestly trying to understand the merry-go-round to, in time, being content to simply go for a ride is a broadly shared experience among respondents. Some do not go through it as easily as Friedman did. It can be a long and challenging process. Clay Garrett, for example, was an only child raised in a Christian fundamentalist family in rural Oregon. His parents' faith never sat well with him, and as he grew older, he became what I have called a searcher:

> I felt differently than how I was being raised. That's why, I think, I looked so hard for answers—so I could feel comfortable with going against what my parents had taught me all along, or even to prove to myself that they were right. Anyway, I needed answers so I could feel satisfied and strong. . . . That lasted through high school and even college. I was tormented, really tweaked. I think that's why I did a lot of drugs—just to turn my brain off and escape for a while. Whenever I was sober, I was constantly thinking about it, you know?
> *So, what did you do? Read books? Or . . .*
> Yeah. Yeah, I read a lot. I looked into different religions and cultures. I just kind of soul searched too. Oh, and I talked to a ton of people. That was really most of it. I'd talk to people—so many people—and ask them, "Hey, are you happy?" "What do you believe in?" "What are you doing, and what's the meaning of it all in your mind?" You know what I mean? I just tried to piece it all together for myself. It's weird. I was looking for answers for a really long time. I was looking for this thing, right? And, after a while it stopped meaning anything to me. I mean I have zero emotion about these questions now.
> *Why not?*
> I guess I got to the point where I don't need an answer to life's meaning and all that. For one thing, I basically decided I don't know the answer, I don't know that there actually *is* an answer, and even if there is, I don't care. The other thing is that I found something that feels good, which I truly appreciate. What I'm saying is that I've taken care of things. I have a career and a family; I do things I enjoy; I've got lots of friendships that have lasted a long time. It's like I know how to live my life in a way that works for me. So, now an answer to the meaning of life isn't one of those things I need. I'm not on that quest anymore.

As with Friedman, Garrett's "I don't know" has opened him up to a new kind of life, one distinguished by an acceptance of and even contentment with his uncertainty about questions that had once badgered him. Further, while acceptance and contentment might at first seem like passive stances, both of these men allude to something more active, something that has required sustained intention on their parts. Friedman, the quintessential inquisitive, finally accepts not having an answer to the "why question." At the same time, he is also quite intentional about taking it upon himself to "make the most" of his life and ride that merry-go-round with an eye toward all the experiences and joy it can provide. Likewise, Garrett, the longtime searcher, has turned away from his "quest" and has finally arrived at a place of contentment that, for many years, seemed beyond his reach. Once again, though, this had lots to do with something distinctly intentional. He took "care of things" such that he now has a life that "works" for him and that he "truly appreciate[s]." In both cases, these men have decided to take responsibility for the quality and meaning of their lives, and in the process of taking that ride, they are also grateful for all the experiences, joys, and accomplishments that come along with it.

These two central themes—responsibility and gratitude—are also implicit in Manahan's remarks. As she sees it, the project of making her life meaningful (in the personal, not capital M, sense) is her responsibility or, as she put it, her "main task." Moreover, as she endeavors to find meaning through dedication to her relationships and her art, she feels "super grateful."

Oftentimes people are much more explicit about how their unknowing opens them up to a way of living for which taking responsibility and feeling grateful are prominent features. "When I was religious, I usually spent more time thinking about the next life than this one," recalls one respondent. "I believed I had a destiny that somehow got me off the hook for choices I made that didn't work out. It allowed me not to pursue certain dreams to the level I'd need to achieve them because I had an 'if it's not meant to be' attitude. But that's a terrible way to live, a cop-out. Now nothing is meant to be. It's all what I make it. Not copping out means taking responsibility for the life I'm making for myself." Statements like this are everywhere, and as illustrated above, people regularly associate taking responsibility with their intention to valorize "*this* life." Another good example is Henry Stengaard, a fifty-something social worker in Milwaukee. Talking about his professional life leads to broader concerns:

> I work to prevent or alleviate suffering to the extent I can. I try to treat my fellow humans with compassion and understanding. . . . I think that this life means more to atheists actually. To the believer, this is a dress rehearsal. To me and other atheists, this life is all I've got, and I feel the need to make the most of it. To give some examples, I see our planet as the only home we have, so I think I cherish it more than many believers who think they're bound for heaven. Suffering is an inevitability, so I meet my obligation to help through my work. I also have a duty to be there for my family and friends to help them get through those tough times. Because all we have is each other. I know it sounds corny, but that's what drives me.

There is no "dress rehearsal" for Stengaard; the curtain has been raised, and he is very comfortable with playing the lead role. This is no passive performance either. He works to alleviate suffering; he tries to be compassionate and understanding; he cherishes the planet; and he is intent on making the most of his life. Just as he has a responsibility to himself for literally giving the performance of a lifetime, he also feels an "obligation" to the people he serves and a "duty" to be there for his family and friends.

Another person who likes to talk about her job is Charise Johnson, a nurse who lives and works in Phoenix. Also employed in a "caring profession," she discusses responsibility in terms of both helping others and taking the initiative to carve out a meaningful life for herself. Yet she mostly gravitates toward our second central theme—how her nonbelief has made her more grateful than she thinks she would otherwise be:

> Looking at life as a lottery of sorts is definitely tougher to swallow when you don't think there's another, better life waiting on the other side. But that's the way I see it; I can't bring myself to ignore it. . . . So, I try to enjoy my life as much as I possibly can. A very lucky life at that! I wake every day with the hopes of enjoying the company of my family and friends and the beauty of the world. I try to help others live happy, fulfilled lives

whatever way I can—whether it's through my nursing career or even just being friendly to the people I meet in passing. For me, though it's terribly cliché, the point of life is to love and be loved during the brief amount of time we have here. It's funny, but I really believe that atheism has given me the clarity to see the light in the world, even during the darkest days. I don't need fairy tales to show me the beauty and bleakness of the world. I simply open my eyes and there it is.

So many other respondents echo Johnson's sentiments, and also like her, they link their sense of gratitude to their appreciation for the fortuitousness ("A very lucky life at that!") and brevity ("the brief amount of time we have here") of human life. Considering the first, Jeff Lollard says, "I'm comfortable with not knowing all the answers. As far as I can tell, we're here because we're not *not* here." Asked to elaborate, he responds, "I'm filled with an appreciation of the life I've been lucky enough to have. Trillions of particles, billions of years, odds stacked so far against the right circumstances for me simply being born means that I'm overwhelmed with appreciation for the way nature worked out, to give me the time I have. Why would I demand more?" Also appreciating this life enough not to need or want "more" is Donna Cizleck. Largely because she miscarried in February and then her youngest child was diagnosed with type 1 diabetes in May, she links her overall feeling of appreciation (during our interview in August of that same year) with the precariousness and brevity of life. "I don't know what happens after death. Most likely nothing. Just nothingness. I must tell you that I find the thought that this is all there is to be comforting. It makes our short time so much more valuable," she tells me while pulling a tissue from her purse. "I have health problems that make it unlikely that I will see old age. But I'm okay with that. Every day I have is a day I can enjoy the marvels of this universe. Each day is a day I can show love to my family. This is enough. I don't desire more."

Openness to Death: Intensifying One's Commitments

Even though Americans' riling anxiety about their mortality usually pushes people in the opposite direction, it is not uncommon for conversations like these, at one point or another, to actually move *toward* the subject of death. This initially caught me off guard, I admit. As anthropologist Ernest Becker argued in his widely read classic *The Denial of Death*, a permeating, at times acute, anxiety about death's inevitability is part of being human and a very large part of what brings us to seek immortality in religious (and other) worldviews that posit truths deemed to be eternal.[17] Since they are all atheists and just about all of my respondents are among the one-quarter of their fellow citizens who say they do not believe in life after death,[18] I suspected they may be especially disinclined to broach this topic.

Yet this was not the case. As it happens, the people I interviewed exhibit an unfraught openness to death as both a topic of conversation and an inescapable reality. This, to be sure, is not a function of their having or claiming any special insight on the matter. Jeff Lollard's comfort with "not knowing all the answers" and Donna Cizleck's disclaimer "I don't know what happens after death" make it clear that their openness to death is very much caught up with their previously discussed openness to mystery. As such, this general "I don't know" about death's mystery is yet another instance of atheists saying "I do know" something about themselves and about the kind of lives they want to lead. This openness to death, in other words, accentuates the new way of living they know they want and that they have chosen to pursue. For both Lollard ("the time I have") and Cizleck ("our short time"), an accosting awareness of life's brevity and finitude makes them value it more than they once did. And because they prize the here and now so much—much more, they usually claim, than do people of faith—their lives feel fuller and thus their lifespans feel like "enough" to them. This is why such this-worldly, life-affirming sentiments as "I get to be part of it for a while . . . that's really good enough for me" (Manahan), "Why would I demand more?" (Lollard), and "I don't desire more" (Cizleck) are heard so regularly among respondents.

So, one might ask, why not demand or desire more? If an awareness and acceptance of mortality makes atheists value their worldly lives more, then why not abide by the poet Dylan Thomas's bracing injunction "Do not go gentle into that good night, . . . / Rage, rage against the dying of the light"?[19] The answer is that they actually do. Their openness to death intensifies their experiences of taking responsibility and feeling gratitude. This in turn makes these experiences seem more legitimate both as affective markers of lives fully lived and as their preferred means of not wasting a moment of them, of raging against the light's inevitable dimming.

First, finitude and responsibility. When Dave Pedroia talks about things pertaining to faith, doubt, meaning, and other such topics, he again and again comes back to all the suffering he sees in the world. As a particularly empathic person, this bothers him quite a bit. "Suffering happens, sometimes indiscriminately, for no reason, and often to good people. That sucks," he says. "As an atheist, this can serve as a reminder that the time we have here is incredibly precious and that a few hundred years ago, most of us would already be dead. All we can do is attempt to live a good life and help others as much as we can to eliminate as much suffering as we can. That's our responsibility—not God's. If we all knew that, we'd care a hell of a lot more about taking care of other people and taking care of the earth too." While many people express versions of Pedroia's outward-looking sense of responsibility for both other people and the planet, others convey a more inward-looking version. Cecil Barron, who thinks a lot about his "obligation to make my life a worthwhile one," is a good example. Asked to say why he feels this sense of obligation so intensely, he, like so many others, brings up his mortality. "Ironically, for me, death is what gives life value. The fact that it doesn't go on forever means that it shouldn't be wasted. If we lived forever, what we do wouldn't matter; we could always correct things later." Reflecting on his own ruminations, he continues, "It's kind of like a millionaire and a pauper both losing a twenty-dollar bill. The millionaire has a lot more, but the pauper may have just lost everything. So, who's going to try hardest to find it and, when found, who will be the most careful on what he spends it on?"

Next, finitude and gratitude. Again, one hears this juxtaposition repeatedly, and one respondent, from a long lineage of Maryland Episcopalians, sums things up quite nicely: "Because life is finite and precious, I am able to treat it with the respect and care it deserves." She continues, "I'm privileged to be a thinking, self-aware entity who can learn, discover, love, and laugh. Isn't it wonderful that there are such things as love and laughter at all? Aren't I lucky to enjoy them for several decades—what anyone would call a pretty long time?" These, of course, are rhetorical questions—to which atheists, probably without exception, would respond in the affirmative. Another respondent, this one a descendent of many generations of Jews from New Jersey (and thereabouts), gave an especially vivid response. "I'm pretty fortunate to be alive, feeling the sun on my face, sipping this coffee, even answering all these damn questions—no offense intended." None taken, I assured him, and partly just to prove it, I questioned him further about this, spurring some additional thoughts:

> As an atheist, I don't believe there is an afterlife, and I'm happy about that. I really don't know what I would do with eternity. I think after a few million years, life would get hellishly boring [we both laugh]. . . . I'm glad life ends. We have only one life to live, so we better live it right, enjoy it, and be thankful for it. Every moment is valuable because, once it passes, it'll never come again. Religious believers often ask me what the point is if we know it will end. I don't think that's a valid question. We go to the movies even though we know that, in two hours, the film will be over. No one asks what the point is in going given our knowledge of the inevitable end credits! We go for the experience and the enjoyment. That's why we live our lives. Hopefully, we will learn stuff and pass that onto others to contribute to the sum of human existence.

Whenever the topic of death emerges naturally within the interview setting, respondents invariably bring it up less to say something about the end of life per se than to provide details about how they have chosen to live.[20] They, as we have seen, raise the topic largely to make the case that, like viewing a movie with an eye toward the inevitable end credits, awareness of the limited "running time" of their days actually intensifies their experience of living, especially in terms of enhancing feelings of responsibility and gratitude. Things shift, however, when they are asked about death more directly. At these moments, interviewees definitely maintain their general openness toward death. Yet they do so by taking one of three discursive tacks: acceptance, forbearance, or reframing.

Due to the influence of Swiss psychiatrist Elizabeth Kübler-Ross's well-known "stages of grief"—purported to be widely experienced among the terminally ill and recently bereaved—many people have come think of death acceptance as the last in a series of stages that include, in order, denial, anger, bargaining, and depression.[21] This is why, even when discussing the issue hypothetically and, to my knowledge, not in the face of either their imminent death or a loved one's recent passing, it still comes as a surprise to hear some respondents, just under half of them, sound so immediately *accepting* of death. It is "just a given," "the rules of life's game," "our small tick on the hands of time," "the way of the world"—they express this nonplussed attitude in all sorts of ways and mostly in counterdistinction to what they take to be others' (usually specified as religious people's) more fearful outlook. As evocative as these phrases are, two other ways of expressing this attitude, both clever one-liners either referenced or directly quoted from well-known historical figures, are especially common. "If I saw a truck coming at me or if I were just diagnosed with cancer, I'd probably experience the same deep animal fear of death as any other vertebrate," explains one young man. "But in the abstract, I don't fear it. I go along with the Greek philosopher Epicurus who said not to be afraid because, 'when we exist, death is not yet present and, when death is present, then we do not exist.' . . . So, I basically feel about death the way a four-year-old feels about bedtime. I don't want to do to bed. But I'm not afraid—I just know I'll miss something good when I go." Along with Epicurus, the other historical notable who is regularly quoted (as in the excerpt above) or misquoted (as in many others) to communicate this sense of acceptance is Mark Twain. "I do not fear death," he once drolly retorted. "I had been dead for billions and billions of years before I was born, and had not suffered the slightest inconvenience from it." Another man, this one much older, affirms this same basic viewpoint. "I didn't mind not existing before I was born, and I'm fairly sure I won't mind or even know when I'm dead again," he chortles, before getting a bit more serious. "For me, this fact really puts the pressure on, you know, to live a good life. Because in my view, when it's done, it's done."

Those who exhibit a *forbearing* attitude toward death, also just under half of all respondents, tend to chortle less and focus more on the conclusion that "when it's done, it's done." Notice a clear difference here. The openness of people who are accepting of death is typically wrought of their sense, illustrated in the excerpts above, that it is essentially a return, a return to a previously experienced state of nonexistence. No big deal. Here, though, it is generally discussed in terms of resisting the temptation to close oneself off from the very-big-deal reality of death—and its attendant feelings of anxiety, sadness, and loss—and, determinedly, unwaveringly, face it head on.

Consider two exemplars of forbearance. The first is Rene Truchi. She never really had to work at becoming nonreligious ("I popped out of the womb as an atheist, and I just kind of stayed that way," she says), and as a thirtyish computer programmer living in San Francisco with lots of secular friends, being an atheist is also easy and, she breezily announces, not something she even thinks much about. The topic of death is another matter altogether. "I have lost people in my life," she says, "my grandparents, a close friend, acquaintances":

> It's the hardest thing to deal with because of the finality, the complete sense of loss you feel. I can understand why people cling to a belief in religion—even against all sense—because of the warm, fuzzy feeling that they will see these people again, that they are not truly lost. But the reality is that the physical person you know is gone. You can't ever see them again. And that knowledge, that reality, is sometimes too great to bear. . . . The thought of losing my husband, my parents, and family is terrifying. The thought of my own death as well. It's a finality we don't like to accept. But regardless of whether we like it or not, the reality doesn't change. I think this makes life infinitely more precious.

Notice three points Truchi makes here. First, she acknowledges the anguish that comes from facing up to death ("the hardest thing to deal with"). Second, in light of this, she understands and even empathizes with those who close themselves off from this anguish and instead opt for the comforts ("the warm, fuzzy") of faith. Lastly, even though she finds the thought of death "terrifying" and "sometimes too great to bear," she is open to what she simply refers to as its "reality." Similarly open and forbearing is Jared Sayoman. A sixty-something retiree living in rural Ohio and an active member of a local freethinker advocacy group intent on, as he puts it, "unbuckling the Bible Belt," his life as an atheist is about as different from Truchi's as one can imagine. Still, when it comes to death, he, like many others, makes the same points:

> We plainly live in a nightmarish world of pain, decay, and oblivion—not only for ourselves but for our loved ones as well. I just do my best to play

the hand I'm dealt in a life I didn't ask to have. I'm frequently left despondent and anxious about this reality. Atheism offers me nothing except the cold comfort that I am living my life with open-eyed honesty. I think this is a very important point as the popular atheist movement presents the rejection of religion as a triumph or some kind of transcendence. Believe me, you don't win anything by acknowledging the terrible truth. I find nothing comforting about that. Religious belief obviously comforts many people in their dying moments, just like a shot of morphine or a swig of whiskey or the hand-holding of a loved one would. I wouldn't deny anyone that. . . . However, I disagree that religion comes to terms with death and suffering. It just whitewashes it.

A final grouping of respondents, about one in twenty of them, express their openness to death in a more tongue-in-cheek manner by ironically, sometimes playfully, drawing upon religious categories to do so. Whereas those with an accepting attitude toward mortality generally perceive faith language as nonessential and those inclined toward forbearance see it (and, as Sayoman notes, its whitewashing atheist equivalents) as nonhelpful, this approach treats faith language as being nonliteral. Some more accepting, others more forbearing, what unites people in this group is their affinity for *reframing* religious categories such that they amplify the uncompromisingly secular dispositions already discussed in this chapter.

One young man, for instance, is very accepting of death. "It's just the admission fee for a life of consciousness and experience," he says. What is most interesting about his remarks is that, in addition to talking at length about his responsibility to make his life meaningful and to treat others decently, he reframes a familiar religious concept in order to accentuate the kind of life he has chosen to lead. "I know that, if I live that way [i.e., responsibly], my life will mean great things to my parents who have watched me grow up, to my girlfriend who knows how much I love her, to my teachers who can revel in the successes I've had and can count those successes as partly their own, and to my friends and community who have all been impacted by my life," he says. "That impact, no matter how big or small, will be my legacy. It will be my heaven." Another man leans more to the forbearing side of things. "I come to terms with pain and death with the understanding that, if you want to live, you have to die," he says. Similar to how the first man reframes the notion of heaven to emphasize the value of a responsible life without God, this man does the same with another religious concept—with the aim of imparting his deep sense of gratitude. "I will mourn the passing of my loved ones, and I mourn my own process of aging and moving closer to the day my life ends. This only makes me appreciate my life and those I love even more." Then he concludes, "Taking each breath as a fortunate moment of life and being thankful for all the blessings I've received is so important because all we have is the here and now."

Heaven? Blessings? Such notions at first seem out of place in conversations with nonbelievers. That would be true if respondents were relying on traditional meanings rather than reframing these persistently resonant symbols such that, for them, they convey new meanings concerning the seriousness of atheist lives. One more, somewhat subtler, example of this practice pertains to a reframing of reverence. Cecilia Leon mostly resists religious language and concepts. When her husband died several years ago and her youngest son suggested that he would still be with their family "like a guardian angel," she explained that he would indeed be with them but in the form of a body in the ground that, over time, breaks down, gets consumed by worms, and ultimately becomes "part of the earth." In a similar vein, when her oldest son was cured of a rare cancer and one of her coworkers blurted out, "It's a miracle!" she responded, as delicately as she could, "Nope, it's doctors and they're awesome!" So, who would suspect that, when addressing life and death in broader terms, even she would engage in some reframing? While discussing her love for nature, she clearly has little use for such symbols as Judgment Day or God's work of creation. Reverence, even holiness, though, is another matter:

> Just yesterday, I read in the paper that the world's rarest tortoise died. He was the last one, a subspecies from the Galapagos Islands. And now his species is extinct. It's just a reminder of how finite things are and how much we need to experience and treasure our world and keep it for the next generation. Because it's finite. There isn't going to be a Judgment Day when we all get lifted off to heaven or hell. This is what we have. You know, I think the idea that we are some sort of special creation and we can do whatever we want to this planet and to other people is the biggest

problem about religion. . . . Another is religious people's misconception about atheists—because we don't see God's hand in it all, that we can't appreciate everything and everyone. But we do. We do see the absolutely beautiful interconnectedness of our world, our universe. . . . We not only appreciate it, we expend the time and effort to understand it. With that understanding, I think, comes a deeper level of emotion or even reverence, piety, whatever—a level deeper than religions seem to go. Coming from an atheist, that may sound like the world's most ironic holier-than-thou bullshit. Maybe it is, but I must tell you that I feel it deeply.

When reframing, people use old religious categories to create such new or freshly expressed meanings as those pertaining to the lasting value of living responsibly (heaven), the fittingness of gratitude (blessings), and the deep sense of interconnectedness with the natural world (reverence). They do this in a nonliteral fashion, obviously. And as Leon suggests, one cannot always know precisely where to draw the line between such sentiments and "bullshit." Not that this is necessarily problematic. Without knowing for sure where to draw that line, she nonetheless feels a deep sense of connection to the world, even in the face of impermanence and loss.

Speaking more generally, unknowing should not be underestimated since, as we have discussed, it often proves to be quite generative for atheists. Their unknowing opens them to a sense of mystery, which helps to hone certain dispositions that in turn tell them *who* they are. Put differently, their "I don't know" is also an "I do know" with respect to envisioning and experiencing themselves as people who are intellectually honest, capable of awe, epistemologically humble, and so forth. Their unknowing also tells them *what* to do. In the absence of an elaborated religious worldview, it goads them to hold tightly to such commitments as taking responsibility for their lives and feeling grateful in the process. Their unknowing even tells them *how* to go about the charge of responsible and appreciative living—with an intensity that would be unavailable to them, they generally contend, were it not for their raging openness to the finality of death. Finally, if saying "I don't know" is facilitative of robust convictions regarding to the organization of meaningful secular lives, then this is likewise the case for when atheists say yes, which is the subject of the next chapter.

The Immanent Root

Progressing by Saying Yes

Scripting Progressive Lives with a Morality Writ Small

As we saw in chapter 4, the science versus religion conflict myth is principally an outgrowth of atheism's deeply embedded *empirical* root, which has long privileged evidence gathering over unsubstantiated faith convictions when it comes to making truth claims about the world and people's place within it. This myth also functions, if we can keep with the same tuberous image, as a uniquely effectual "root metaphor" for atheists in the United States.[1] In other words, by naturalizing sets of oppositional categories, it serves as a "model for" the honing of inner dispositions that get reinforced by people's appropriation of Western atheism's other roots. Accepting the conflict myth's opposition between faith and integrity, they, true to the *critical* root, say no to certain theological, doctrinal, and institutional features of religion in order to better establish themselves as people of integrity. Similarly accepting the presumed opposition between being religious and being open, they tap into the *agnostic* root in acknowledging that "I don't know" is both a legitimate thing for one to say vis-à-vis life's perduring questions and, at the same time, reflective of their openness to such things as mystery, lives marked by responsibility and gratitude, and even to the reality of death itself.

Another way of putting all this is to note that the conflict myth became culturally possible and then compelling to many people because of the objectification of Western religion, a process that, as we have seen, often cast it as being at loggerheads with scientific developments. As such, for the lion's share of American atheists, the supposedly conflictual relationships between science and religion, reason and faith, fact and belief, and so forth have become internalized as a kind of tacit knowledge, or what the philosopher Michael Sandel calls their "unreflective background."[2] In order to elaborate upon this taken-for-granted sensibility, they draw upon other atheist roots—or different styles of atheist thinking and discourse—to articulate an even more detailed account of why they think in the ways they do, how this sets them apart from religious believers, and what this says about the kind of people they have become. As I have been trying to show, these other roots matter because they enable people who do not believe in God to better convey both to outsiders and even to themselves that they nevertheless still very much believe in having integrity, living responsibly, and feeling grateful for the good things in their lives. These convictions in turn are crucial for helping them to develop the dispositional traits that define their inner selves. Observing that human beings are essentially animals who both make and are made by myths and other narratives, sociologist Christian Smith gets it just right in contending that "we tell and retell narratives that themselves come fundamentally to constitute and direct our lives."[3]

Direct, how?—one might ask of specifically atheist lives. The conflict myth addresses this question well. As we also saw in chapter 4 with respect to this myth's "religion : science :: regression : progress" binary, it sets religion's presumed regressive character in opposition to the progress that flows naturally from science and from those whose worldviews are informed by it. Progress, huh?—one might further query, maybe with some head-scratching. Some skepticism here would seem appropriate in light of the ever-gathering sense that, in today's postmodern world, buying into overarching "metanarratives"—such as the Enlightenment-tinctured one that foresees a future of inexorable progress—now appears somewhat quaint, if not intellectually naïve. It also appears to commentators of various ideological positions to be extremely problematic for sustaining atheist identities. When such hallmark certitudes of modernity as the rationality-derived and universally applicable nature of truth claims come under assault, they contend, then the foundations of atheism, especially the predominant "scientific atheism" one finds in the United States, begin to crack quite portentously.

This is the view expressed by the Christian theologian and apologist Alister McGrath in his tellingly titled *The Twilight of Atheism*. Now that the last century's lamentable unfolding of tragic events and the unsquelched expression of disparate worldviews have undermined many people's confidence in rationalism, universalism, and perhaps most especially, social progress, he writes, there is precious little left for atheism to champion. "The failure of atheism to capture the public imagination in the West is a reflection of its failure to articulate a compelling imaginative vision of a godless future. . . . Atheism is wedded to philosophical modernity, and both are aging gracefully in the cultural equivalent of an old folks' home."[4] Those who would be tempted to rebuff this perspective as evidence of wishful thinking on McGrath's part should realize that it is not infrequently shared by outspokenly atheist commentators as well. Historian Ronald Aronson is among the more thoughtful of them. He is concerned about atheists' (and others secularists') prospects for developing meaningful narratives that are "no longer explicitly or implicitly tied to the belief in human and societal advancement." Not necessarily at "twilight," yet the hour is still getting nigh, in Aronson's glum estimation. "No longer hitched to the star of Progress," he informs his readers, "atheism, agnosticism, and secularism have lost conviction and optimism, and thus a main source of their missionary energy."[5]

The problem with this perspective, a problem that we have seen previously, is that it reflects a view more from the penthouse than the ground floor. What may be true for intellectual elites—whether they be atheism's naysayers or hurray-sayers—tends not to be the case among the rank and file. Take, for instance, the highfalutin postmodern discourse that is so assuredly dismissive of progress as a resonant category. Many scholars may equate postmodernity, as the philosopher Jean-François Lyotard did quite famously, with an "incredulity towards metanarratives."[6] But the reality is that most people in most settings remain resiliently credulous toward narratives ranging from the meta- (how God is bringing about salvation) to the micro- (what it felt like for me to become an atheist) varieties. This includes countless people working in academia's "ivory towers," by the way, for whom the transition from a modern to a postmodern world is itself a coherency-conferring metanarrative typically founded upon something more akin to faith than fact. This self-contradiction notwithstanding, the on-the-ground reality is that the current situation is better defined not by the demise of such narratives but by their proliferation. The American dream narrative, the romantic love narrative, the expressive individualism narrative, the good citizen narrative, the cultural Jew narrative, the working mom narrative, the party animal narrative—these, and so many more, are readily available to us as cultural templates we use to organize and direct our lives in individually satisfying and publicly recognizable ways. It is the pluralization and often incommensurability of these narratives, experienced both within a single individual (think of the relatively new and now widespread phenomenon of the "identity crisis") and certainly among them, that is a key feature of our time—not our incredulity toward them.

As we have seen, the conflict myth functions as a kind of template or narrative for American atheists, which counterpoises religion's comforts with their own desire to live with integrity, religious faith with their own openness, and the social regression wrought of faith traditions with their aims to help bring about progress in the world. Here I would like to make two additional points. First, this science versus religion narrative is truly influential even though, as we have seen, it is not necessarily true. In keeping with sociologists William Isaac Thomas and Dorothy Swaine Thomas's well-known maxim "If men define situations as real, they are real in their consequences," the proclivity of atheists to treat these sets of oppositional categories as real has indeed produced real consequences in terms of helping them to first desire and then craft identities marked by such dispositions as integrity, openness, and a concern for others.[7] Second, regardless of what many commentators and intellectual elites define as real about everyday atheists—which unfortunately, often produces the all-too-real consequence of mischaracterizing them—the idea of progress actually remains extremely salient for them. However, in their case, one should not conceive of progress in the usual manner, as advancement toward some utopian ideal or antecedently fixed goal. Rather than *progress to* some "imaginative vision of a godless future" (McGrath) or a fixed "star of Progress" (Aronson), the atheists I spoke with generally think in terms of *progress from* a situation riddled with problems associated with religious belief and authority.[8]

In thinking about progress this way, they draw upon what we earlier described as Western atheism's *immanent* root. Just as they say no to specific dimensions of religion and "I don't know" to some of the knottiest questions facing humanity, tapping into this root entails their saying yes to living well and doing good within the worldly, sometimes prosaic round of their everyday lives. They seldom go about their lives in accordance with carefully worked out and internally consistent philosophical positions, as was evident with the Cynics, Stoics, and Epicureans of the Hellenistic age. Rather, they do it by endeavoring to be courteous neighbors and responsible employees, caring siblings and loving spouses, occasional volunteers, and friends who are dependably "there for you." They, in brief, nudge the needle of progress by meeting their quotidian obligations and living in accordance with norms associated with plain, common decency. Labeling it "morality writ small," this is essentially what sociologist Alan Wolfe sees as the dominant ethical sensibility among contemporary middle-class Americans. "Not only should our circles of moral obligation never become so large that they lose coherence," he writes in clarifying this overall view, "but morality should also be modest in its ambitions and quiet in its proclamations, not seeking to transform the entire world but to make a difference where it can."[9] Saying yes to this conceptualization of morality in the face of their busy schedules may not be rigorously demanding. Nor does it guarantee measureable progress toward some utopian, perhaps transcendent, ideal or sought-after goal. It instead means doing one's part to ensure the steady *progress from* situations in which dogmatism and authoritarianism have held sway and thus common human decency has been harder to come by.

Ken Preston: Searching for Faith, Finding Something Better

Ken Preston is a good example of someone who, while not having an especially clear destination in sight ("My personal philosophy is still evolving," he admits), is sure he is making significant progress in his life. Looking back, he sounds a lot like what, in chapter 2, I called inquisitives, people who basically grew out of religious belief and belonging as their questions went largely unanswered. Like them, he has no lack of stories to this effect particularly since, he is quick to add, the Missionary Baptist church in which he was raised (in Murfreesboro, Tennessee) was strictly fundamentalist. To give just one example, he recalls asking his eighth-grade Sunday school teacher why it is that, if his own father would never condemn him to hell, his heavenly Father, whose love reportedly surpasses that of all others, seemed more than willing to do so as punishment for a whole slew of possible, even seemingly slight, infractions. "She was like, 'Um, let's talk about something else,' and all I was thinking was, 'Holy shit, I have to do this work on my own!'"

"Work" is the operative word here, which is why Preston actually became a dedicated searcher. Not simply outgrowing his faith, he devoted
considerable effort in asking more questions (and, in response, hearing
more "Ums" or its theological equivalents), reading the Bible and whatever books about religion he could get his hands on, and praying for the
kind of faith that could make sense to him. The turning point came when
he matriculated into a nearby Methodist College that, being more liberal
than either he or, very much to their chagrin, his parents had realized,
introduced him to liberation theology and to critical (read nonliteral)
approaches to biblical interpretation. "This was a really important experience for me," he says with respect to legitimating both the questioning
attitude he had long held and the long quest upon which he was then
ready to embark. His first stop was to join a liberal Methodist church
while in college. Then, after earning his degree in communications, he
converted to Catholicism and became a regular churchgoer at a parish in
Nashville, where he moved for a job. Then, after several more years during which he came to find certain Catholic doctrines to be intellectually
dubious, he discovered Buddhism and became a Zen practitioner. This
in turn was followed by still another few years of exploring all kinds of
"New Age-y" offerings, which included dream analysis, crystals, past-life
regression, and more. Preston still believed in "a God or at least a divine
force of some kind" during this entire time. But at each station along the
way, he realized that he needed the supernatural less and less to provide
a foundation for organizing his life (à la his time as a Methodist), community and tradition (as a Catholic), awareness-enhancing practices (as
a "Buddhist of sorts"), and an overall sense of mystery (his New Age
period)—until he clung to his theism solely as a way to understand the
source of what he calls a "cosmic notion of goodness and justice."

That, he was sure, would be his last stop. This moral sensibility made
his beliefs, while admittedly vague, seem right until one day—September
11, 2001, to be precise—when things shifted yet again. In contrast to
many atheists who saw these terrorist attacks as singularly damning evidence of religion's nefarious influence, case closed, Preston's experience
was different. He recalls watching a television news program on which
appeared a self-identified atheist spokeswoman for the Freedom from
Religion Foundation (FFRF). "She was so reasonable and expressed my
own views so well," he remembers, "and she was clearly this ethically se-

rious person who spoke with such sophistication and moral conviction." This opened his eyes to the possibility of grounding notions of goodness and justice in purely secular terms. Within a day or two, in fact, he became a FFRF member, and about a year later he actually co-founded a Freethinker group in Nashville.

Now in his late fifties, Preston has found an intellectual and even spiritual home with this eclectic group of atheist activists. Some are more focused on debunking religious traditions and some are passionate about church-state separation issues, whereas he is much more interested in secular philosophies that explore possibilities for living with purpose and "without a bunch of dogmas or trying to please some deity." This is very spiritual for him, a term he applies to denote his abiding desire to "transcend my own self" as a means for better appreciating the interconnectedness of all people and their resulting obligations to one another. It is not at all religious, he insists. Religions "hold people back morally," a contention he illustrates by telling stories about his relationship with his born-again sister. In one, he describes how he and she are both opposed to the practice of fracking as a means of natural gas extraction. Yet since they also both own land in western Tennessee where this occurs, the state provides them with land-use royalties. Out of principle, he has donated this money to a local charity and says he was "completely floored" to hear that she, without much consideration at all, keeps the money. In another, she tried to convince him to give to an India-based charity she supports, which buys destitute children out of servitude and sends them to a tuition-free Christian school. Roughly equivalent to "using the parents' poverty as a means to indoctrinate their children out of their family traditions," this was "unbelievably unethical," in Preston's opinion.

Especially since he loves his sister and, in any case, is loath to "get all preachy," Preston tries not to blame her for what he sees as undeniable moral shortcomings. Not everyone, he concedes, has the time and ability to do the sort of searching and reflection he has done. "When I was doing all that religious exploring, I was just looking for prefabricated answers about how to live," he says. "Since then, I've taken upon myself to think through what I consider to be right." Plus, he notes, despite causing difficulties early on in his conservative upbringing, he suspects that his being gay may have afforded him the critical outsider's perspective that many people lack. Still, he does get frustrated sometimes—with his sister and with other religious people. Their main fault, he thinks, is that they needlessly "mystify" what is actually quite clear: human beings are profoundly connected and thus have rights that others ought to respect. "You can complicate it and mystify it all you want, but it really isn't rocket science!" he blurts out. Asked to explain this a bit, he is happy to oblige:

> A few years ago, I read this book *The Ancestor's Tale* by Richard Dawkins. Don't get me wrong: I understood evolution, but I didn't understand how beautiful it was until then. It's really beautiful to think how we have a common ancestor. We're told endlessly how we're all separate, you know as separate individuals, separate groups and nations—all that. In reality, you realize that's the lie. The truth is that we're all connected. It's awe-inspiring to view the world and other people that way. . . . One person who really got this was Eleanor Roosevelt who came up with the "Universal Declaration of Human Rights" back in the forties. She doesn't always get her due, but she was really brilliant and came up with this framework, which you can use to analyze and then make ethical decisions. The thing is that they're not esoteric. You don't need to go to church or get an advanced degree in philosophy to figure these out.

You also do not need to be an award-winning evolutionary biologist like Dawkins or a brilliant former First Lady like Roosevelt, suggests Preston. Just to be mindful both of our deep connections with one another and of everyone's inherent rights, he says, is to be more than aptly equipped to live morally and with purpose. "I don't think the world comes with some ready-made purpose," he elaborates. "I think we have to organize a sense of meaning for ourselves based on the kind of interconnected beings we are. So, we create our own meaning. For me, it's to add a little, small raindrop in a sea of humanity, which might not make a dramatic change. But it'll send ripples that might change the course of one or two things, which then might change the course of one or two things, which might change the course of one or two things, and so on. That's enough for me."

Stepping back a bit, it is worth noticing a commonly heard refrain highlighted in the last chapter. Immediately reminiscent of Sheryl Manahan's this-worldly affirmation, "I get to be part of it for a while . . .

that's really good enough for me," I asked Preston to take a moment to clarify this. "It's hard to explain," he confessed, "but a good way to illustrate what I'm trying to get across to you is the story of that photo-journalist who was working in Sudan during a famine years ago. And he took that Pulitzer Prize–winning picture of a vulture standing next to an emaciated child." From there, Preston described the photo in detail, why the image has stuck with him over the years and then disclosed that, when he imagines it, he mostly thinks about the photographer who, so distraught about what he had seen during his assignment in Sudan and elsewhere, ultimately committed suicide. I pushed him a little here:

> *When you're reminded of that photo, why do you think so much about him?*
> I guess it just makes me sad. Obviously, thinking about that child and about all the children who suffer isn't easy either. Thinking about that guy, though, really gets me. I keep thinking that he wanted too much, more than this world can give at any one time. You know, some grand divine intervention to help that child and maybe even to provide some comfort, some peace of mind for himself.
> *Would you blame him if that's what he might have wanted?*
> Oh, no, not at all. It's just that he was really young. And you know, he was already a person of conviction and doing something positive— you know, really feeling the injustice, taking those photos and alert-ing the world to what was going on. From there, as I said before, who knows what king of ripple effect that could have had. That's what I'm saying—that would have been good enough for me, and I wish it could have been good enough for him too.

Not expecting "more than this world can give" while, at the same time, being a "person of conviction and doing something positive" is a good summation of what it means to draw upon and exemplify athe-ism's *immanent* root. This term, used in the present context as distinct from things transcendent, fundamentally denotes a life project con-ceived as meaningful and worthwhile in all its worldliness. I borrow the term from philosopher Charles Taylor, whose important book, *A Secular Age*, incisively explores what he calls the "immanent frame," his phrase for the increasingly preponderant paradigm by which modern people imagine their everyday worlds in a manner that precludes expectations of transcendence.[10]

Although this is how I also use the term, my intent is far more focused than his. For example, his work is largely historical—asking why belief in God was commonsensical in the West five hundred years ago whereas now it is but one option among feasible others—but mine, of course, is primarily set in the present. Second, Taylor attends mostly to the altered "conditions of belief" and thus to the truncated possibilities for religious conviction within the modern context. However, the present study focuses on that segment of the American public for whom these altered conditions render belief completely untenable and who, content to trade religious belief for upright behavior, say yes to living decent, conscientious lives as well as they can. Lastly, even though Taylor is extremely sensitive to many people's felt experience of living within the immanent frame, this is primarily explored from the perspective of believers of various sorts. He is at his best, for instance, when he discusses the experience of "fragilization," the feeling that, in the face of so many other options, one's own faith convictions seem uncomfortably fragile or even dubitable.[11] American atheists are not immune from such feelings, certainly. As with Max Weber, the experience of solving life's puzzles to one's complete satisfaction and thus being "satiated with life" likely eludes many, if not most, of them. Yet this is hardly all they feel. As we will see, their saying yes to meaningful lives of immanence generally feels like real progress to them because, albeit typically "writ small," their moral stances are generally experienced by them as being free from illusion as well as from both undue complexification and deference to religious (and other) "experts" when it comes to discerning ethical matters.

Morality Immanently Framed: Progressing from Illusion

Another way of saying that atheists think of morality in immanent terms is to point out that they give a very definitive answer to a very old question. About twenty-four centuries ago, Plato depicted Euthyphro, an Athenian teacher and soothsayer, happening upon his friend Socrates at the city's courthouse. Socrates learns that he is there to present charges of manslaughter against his own father (who inadvertently killed one of his workers), which surprises him because Athenian law typically allows only relatives of the dead to file manslaughter and murder suits. Even more startling to him is that Euthyphro's decision to go beyond the law is born of his brash overconfidence when it comes to matters pertaining to ethics and to discerning between what is pious and impious, a topic of considerable interest to Socrates, who was then facing capital charges of impiety. Ostensibly intent on learning from Euthyphro and thus better preparing himself for trial, Socrates asks his friend about this. "Piety, then, is that which is dear to the gods," responds Euthyphro at the dialogue's key moment, "and impiety is that which is not dear to them." At this, Socrates, to put his question in the modified form philosophers have preferred ever since, further prods: "Is that which the gods love good because they love it, or do they love it because it is good?"[12]

Very much the latter, insist my respondents who, to a person, are adamant that the widespread conceit that religion is the primary source of goodness and morality is actually an illusion. To demonstrate this more fulsomely, the people I interviewed look back, look around, and look within. When they *look back*, they sound like, and often make reference to books written by, the growing number of anthropologists, evolutionary biologists, and primatologists who are discovering that cooperation, altruism, and other forms of ethical behavior are actually adaptive traits that, when passed on by natural selection, have proven to be key to our success as a species.[13] Many respondents talk about this kind of scientific work, but one cleverly sums up the basic insight with a "little fable" he recounts:

> So, a huge man-eating tiger is stalking the jungle. In this jungle live two tribes: the Droppos and the Grabbos. One day a Droppo comes running into his camp screaming, "The tiger is coming! Drop the kids and run!" Everyone does. A week later a Grabbo comes running into his camp screaming, "The tiger is coming! Grab the kids and run!" Everyone does. My point is that the basic premise of evolution by natural selection is that certain traits will lead to the survival of more offspring and, over the long haul, this will favor the species that exhibit those traits. Which trait do you suppose evolution favors in that tiger-infested jungle, the selfish behavior of the Droppos or the altruistic behavior of the Grabbos? Evolutionary theory provides a perfectly understandable explanation for the rise and success of morality among humans—nothing at all supernatural about it.

Those who *look around* are less focused on evolutionary origins and more on making the case that, if the source of morality were God or, in Euthyphro's and Socrates's phrasing, "the gods," then it would not be so temporally and culturally variable. "You just need to open your eyes and look," one young man told me, actually widening his eyes and looking around for what I took to be dramatic effect. "If God or any one collection of scriptures provided the foundation for morality, then how does one explain that we no longer stone people to death and that we treat women with more respect than just fifty years ago? A morality that comes from God would be immutable over time—and from one culture to the next too. It's clear that what people consider moral varies greatly between, say, modern societies and developing or tribal ones, and between Western societies and the East." Finally, those who *look within* are people who provide some accounting of the nonreligious sources of their own ethical sensibilities. "What I consider to be moral is pretty predictable really," said this same young man; "it's a reflection of this particular time and this particular culture." "I get my morals from the same place as everybody else," said another, "about 60 percent from my parents, 30 percent from other people, and 10 percent from thinking about it myself." "My morality comes from my parents, my teachers, my peers, and from everything I've experienced up to this point," said a third.

One hears statements like these a lot. Just as frequently, people respond to Socrates's question by going still further. Not only is religion neither the source of morality in general nor a source for their own ethics in particular, but also they maintain that, when all is said and especially done, it does not truly regulate the moral lives of even most believers. Indeed, many note, it would be a sad state of affairs if religion were the source for morality and ethics. "The possibility that some people wouldn't know right from wrong without God is absolutely terrifying to me," gasped one woman. "If you need some make-pretend being to tell you that murder and rape are bad, then you're most likely an amoral sociopath!" Many more of them are well aware that most believers are not sociopaths and, in fact, that the vast majority of religious people have internalized societal norms and values to the same extent as everyone else. These norms and values, they inevitably add, typically prevail when contradicted by religious teachings, which only proves the greater ethical weight of the former over the latter when it comes to shaping attitudes. As one woman explains:

> Moral codes and philosophies predate religion. Otherwise we wouldn't have survived as a species and then created religions. . . . Survival of the species is our most basic instinct, and that is more likely in a cooperative community than in an individualistic free-for-all. Most people are more moral than their religions dictate. People will, and have, abandoned positions—even if outlined in one of their sacred texts—that they find morally obsolete. Churches will have to reconsider their positions on the LGBT community, for example, because society is coming to the conclusion that discriminating against them is no longer acceptable. If they continue to go against the flow of society, they'll become irrelevant.

Another respondent, focusing on scripture this time, offers a similar view:

> Nobody I know bases their morality off of what's written in the Bible. Every one of them finds the things they already believe and then picks out Bible verses to justify their belief. Here's an exercise for you. Take three pens: red, green, and yellow. Go to the rules sections of the Bible such as the ones in Exodus, Leviticus, and Deuteronomy. Mark the good laws that are reflected in our modern law codes in green, the ones that are now irrelevant in yellow, and those that are considered bad laws or morally unacceptable today in red. You'll see lots of yellow and red, and very little green. So you can't tell me people derive what's right and wrong from the Bible.

That the everyday ethics of even people in the pews are actually based more on the openness of secular reason than the obsolescence of religious traditions all suggests significant progress, according to atheists today. The majority of them are not reticent to make an additional point. Not only is religion neither the source of morality nor what actually informs most believers' sense of right and wrong, but also they claim that, when taken seriously, it generally makes people less moral than they would be otherwise. To substantiate this point, they engage in a good deal of list making. They list what they see as the highly immoral events and mindsets that appear in religious scriptures, especially in the Old

Testament of the Bible: "Kill your disrespectful children, dash heathen babies against rocks, commit mass murder and keep slaves? Are you kidding me?" They list historical events that reflect badly on religion: the crusades, the Inquisition, witch-hunts, sectarian violence, 9/11, religiously legitimated discrimination, clergy pedophilia—let's just say that this one can get pretty long. And from the other side of the ledger, they sometimes list exemplars of secular morality: "The fallacious assertion that, without God, there can be no morality is refuted by the lives of Carl Sagan, Richard Dawkins, Robert Ingersoll, Margaret Sanger, Noam Chomsky, Peter Singer, Thomas Edison, Erich Fromm, and so many others who lived eminently admirable lives untainted by the stain of religious morality."

More than anything else, atheists come to this conclusion by reflecting on their own experience, making comparisons between how believers and nonbelievers go about their lives. These comparisons are usually of two kinds. Similar to Ken Preston's description of how he went from relying on "prefabricated answers" to taking it upon himself to "think through" moral issues on his own, many compare their former religious or religiously influenced selves with who they are presently. This is what Neal Kamenetz does. He gets "kind of cringe-y" when he thinks about growing up in the St. Louis suburb where he was one of the main leaders of a high school youth group sponsored by the Evangelical church he attended regularly. "Righteous living" and "purity of body, mind, and spirit" were the much-discussed watchwords that animated that group's ethos. Nevertheless, he confides, when it comes to moving beyond watchwords to actual living in the world, his past self pales in comparison with its present iteration:

> I was never a Bible thumper or a judgmental type. I was never *that* guy, you know? At the same time, I have to admit I was pretty immature morally. From the outside, I know people looked at me and thought I was this upstanding, good, and even devout person. But on the inside, it was all about me. Am I checking all the religious boxes? Am I following the rules? Am I following the path to my salvation? It's embarrassing to admit all this. . . . Now I get it that there are no set boxes or rules or paths, so it's like I have to figure out what's right all by myself—you know, every day, every unique situation. So, when I see people on other paths, I respect

that more. Not everyone is doing a second-rate job trying to be who I am. They're doing their own thing the best they can. Because they have challenges and hurdles that my one, narrow perspective probably can't even grasp, I just feel this sense of empathy—much more empathy than I had when I was religious. I'm just being honest. I wasn't a complete jerk, but I definitely wasn't where I am today.

Second, similar to how Preston compared himself to his sister, others are also prone to observing the religious people in their lives. Doing so usually indicates to them that they are on the right track. To use concepts derived from developmental psychologist Lawrence Kohlberg, they generally see their own secular morality as representing progress from preconventional ("How can I avoid punishment?") or conventional ("How can I conform to society's expectations?") levels of morality to a postconventional level marked by their willingness and ability to critically evaluate situations and then come up with the principled, ethical responses that make most sense to them.[14] People of faith, on the other hand, seem to be stuck at these lower levels. "As far as I can tell," observes one woman, "when belief in God is the basis of someone's morality, then they aren't moral persons. They're simply acting in whatever way they think will keep them on the good side of their godly parent. Religion impedes true moral development by keeping them on the emotional level of a child who thinks doing the right thing is just about not getting punished." "Religion seems to lessen people's morality," notes another. "It instills a criminal mentality that basically says, 'I'm only good when the cops are watching!'" Progressing from moral immaturity, or mere authority pleasing, means acknowledging that one is, in fact, an autonomous adult and then, as described in the last chapter, accepting the responsibility to determine for oneself how best to live. It would be difficult to find an atheist who does not hold to some version of this basic conviction. "Without religion, one must rise to the occasion and provide some reasoning to define right and wrong," explains one man who sums up the perceived superiority of secular to religious ethics quite succinctly. "But establish those concepts based on what's claimed to come from a deity, and then you no longer bear that responsibility. You merely have to say, 'It's because God said so.' The results are usually less than truly moral and, historically speaking, often really tragic."

Morality Immanently Achievable: Progressing from Ethical Abstraction and Heroism

Notice, once again, the emphasis on assuming personal responsibility, which is absolutely at the core of atheists' moral bearings. Since taking responsibility means they are as willing to think for themselves as they are completely unwilling to outsource ethical matters in deference to God's will, scriptural mandates, or religious authorities, it denotes for them the superiority of secular ethical perspectives to faith-based ones. It is also the linchpin of Wolfe's morality writ small, emphasizing obligations to others that are relatively modest in their ambitions and scope. The reason responsibility is so central to this understanding of morality is relatively straightforward. Some people, as we all know, are smarter, richer, or better looking than others. No argument there. In contrast, Americans generally presume a considerable degree of moral equality, the sense that we are all capable of taking responsibility for ourselves and living decently in the ways we see fit. To do too much, to go beyond morality writ small and assume an inordinate responsibility for other people, the thinking goes, could result in their not taking responsibility for their own fates, and to be sure, it would imply a hierarchy of goodness that runs counter to notions of equality.

Morality writ small is exactly what Ken Preston subscribes to when he talks about adding "a little, small raindrop in a sea of humanity" and about his hope that this, even if not resulting in "dramatic change," would be enough to "send ripples that might change the course of one or two things." He wishes that that photographer could have thought similarly about his own work. He was, after all, "doing something positive" by addressing what was in front of him, doing what he did best, and trying to alert the wider world to a humanitarian crisis. This, in Preston's view, would have been "good enough."

It may be tempting for some to write off morality writ small for being of equally small account, for representing the sort of "moral mediocrity" that, seemingly burgeoning within modern societies, so perturbed Emile Durkheim about a century ago.[15] That would be short-sighted, in my view. For one thing, to focus on atheists specifically, many are without doubt genuinely concerned about leading meaningful and upright lives. Accordingly, they often get justifiably irate when their fellow citizens suggest otherwise, as did the late Supreme Court justice Antonin Scalia a few years back, who said that atheists are predisposed to "the devil's desires."[16] None claim to be angels, certainly, but their everyday lives are generally as good as anyone's. It is not uncommon for them to talk about their charitable giving, political involvements, not-so-random acts of kindness, or in Preston's case, their socially beneficial jobs. He now works as the development director and chief fund raiser for an inner-city charter high school attended primarily by poor and working-class students. "It's not saving the world," he offers modestly, "but at least I'm making it a little better, and so I get to feel like I'm contributing somewhat."

Another argument against writing it off is that a morality writ small is also more likely to be a morality with legs. If everyone is equally responsible for leading good lives, then it stands to reason that ethical standards cannot be set too high. And if that is the case, the moral life comes to be envisioned as something broadly expected and, more important, actually achievable by ordinary people. None of the people with whom I spoke state this implied logic explicitly. However, just about everyone, in one way or another, suggests that their moral convictions are indeed realizable in terms of both the *thinking* and the *doing* these convictions demand. They are writ small insofar as they require neither abstract theorizing nor a heroic level of obligation, which, being more achievable for more people amid the hubbub of busy lives, counts as definite progress among my respondents.

Let us first focus on thinking. Intellectually speaking, atheists lower the ethical bar in a couple of ways. The first is that they do not conceptualize morality as the sort of internally coherent systems that one finds in the theological ethics of particular religious traditions or, for that matter, in such secular moral philosophies as Immanuel Kant's deontological theory or John Stuart Mills's utilitarianism. They have not, in other words, "done the math" with respect to integrating revealed truths with corresponding ethical precepts and commandments or by delineating axioms in support of some logically consistent moral framework. Instead they are content to be ethical *bricoleurs*, to use the word anthropologist Claude Lévi-Strauss chose to denote a willingness to assemble meaningful outlooks out of whatever cultural resources, often unmoored from their original meanings, one finds on hand.[17]

So, when asked about the sources of their ethics, just about every-body points to their socialization. They have been taught to be good by their parents and teachers, by society's laws and mores, and by the books they have read and the movies they have seen. No surprises there. When queried a bit more about the principles they have learned from those sociocultural sources, they have a much tougher time. Most people are not accustomed to being so self-conscious about being good—it is just something automatic, they insist, something they just *are*. As conversa-tions proceed and deepen, and when prodded still further, their à la carte style of morality construction comes clear. At that juncture, one hears them talk about respecting other people's rights, weighing conse-quences of prospective actions, interrogating their feelings, abiding by the dictates of natural law, paying attention to the Golden Rule—or any combination of these. On the more erudite side, one person talks about how he draws upon Plato's moral absolutism, Aristotle's *eudemonistic* (precipitous of "well-being") ethics, and Nietzsche's nihilism, each of which, incidentally, reflects very different approaches to moral reason-ing. Another person says she draws upon lessons her Wiccan friends have imparted to her (especially the Law of Return: whatever good or bad someone does will return to them either three- or tenfold); words of advice she collects from famous figures; and especially "the rule of thumb that my rights end where your rights begin." These are particu-larly glaring examples of this pell-mell, bricoleur style. Still, no one I in-terviewed is the least bit persnickety about snatching whatever concepts and insights that are available to them—even contradictory ones—to make sense of their ethical positions.

If their sources can be internally inconsistent and indeed sometimes dizzyingly eclectic, a second way atheists resist unnecessary abstraction is by insisting upon the fundamental simplicity of the ethical positions at which they ultimately arrive. While they often go on and on about all kinds of captivating insights and anecdotes related to the conscien-tious ways they try to comport themselves, when it comes to expound-ing upon their overall moral viewpoint, they turn parsimonious very quickly. Here is just a glimpse:

Hector: There's really no need to overthink ethics as it pertains to the
real world. And there are very few situations that require a person to

actually contemplate what the right or wrong thing would be. I just try not to hurt anybody or be an asshole.

Kelley Anne: Nice matters. That's my moral compass: Be nice to people. Don't kill. Don't steal. Don't be horrible to others. Basically, do what you want as long as you leave no victims. I don't think morals are that hard. Be nice. From there, it's kindness, consideration, and no victims.

Gary: Turns out, it's not that difficult. Just don't be a dick. It's really that simple.

Dieter: I decide what things are good or bad, right or wrong, based on what impact they have on others. I can do whatever I want to myself, but I try not to cause harm or inconvenience to others.

Tyler: The foundation of my morality is the simple test of asking, "Will a given action make the world a better place?"

Sally: I really, really don't think many people pay attention to commandments or tenets or whatever to make choices. For me it's just basic: do the best you can.

Eleanor: I base my morality on an inherent sense of right and wrong and an understanding of equality. I can't explain it. Simply put, I treat others the way I want to be treated.

Why elaborate, they seem to be asking in chorus, when morality is so basic and therefore requires so little by way of intellectual heavy lifting?

Of all these summations, it is the last one, Eleanor's, that plucks the single most commonly heard chord. This is the Golden Rule, the idea that you should treat others as you would want to be treated. Whereas its most familiar iteration comes from the Bible—"Do to others as you would have them do to you" (Luke 6:31)—other, often older, versions appear within the venerable texts of many religious traditions and secular philosophies, and as Eleanor rightly suggests, it makes good sense from an everyday atheist perspective as well.[18] What is often missed about the Golden Rule is that, while eminently sensible, it is not exceptionally rigorous. It seems to require less of Christians, for example, than such other, far more supererogatory, biblical injunctions as loving thy neighbor as thyself, turning the other cheek, divesting oneself of all one's possessions in order to be saved, and most certainly, "Be perfect, therefore, as your heavenly Father is perfect" (Matthew 5:48).[19] The same can be said for what it requires of atheists. Rather than enjoining them to undertake specified, perhaps personally challenging actions, they (not unlike many Christians and people of other faiths) generally interpret it in a more psychological sense, as a reminder to simply avoid self-absorption and do one's best to cultivate a greater awareness of and sensitivity toward others. As such, it represents another facet of morality writ small in that, just as atheists render ethics more user-friendly intellectually, they do the same with respect to practice—the everyday obligations it entails. By framing the Golden Rule as a gentle goad toward this very general sort of other-directedness, it comes to represent for atheists an ethical sensibility that, although not especially heroic in its rigors, is still deemed valid in that it is actually achievable within daily life.

Many people explicitly mention or at least vaguely allude to the Golden Rule when thinking about their morals. What is most interesting is that, when doing so, they almost always, in some fashion, touch upon the same three themes. These are their shared view that the Golden Rule is (1) quite simple; (2) superior to the unnecessary and often problematic ethical complexifications wrought of religious traditions; and (3) less about mandating the performance of specific moral actions than moving people toward an overall attitude of other-directedness, reciprocity, and empathy. "This is not a Christian concept and, frankly, Christians seem like the group of people least likely to walk the walk [theme 2]," observes one woman after mentioning her adherence to the Golden Rule. "It's as basic as it gets [theme 1]. I don't need an ancient book to tell me to treat others with fairness and dignity. It's what I want for myself, and it's what we're all equally worthy of. We all bleed, we all have the same needs, and we all sink or swim together [theme 3]." Another respondent covers essentially the same ground by reflecting on the rule's inverse or prohibitive form, sometimes called the Silver Rule. "I base my morality on a strong allergy to prison and an overblown sense of empathy [theme 1]," he says. "The law states what's right and wrong fairly well. That, combined with my automatic tendency to put myself in the place of the other guy, gives me a good guide ethically [theme 3]. I've also adopted the inverse of the Golden Rule: I won't do to others what I don't want done to myself. It's easy to apply, and it doesn't confuse things with a lot of unnecessary doctrines and other thou-shalt-not bullshit [theme 2]." Finally, Dan Stein, an "escapee from Judaism" now living in western Pennsylvania, repeats these same three themes as well as the earlier discussed point about the nonreligious, evolution-based source of morality:

> I think morality is based on nothing more than the preservation of oneself [theme 1]. Altruism doesn't exist, in my opinion. And that's not a bad thing. The fact that we're selfish beings gave rise to what we now call the Golden Rule: "Do unto others as you'd have them do unto you." This has guaranteed the survival of the species. Why shouldn't we kill others? Because we ourselves don't want to be killed. Why not steal from others? Because we don't want to be stolen from. The best hope for cultural harmony is that we all see each other as equals. And seeing ourselves as vulnerable should open us up to others, to see that they're vulnerable too [theme 3]. . . . This form of morality requires no higher power to govern our behavior. In fact, that just distracts us from the simple reality I'm talking about [theme 2]. If the only thing keeping society from chaos is the threat of eternal damnation, then we're in desperate need of an ethical overhaul!

Treating others with "fairness and dignity"? Sustaining a "sense of empathy"? Seeing others as equal to oneself and equally vulnerable? Sounds good. In fact, such dispositions are both obviously good in themselves and, respondents claim, considerably better than religiously informed moralities because, while are not excessively demanding, they are shorn of complexity, manageable for busy people, and thus actually realizable in the real world.

Add to this yet another aspect of morality writ small that ensures its feasibility. When Dan Stein privileges the preservation and interests of the self over altruism, he speaks for many in suggesting that ethics need not entail a level of self-abnegation that would ultimately prove untenable in a society—such as ours—that so values individualism. Here they echo the social theorist Alexis de Tocqueville who, upon visiting

Jacksonian-era America, found that, at their best, citizens did not make an either/or decision between the needs of the self and those of others.[20] They chose both. Due largely to the quality of their institutions and culture, he noted, they exhibited a more ethically attainable "self-interest rightly understood" whereby actions intent on enhancing the self could often also prove beneficial to the larger community, and vice versa.

This understanding seems very convincing to atheists today. Take Dan Stein, for instance. He concedes that one of the very few things he likes about his job as a mortgage broker is that it has given him the skills to become an indispensable member of the board of directors for a nonprofit organization specializing in low-income home construction. Many of his fellow volunteers are motivated by their religious beliefs, he says. For him, it is different: "Sharing what I know just seems like the right thing to do. Plus, I get a lot out of it too—believe me." Believing him is easy because he is so forthcoming about the friends he has met doing this work; the social status it has conferred to him ("People look at me differently, you know?"); and even its importance for enabling him to model good social engagement for his eleven-year-old son. "I'm really proud that he's proud of me," he says, with his voice cracking just a bit. Or listen in on Eleanor again. She thinks that morality in itself is good and, like Dan, she gets plenty from it as well. "Not hurting people is good, and helping them is even better," she says. "Every living thing experiences hunger, pain, loneliness. These things are part of being alive, so it's good to do something if you can. There's no way to refute the positive feelings that come with helping a homeless person or feeding a hungry dog or watering a drooping plant." To give one more example, consider Sally, whom I also quoted above. Currently enrolled in a graduate program in geriatric social work, she, too, thinks that being good is as much about getting as it is about giving. In her case, rather than social status or a good feeling, she gets the confidence of living in a world where, when she finds herself in a pinch, others can be counted on to help her out. "When I think through things morally, I just ask myself, 'Is this something that I would want somebody else to do to me or for me?'" she explains, referencing the Golden Rule. "It's not about altruism. It's more interdependent for me. It's really that I'm studying to become a geriatric social worker because I really hope that, when I'm ninety-two, somebody's going to come along and look after me."

Morality Immanently Accessible: Progressing from Ethical Incompetence

Taking stock for a moment, atheists associate secular morality with progress because, when compared to religiously informed moralities, it seems to them to be both inherently superior and, since it is writ small in terms of the theorizing and behaviors required, far more achievable by most people today. In addition, as Dan, Eleanor, and Sally all suggest, people's interests in such things as social status, good feelings, and expectations of reciprocity are not necessarily at odds with the good of others, especially when self-interest is "rightly understood" with respect to being steered in community-serving directions. From Tocqueville's perspective, this often occurred because the United States—especially in light of the various institutions that comprised its robust civil society— was organized in such a way that the good of the individual and of the broader society could frequently align.

This warrants mentioning because a version of this perspective is apparent among atheists today. There is much that is good about society, they claim or sometimes just suggest, which renders the specific requirements of the moral life accessible (literally, *able* to *access*) to them. As we have seen, they are unreserved in insisting that they are unquestionably *able* to discern how best to live. They do not need, as Ken Preston finally realized, "to go to church or get an advanced degree in philosophy." They, as we have also heard in this chapter, do not need "an ancient book" or a "lot of unnecessary doctrines and other thou-shalt-not bullshit" or "the threat of eternal damnation" to be good and respectable people. Partly because they alone bear the ultimate responsibility for their lives, partly due to their sense of morality's sheer basicness ("Just don't be a dick," "Be nice," and so on), and partly a reflection of the critical thinking they so often exhibit, they do not consider it necessary to outsource their moral discernment. No clergy or gurus or bodhisattvas need apply. They are perfectly able to take care of this on their own.

Often unnoticed is another reason for atheists' sense of ethical competence, which harkens back to Tocqueville's insight about the alignment of individual and community interests. In addition to being able to be moral on their own, they also have *access* to the particular requirements of morality by dint of participating within what they usually con-

THE IMMANENT ROOT | 217

sider to be a fundamentally good society. No Pollyannas, they are well aware of the innumerable social maladies—racism, class divisions, gun violence, and all the rest—that continue to plague the nation. They are nevertheless convinced that, supplementing their innate moral capacities, there are the specific, socially embedded contents that constitute the substance of being good and to which they have ready access. The narratives, the values, the norms, the social roles: all the sources of moral reasoning and behavior are simply, as it were, given to us. Or to use a long-standing philosophical distinction, atheists are inclined to take a pass on abstract or systematized propositions (*Moralität*) and center their ethical sensibilities within their society's *Sittlichkeit*, the concrete beliefs and practices that make up its distinctive "ethical life."[21]

This has been Ken Preston's inclination. *Moralität* seems "esoteric" to him and tends to "mystify" the ethical life. He has the very strong feeling that being a good person "really isn't rocket science!" His experience was one of simply opening his eyes and accessing the moral information and cues that had been available to him all along. These were sustained by institutions like his Methodist college and the Freedom from Religion Foundation that inculcated, respectively, a "questioning attitude" and an atheism marked by "sophistication and moral conviction," as well as by such public figures as Richard Dawkins and Eleanor Roosevelt, who deepened his understanding of human interconnectedness and rights.

Indications that others are similarly confident in the moral worth of the normative frameworks bequeathed to them by society are everywhere. Since they are so omnipresent, allow me to give just a few examples. The most general of these stems from the fact that a full 95 percent of the atheists in this study say the term "humanist" describes them well. When asked to fill this in and specify more precisely what this very amorphous term actually entails, they inevitably draw upon what sociologist Robert Wuthnow calls the "deep meanings" of American culture, those publicly accessible and broadly salient symbols that both emanate from a people's common experience and assist them in making sense of it.[22] They talk about being free to be individuals—thinking for themselves and living in ways that seem authentic to them. They talk about being able to make something of themselves and, at the same time, give back to the community. They talk about entering into whatever loving relationships feel right to them and finding happiness in whatever ways they define it. They talk about growing and learning and realizing one's potential. In short, when filling in the details of what it means to them to be fully human, they trust and appropriate the "usual suspects," the deep meanings that have come to seem most fitting to contemporary Americans and that they draw upon to organize their experience.

Trust is essential here. Atheists trust the *Sittlichkeit* of which they are a part as being sufficient for conveying deep meanings and constituting them as moral selves. This becomes clearer when, getting somewhat more focused, conversations turn to what it means exactly to be moral. Randy Schimmel, a graduate student in North Carolina studying to become a public schoolteacher, is exceptionally precise on this topic. At the same time, though, his emphasis on the social origins of personal morality is typical among respondents:

> Morality is based on innate social morality, which is evident among even our apelike ancestors, and societal rules. So, when you get to specifics, whatever is bad for society is a bad thing. And whatever is good for society is a good, moral thing. God and religion aren't requirements for this. Don't kill each other, don't cheat with your neighbor's spouse, don't steal—these are just basic codes for any society to survive. . . . So, yeah, I definitely consider myself to be a moral person, but I don't expect a prize or anything since I'm just doing what I learned to do. I treat people with respect, I try to be honest and, you know, to help others when I can. I also want to make something of my life. The way it's playing out now is that I'm trying to get a good education, love my family and friends, make them laugh, work hard, learn as much as I can, and then pass on what I know to the next generation. I'd like to leave this a smarter, better world than what I was born into.

Notice two basic convictions that reliably emerge from discussions like this. One is that Schimmel is positively unyielding when it comes to designating society as the source of his ethics. He hardly deserves a prize, he says, when he is simply doing what, through socialization, he has learned to do. The other is his trust in the moral sufficiency of the deep meanings he has internalized. Working hard, loving the people around him, making something of himself—it is all making him better, and as a result, he trusts that he is doing his part in making the world smarter and better as well.

These two convictions show up again when, getting even more focused this time, conversations sometimes turn to the specific topic of child-rearing.[23] The majority of atheist parents in this study are resolute about not exposing their kids to any degree of religious influence. As with atheist parents nationally, only a small percentage of even these parents say they are intentionally raising their kids to adopt an atheist worldview, preferring that they make up their own minds when ready to do so.[24] Other parents in this study have a somewhat looser attitude, and treating faith traditions like any other cultural tradition, they are fine with exposing their kids to the religious ideas and rituals that are so meaningful to the friends, family members, and other people in their lives. These parents are more like the one in four atheist parents nationally who enroll their children in some kind of religious education program, which once again, is generally understood as a means for better enabling them to make up their own minds about God, faith, and so on when the time is right.[25] The point is that, when discussing child-rearing, respondents range from considering religion "a form of child abuse" to thinking of it as something they can abide introducing their kids to as a "fascinating window into American culture and into what animates *other* people's lives." Either way, what nearly all of the people I spoke with have in common is their view that religion is absolutely unnecessary, and oftentimes detrimental, when it comes to the specific issue of children's moral development. Albuquerque dental assistant Maria Lozano provides the representative voice here:

> If you compared my atheist son with his Christian friends, you'd get a pretty clear picture. My husband and I have raised a thoughtful, loving, generous, tolerant young man. Unlike with his brainwashed friends, we've taught him to think for himself! . . . I've always thought that spending Sunday morning on a bike ride with his parents is better than sitting silently next to them in a pew. Rather than asking, "What would Jesus do?" we've wanted him to ask, "What would Mom and Dad do?" Not that we're special or anything. It's just that we've tried to set a good example. So, rather than praising the Lord, we've tried to teach and show him how to be good and honest and kind to others. We've encouraged him to find a good job that'll make him happy, find a spouse that will make him happy. Shoot for your goals, work hard, have fun. I see him heading in that general direction for sure.

Again, pay attention to her reliance upon the two convictions that Randy Schimmel also expressed. The first one about the societal source of people's ethical lives? Check. She and her husband are not special; they *are* society in a sense. As parents, they simply inhabit a social role and pass on what they have themselves learned, perhaps during Sunday morning bike rides with their own parents. Nor, they imply, is their son necessarily special, at least in the ethical sense. Per the second basic conviction, all he has needed to do is "think for himself" and trust, as Lozano and presumably her husband does, that society's moral signposts will do the rest. That these are sufficient and worthy of that trust, she notes, is abundantly clear. The proof of the efficacy of America's deep meanings—"Shoot for your goals, work hard, have fun," "be good and honest and kind"—are in the pudding. She is well pleased with what she and, most especially, since she makes no claims to specialness, the moral order of society have produced.

The Real Consequences of Saying Yes to Immanence

America's morality writ small is obviously not the only thing atheists affirm. They also say yes to family life and plenty of close friends, to great books and great (and guilt-free) sex lives, to meaningful jobs and vibrant communities, and to the awe-inspiring wonders of the natural world. News flash: they are very much alive, and hence they affirm much what most of their fellow citizens living today, religious people included, also appreciate and desire. In that sense, the topic of their saying yes to leading good, decent lives is not exceptional. What sets it apart is that it is the topic that engenders the most (and usually most energized) conversation and one that they, perhaps in the hopes of preemptively fending off the immoral atheist stereotype, so often broach on their own, even before being asked. Of all the ways one says yes to life, the topic of morality also seems to best mirror for atheists the faith in progress (religion : science :: regression : progress) encoded in the religion versus science conflict myth. As with that myth, however, the commonly held understanding that atheist morality represents *progress from* its religious analogue—from how people of faith have attempted and do attempt to lead good lives—should raise some questions.

For one thing, in spite of the impressive amount of empirical research done in the area, it is not at all certain that atheists are actually more moral than believers, or vice versa. Studies that claim to be definitive one way or the other are usually replete with all sorts of methodological problems.[26] Some that isolate worldviews, either secular or religious, as the *cause* of people's moral responses often overlook the reality that these are frequently not causes at all. Such worldviews can, in fact, be the *effect* of psychological or political predispositions that then shape both whether or not people identify as religious and their attitudes on various moral issues. Other studies reflect an "apples and oranges" problem in that they do not sufficiently control for demographic and other differences between the religious and secular people in their sample. For example, investigations suggesting that the religious are exceptionally charitable sometimes neglect to account for the fact that many of them are also "churched"—and thus exposed to social cues from the pulpit, community networks, opportunities for giving, and so on—whereas secular people are much less likely to be affiliated with comparable groups that function for them in these same ways. Beyond methodological issues, there is also the more foundational issue about whether studies in this area exhibit a sufficient degree of reflexivity about what presumably constitutes any given morally superior position.[27] Is being pro-life more moral than being pro-choice? Is supporting increases in state-funded welfare provision more moral than not? Which attitudes toward divorce, capital punishment, or school vouchers are the right ones? These are difficult questions because the factors to which people attend when making ethical decisions vary so widely. For instance, psychologist Jonathan Haidt has helpfully identified five general domains of moral concern upon which people, usually unconsciously (and only rationally justified after the fact), focus when making these kind of decisions: (1) harm/care; (2) fairness/reciprocity; (3) authority/respect; (4) in-group/loyalty; and (5) purity/sanctity. As opposed to being more or less moral per se, he found that people are actually differently moral from one another, with the secular among us being more likely to base moral decisions on the "individualizing"-leaning domains (1 and 2) whereas people of faith generally attend to these two domains as well as to the other "binding"-related ones (3, 4, and 5).[28]

Next, just as atheists are not necessarily more (or, of course, less) moral than believers, their ethical frameworks are not always more achievable. Their presuming as much is often a reflection of their own stereotypes of religious people. Perhaps some religious leaders pine for the days when their flocks simply, as the hackneyed Catholic saw once had it, "payed, prayed, and obeyed," and the faithful assiduously adhered to a theologically nuanced and rigorously demanding moral system. If those days ever truly existed, they are now long gone. Instead of working through their ethical frameworks in a considered and coherent manner, both secular *and* religious Americans alike tend to be bricoleurs in that they mix and match what philosopher Alasdair MacIntyre calls moral "fragments," and then rely upon these in whatever ways seem right to them at any given time.[29] Moreover, for good or for ill, the actual ethical demands associated with religious commitment have come to be imagined by many believers to be less-than-onerously achievable. They typically interpret the Golden Rule as the same gentle reminder to be more caring, as do atheists. And, if anything, the user-friendly ilk of religiosity that sociologist Robert Bellah and his colleagues identified more than three decades ago is significantly more prevalent today. "I believe in God. I'm not a religious fanatic. I can't remember the last time I went so church," explained a young nursed named Sheila Larson to one of the interviewers. "My faith has carried me a long way. It's Sheilaism. Just my own little voice." Asked to define this, she did so by continuing, "It's just try to love yourself and be gentle with yourself. You know, I guess, take care of each other. I think He would want us to take care of each other."[30] Whatever else this might suggest, neither "Sheilaism" nor its individually named equivalents among the broader, religiously identified populace appear to be either incompatible with a morality writ small or in any way less readily achievable in a day-to-day, practical sense.

Then what about atheists' third widely held contention that they better exercise their individual moral competence by dint of embracing the values and norms of American society to which they have easy access? Readers should question this too. Sheila Larson, whose faith is based largely on trusting her "own little voice," certainly would. So, too, would an increasing number of churchgoing Americans whose locus of moral authority, starting after about the Second World War, has decidedly shifted from religious leaders (and scriptures, teachings, and so forth) to the individual self. The reality is that, despite the prevailing idea that atheists and believers are so different from one another, both groups exercise plenty of moral agency. Both groups abide by their own little voices, which tend to be profoundly informed by the *Sittlichkeit* of American society. In his recent *Secular Faith*, for instance, political scientist Mark Smith makes this point very definitively. He writes compellingly about how "culture has trumped religion" with respect to Americans' views on various moral issues throughout the nation's history—and especially today. "The best predictors of people's moral beliefs are not their religious convictions or lack thereof but rather when and where they were born," he argues in the book's final pages. "Christians in America today hold more in common morally and politically with their atheist neighbors than their Christian predecessors in the America of 1800."[31]

If not with respect to the sociocultural sources of the moral and political attitudes they hold in common, atheists do often differ from many believers in their assessment of the moral sufficiency of those sources. In other words, they are without doubt ethically competent to the extent that, rather than outsourcing their moral deliberations to religious leaders and other "experts," they assume the responsibility to discern for themselves how best to fashion their moral lives. They also demonstrate competence in the sense that they draw freely and confidently from the norms, values, and narratives of their society in advancing their aim to be, or at least one day become, the persons they want to be. Yet, especially for such generally thoughtful people for whom critical thinking is so esteemed and usually more than abundantly evident, they are surprisingly less competent with respect to understanding the moral limits of their society's normative frameworks. They trust the normative features of their society, but everyone I asked seems to have an enormously difficult time explaining why they should be so trusting when societies change and are so different from one to the next. While, again, just about *everyone* has trouble here, my exchange with Gary, whom I also quoted previously, demonstrates this particularly well. When asked to elaborate upon his "Just don't be a dick" axiom, he talked about obeying the law, respecting others, doing his part within his local community, and basically making sure that "everything's not all about me, you know?" Yes, I said, but:

How do you know that all this is what you should be doing?

Well, as I said earlier, I think our morals come from the society we live in. So, I really just try to live out what I learned from my parents, my schooling, from the whole culture—from everything. It's all informed me.

Right. But here's what I think is a tough question, one I think about sometimes. That is, if society changes all the time, why are the morals it conveys at any one point in time trustworthy?

I don't really know the answer to that. Honestly, where we are now works for me. It's what morality means for me. That is tough!

I know. Here's an even tougher version. If you were born a couple of hundred years ago when slavery was legal and women couldn't vote and children were expected to work long hours and so on, would that alter what morality means for you?

Yes, I have to say it probably would. People weren't assholes or anything back then; they just lived in a different time so saw things differently. Maybe two hundred years from now people will question my morality because I walk by homeless people on my way to work or live in a big house with a furnace that burns natural gas. So, maybe they'll think I'm the asshole for just imbibing the values and customs of my society.

And me too, I must admit. Then what's the moral worth of those values and customs if they change over time and even from place to place?

Dude, you're killing me! I really don't know the answer to that one. Society makes me better than I'd be without it. That's for sure. But is it moral in that larger sense? Hard to say.

It *is* hard to say—for Gary, for other atheists, and for most Americans. Most people, notes Charles Taylor, have internalized the "modern moral order" to such a degree that, forgetful of its socially constructed and historically contingent character, its normative codes and practices come to be "unthought," defined as real, and thus shape our deepest convictions from behind our own backs.

Hence that Thomas theorem again. True, one could look askance at atheists for reifying the modern moral order or, at the very least, for not demonstrating the kind of critical perspective toward it that one might expect of people who generally, as a well-known bumper sticker puts it, "question authority" of all sorts. One could even chide them for misrecognizing the pervasive and, for them, often *unquestioned* authority that the surrounding culture actually wields over their ethical lives and thus significantly undermines their claims to moral superiority. Like anyone (including, as is likely evident, sociologists), atheists have their blind spots. As I have pointed out throughout this book, they also tend to adhere less than critically to the science versus religion conflict myth as well as to their broad-based presumption of religious believers' irrationality. Again, these are real blind spots.

Even though critiques like these are warranted and, in this case, intended entirely to be helpful to readers, leaving things there could also leave ourselves blind to an important dimension of atheists' ethical discourse. That is, as with their acceptance of the conflict myth and their presumption of believers' irrationality, their views concerning secular morality may have less to do with reflecting objective realities than engendering subjective consequences. If their moral lives are defined by them as superior to and more achievable and accessible than those of their religious counterparts, then, for atheists, such convictions are "real in their consequences." The notion that their moral sensibilities represent progress from religious ones enables them to push back against many of their fellow citizens' stigmatizing presumptions about their immorality. It also provides them with the confidence that—in the absence of religious leaders, scriptures, and traditions, as well as assurances of transcendence, all functioning as ethical road markers for believers— they are still on the right track ethically, even if they are not necessarily always taking a higher road.

Conclusion

As I hinted at in the preface, this book's title is a play on William James's 1902 classic *The Varieties of Religious Experience*. Though I generally like playful titles, choosing this one in the early stages of this project had much less to do with playfulness than with my desire to emulate the spirit of James's important work. The founding stipulation of the prestigious Gifford Lectures, which he delivered in Edinburgh, Scotland, and upon which his twenty-lecture book is based, was that all addresses should draw upon publically accessible evidence in their treatments of religion. No problem there. A distinctly empirical approach is precisely what James had in mind all along. Many of his lectures, and therefore much of his book, present one testimony after another from people of various historical epochs and seemingly all walks of life (though almost entirely Christian) concerning their often life-changing encounters with what they consider to be "the divine." Moreover, he took these accounts very seriously. Rather than privileging what he called the "second-hand" religion of official doctrines and rituals, he explored the psychological contours and practical consequences of people's "first-hand" religious experiences in a thorough and impressively balanced manner.

Trying my best to emulate James's empirical grounding and interpretive generosity has been my primary strategy for, as Sir Isaac Newton once described his own work, "standing on the shoulders of giants." Looking about and paying attention—through in-person and telephone-based conversations, and e-mailed questionnaires and surveys—to the firsthand experiences of 518 atheists was no mean feat, but I will leave it to readers to determine the extent to which this effort has been a success. No doubt such assessments will reveal one, patently obvious, way that my work, in terms of overall quality, differs from the unquestionably successful effort of this particular giant. To this, I want to conclude by directing readers' attentions to four other ways.

First, and most obviously, my topic is different from James's. He makes a seldom-noticed point when mentioning that "to find religion is only one out of many ways of reaching unity" and, as he illustrates with the three examples of conversion to nonreligious worldviews that appear in his book, "new birth may be away from religion into incredulity."[1] Still, his driving concern, of course, is with religion whereas I have introduced readers to American atheists. In doing so, I have attempted to unearth what, in the preface, I described as valuable nuggets that should enhance our understanding of this topic. One of these is that we use one word, "atheist," to denote a grouping that is actually rife with myriad and often intriguing *varieties*. Also, more important to most atheists than in-person or online communities is an "imagined" one that they symbolically construct to differentiate themselves from people of faith. Next, New Atheist authors are widely read but not roundly emulated by rank-and-file atheists in terms of these authors' scientism and heavy-handed attitudes toward religion. And the final nugget is that atheism is not simply about *not* believing in God. It is very typically something more positive, more substantial, and at its best, much more about life projects defined by being rational, having integrity, exemplifying openness, and standing for progress. I hope these nuggets—along with the others I discuss a bit more fully below—have been sufficiently dusted off and examined closely enough for readers.

Second, not unexpected from one of the founders of modern psychology, James's focus is entirely trained on the individual psyche. For him, community-based institutions, rituals, and creeds are not at all what are most fundamental to religion. Reflective of his singular attention to the self, he defines religion as "the feelings, acts, and experiences of individual men in their solitude, so far as they apprehend themselves to stand in relation to whatever they may consider divine."[2] Some may be optimistic "healthy-minded" people, and others, whom he labels "sick souls," may be prone to despair and, so being, struggle to discern the sacred "unseen order" of the world. Yet in both cases, the religious experience, the experience of moving from a sense of "something wrong" to "something made right," and the moral transformation that ensues from this are deemed by James to be universal, essentially the same across cultures.

In this book, however, I have attempted to show that being an atheist is not a single, universal experience. As we have seen, people vary enormously with respect to such matters as their process of rejecting faith, the salience of their nonbelief vis-à-vis their overall identities, their attitudes toward religion and religious people, and their views concerning what is meaningful in life. Perhaps more importantly, I have given pride of place not to psychological considerations but to the socially constituted aspect of nonbelief. Throughout this study, I have emphasized how American atheism is, to use a spot-on German word, *Standortsgebunden*, meaning inextricably linked to a particular time and place. If the United States were not so "awash in a sea of faith," then it would likely not occur to a subset of its citizenry to identify themselves as atheists. If American culture did not so regularly conflate religious adherence with moral rectitude, then atheists would face little or no stigma and hence their identities would almost certainly entail a fraction of the (either modest or considerable) effort and ongoing "role making" they actually require. And if religions in the West were not so frequently conceptualized with respect to their most objectified, cognitive dimensions, then a specifically "scientific atheism" would likely neither emerge as the predominant type nor seem, for many, so credibly underwritten by the science versus religion "conflict myth." In sum, this book deals in no universal Platonic forms. It is about specifically *American* atheists as they go about living within *American* society at a particular juncture in its history.

Third, in James's view, religions are always and everywhere "founded on feeling." At their core, they are based primarily upon emotionally charged experiences of conversion after which individuals become motivated and energized to live in harmony with the unseen order of ultimate reality. Theological concepts and creedal systems—what James calls "over-beliefs"—are merely secondary, culturally variable constructs that reflect different people's attempts to organize and make sense of that initial, powerfully affective experience. "When we survey the whole field of religion," he reflects at the conclusion of his work, "we find a great variety in the thoughts that have prevailed there; but the feelings on the one hand and the conduct on the other are almost always the same."[3]

I have discovered the opposite to be the case among American atheists today. Most common among them is a single "over-belief," their almost uniformly shared belief in the conflict myth. Rather than being primary, feelings function after the fact, as a kind of affective validation for an identity that is generally accorded scant legitimacy among the wider populace. This, as we have seen, occurs in a couple of ways. Narratively speaking, feelings provide a sense of autobiographical periodization. Similar to how society has changed—from religious domination to scientific ascendency—so, too, do most of the people with whom I have spoken claim to have changed. Accounts of what the process of becoming atheists felt like to them, feelings of regret concerning their religion-tinctured pasts, feelings of freedom and gratitude in the present, and feelings of profound responsibility for shaping an indeterminate future all provide a felt confirmation of the reality of this change, which again, atheists experience as being aligned with the trajectory of societal betterment. Next, dispositionally speaking, feelings also provide for atheists' assurances that their lives are on the right track in ways analogous to how doctrinal assent, ritual performance, and communal ties commonly function for the religious. Encoded within the conflict myth as oppositional categories, feelings of having chosen integrity over comfort, openness over closed-mindedness, and of contributing to progress instead of inhibiting it all serve to legitimate their identities as nonbelievers and assure them that they, if I may be permitted a line from Luke's gospel (10:42), have indeed "chosen the better part" among these sets of binaries. Appropriating the styles of nonreligious thinking and discourse from Western atheism's other deeply embedded roots further naturalizes these binaries and provides people with additional ways of expressing their atheism as they reflect on various issues and aspects of their own lives. Another way of putting this is to say that drawing upon these roots broadens their repertoire of atheism-related discourse—especially in terms of highlighting themes of integrity, openness, and progress—and allows them to speak about their atheist identities in a more elaborated manner.

Lastly, in the final few pages of his book, James provides his readers with a glimpse of his own "over-belief." As a Christian, albeit a congenitally nondogmatic one for whom faith feels akin to an uncertain "personal venture," he claims that believing in the existence of God is the best way for him to account for the unseen order. Ever the pragmatist, he also confides, "By being faithful in my poor measure to this over-belief, I seem to myself to keep more sane and true."[4]

In contrast, although aspiring to sanity when necessary and truth whenever possible, I have no such interest in self-disclosure. It was, after all, the yearning to get outside of myself that originally spurred my hopes of one day becoming a sociologist. As such, I consider whatever success I have displayed in these pages in terms of practicing *Verstehen*, understanding the other on the other's own terms, to comprise the totality of why writing (and, one hopes, reading) this book has been profitable. Of course, never having been mistaken for an intellectual giant myself, my refraining from musing autobiographically probably disappoints few, if any, readers anyway.

So, let us settle for just a smidge of outward-looking musing. Throughout this book, true to my aim of respecting others' own terms, I have employed Americans' oft-used distinction between the religious and nonreligious, between believers and atheists. Yet, as I have noted repeatedly, the boundary that purportedly separates them is quite porous, and people in these supposedly vying camps frequently have much in common. They also, I contend, have much to say to one another. For instance, many people of faith have little trouble dismissing the stereotypes and reductionisms of the New Atheist authors with hardly a second thought. But they should resist whatever temptation they might feel to do likewise with the everyday atheists in their midst who, it turns out, have extremely nuanced things to say about faith and reason, images of God, religious communities and institutions, and so forth. People of faith would do well to listen. I say this because, despite many of my respondents' claims to the contrary, believers generally do not eschew critical reasoning, and in fact, they continually rely on it as they think through and reimagine what it means to be religious today. This process could be greatly enhanced if they were to consider the perspectives of atheist "outsiders" with the high degree of seriousness that, in my estimation, they clearly deserve.

For their part, atheists would do well to consider that, just as they do not have the corner on rationality, believers are not the only ones who "walk by faith" to some extent. Even as they emphasize critical thinking, atheists have also internalized the deeply engrained cultural values and norms that enable them to operate in the world in conjunction with others doing the same. It is in this respect that they, too, are "believers" or, as sociologist Christian Smith put it, *homo credens*.[5] They believe in things that are "personally meaningful" to them. They give fulsome assent to the myth that science and religion are necessarily at logger-heads as well as to the notion that their reasoning and even their feelings provide them with valid information about the world. They exhibit a nearly unwavering fidelity to the normative sensibilities associated with the "modern moral order" and to the belief that these are sufficient for shaping ethical lives.

Less a critique *of* American atheists, I make this final point to high-light a missed opportunity in terms of a potential critique that could be made *by* them. In other words, they say no to God and to key compo-nents of religion. They likewise say "I don't know" to perplexing ques-tions. But are they perplexed enough? Are they unknowing enough to truly say yes to something new and not, as unquestioning "believers" in the "truth" of cultural mores, to something that smacks more of an un-acknowledged fidelity to un-interrogated meanings and norms?

A decade or so before James delivered his famed Gifford Lectures, the philosopher Friedrich Nietzsche wrote his remarkable atheist myth titled *Thus Spoke Zarathustra*.[6] In it, he describes three metamorpho-ses of the human spirit. By accepting Christianity, it becomes a camel heavily burdened with the mortification of its pride, the denigration of its own wisdom, and the weight of moral obligation—all of which com-mand to humanity, "Thou shalt." Then the camel enters a desert, and in time, a second metamorphosis occurs. The human spirit becomes a lion. It then casts off the burdens imposed upon it, slays the dragon of obligation, and instead of abiding by "Thou shalt," it now growlingly declares, "I will." The lion rises up, but even after proving victorious, it finds itself in a bleak and barren desert. It overcomes the burdens of obligation but cannot burgeon forth new values and insights until it, too, is transformed. This time, the human spirit becomes a child whose imagination, marked by "innocence and forgetting," is not shaped by the past. The child is creative, he "wills his own will," and simply utters, "I am." Ultimately, says Nietzsche, only the child is truly able to express a "sacred Yes" unto life because it is unencumbered by the strictures of the past, which have weighed down and contorted the human spirit.

I mention this myth because so many American atheists seem like lions to me—authentically discerning, morally decent, intellectually astute lions. Yet, as Nietzsche imagined, while the lion's fierce defiance is necessary for the "creation of freedom"—a freedom, as we have seen, emphatically acclaimed by atheists to this day—something more could come from this. Put differently, atheists still possess a kind of faith in the cultural values, norms, and narratives that shape their thinking, their behavior, and even their core sense of self much more than they seem to know. If they were to become more self-consciously reflexive about this reality, they could offer an even more incisive critique of all we presume to know and of the taken-for-granted ways in which we live today. This, I think, might enable them to make a much-needed and even more significant contribution to American public life than they are presently. Why stop at rejecting God when the burdens of so many lesser gods— our consumerism and other distraction rituals, our violence in all its manifestations, and our practices of obligatory happiness and yet relentless striving—all continue to be borne without complaint?

To make this contribution, to become the child Nietzsche envisions, American atheists would need to do more than rear back and roar at religion, even when they do so in the generally thoughtful ways I have recounted. Many among them are starting to come to a similar conclusion. Especially interesting, and quite ironic, is that efforts to articulate a more positive, socially engaged face of public atheism usually veer off in the direction of religion in some manner or another. For instance, the newly emergent Atheism + (meaning atheism *plus* social justice) movement promotes a variant of atheism dedicated to promoting justice and countering sexism, racism, ableism, and other forms of bigotry. Insofar as this movement weds atheism to a strong belief in the values of the "modern moral order," which are typically espoused by progressive faith communities as well, it actually reflects the sort of fidelity to prevailing cultural values and norms I have been describing. Another, more explicit example is atheist author Alain de Botton's baby-*sans*-bathwater contention that, as they throw out theism generally, secular people should salvage such specific dimensions of religion as a more holistic type of education and a thicker understanding of community, an emphasis on kindness and tenderness, and even inspirational forms of art and architecture. He suggests that religious bestowments such as these may be needed now more than ever, especially since contemporary life feels much like a desert of alienation and meaninglessness to so many people.

"God may be dead," he cautions his readers, "but the urgent issues which impelled us to make him up still stir and demand resolutions which do not go away when we have been nudged to perceive some scientific inaccuracies in the tale of the seven loaves and fishes."[7]

Undoubtedly helpful sometimes, expressing a collective faith in certain progressive values and appropriating certain dimensions of religion still do not seem like approaches that would enable atheists to contribute to the public conversation as critically as they might. A more valuable contribution would be for atheists to question God *and* the myriad lesser gods; to question the "unseen order" *and* the "modern moral order"; and to question the religious dogmas articulated from American pulpits *and* those enjoined by the *Sittlichkeit* of American culture. This is no easy task, and the way to go about it is definitely unclear. Nevertheless, instead of appropriating specific values or dimensions, one way to grow into Nietzsche's child might be for atheists to embrace something far more basic to religion, something at its very core. Philosopher Tim Crane calls this the foundational religious "impulse" or the very vague, always personally unsettling sense that there is "something beyond all this."[8] Another philosopher, Chantal Milon-Delsol, prefers the phrase *désir d'éternité* ("desire for eternity").[9] And William James famously referred to this basic, foundational element of religion simply as a deep longing for "the more."

Perhaps embracing something like this could enable atheists to take a next, bolder step in American public life. It could be that purposefully honing this unsettling sense, acutely feeling this *désir*, and truly accepting this longing as viscerally constitutive of the human condition—all possibilities open to secular people as well as being intrinsically related to firsthand religion—is what could best enable atheists, as unabashed atheists, to recognize the desertlike features of our present situation, to move beyond criticizing religions for, among other things, their frequent misrecognition of this situation, and then offer a more penetrating critique of it. Taking this step may even engender sensibilities not unlike such characteristically religious ones as prophetic denunciations of things inimical to full human flourishing, priestly smashings of idols, honoring untamed moments of mystery and wonder, and an unremitting urge to move from "something wrong" to "something made right." The great irony in all this is captured by Nietzsche in the child's distinctly "*sacred* Yes." One can only speculate here. Yet, perhaps sensibilities like these as well as the honest acknowledgment that we seem to ceaselessly desire more than the present can give are what could help to turn atheism's yes to immanence in the direction of a future less delimited by imaginative constraints inherited from the past. Maybe this would also enable American atheists to cultivate what James extols as the profound "feeling of being in a wider life than that of this world's selfish little interests."[10] They, as we have discussed, already rely on various feelings for assurances that they are on the right track as atheists. This additional one could remind them to take newer tracks. If they could nurture this feeling, then perhaps they could bring an important and uniquely critical perspective to the American public square, and since this also happens to be James's description of saintliness, in doing so they might find themselves in better (or at least different) company than they ever imagined.

ACKNOWLEDGMENTS

Book writing can feel pretty lonely sometimes. In the office, door closed, poring over books and notes and transcripts, trying to get the story right. This is why acknowledgments sections are so helpful, at least for me. They prod me to take stock. Even though I tend to write them, like right now, when I am really drained—at the end of a challenging intellectual journey—they make me look back and then remind me that I have not been so alone after all. I have actually been helped and supported along the way. And I am truly grateful.

First, I am grateful to this study's respondents, the 518 atheists who took the time to share their musings, convictions, and wisdom with someone who was, for most of them, a complete stranger. If, in these pages, I have indeed gotten their story right, then this is simply because I was spurred to do so by my respect and, not uncommonly, by my admiration for these people.

I am also thankful to my scholarly home, Santa Clara University. I would likely still be at a much earlier phase of this project were it not for two half-year sabbaticals granted to me. The first was primarily dedicated to conducting interviews, whereas the second gave me the time to really bear down and complete the writing process. The university's Markkula Center for Applied Ethics also awarded me a Hackworth Grant that, among other things, enabled me to hire research assistants and interview transcribers to work with me. Speaking of whom, I want to thank my two research assistants, Sara Brabec and Troy Mikanovich, as well as the students who worked so diligently to carefully transcribe the taped interviews for this project: Nabilah Deen, Chanel Gad, Hunt Hoffman, Claire Overholt, Nicki Steinmetz, Elizabeth Mueller, and John Michael Reyes.

Other students deserving of a shout-out from me are the ones who participated in the graduate-level "The 'New Atheism' in American Culture" course I have taught every so often at Santa Clara University's Jesuit School of Theology. I truly appreciate their studiousness, liveliness, and willingness to assist me in honing my ideas from their sometimes half- (or less) baked iterations to what has been published here.

Next, I want to thank all the people at New York University Press who contributed to the detailed process of transforming my manuscript into the book you are currently reading . . . or maybe just thinking about reading. I especially want to express my appreciation to senior editor Jennifer Hammer, editorial assistant Amy Klopfenstein, and production director Martin Coleman for the abundance of professionalism and care they contributed to this project. I also send my thanks to the three anonymous reviewers who read, thought hard about, and without question, helped me to improve my manuscript. And I am absolutely falling over myself with gratitude for the encouragement and incisive critiques I have received from the general editor of NYU Press's Secular Studies series, Phil Zuckerman, whose scholarship I have long admired and whom I have also discovered to be an impressive colleague and person.

Finally, I am so grateful to my wife, Sheri Hostetler, and our son, Patrick Baggett, for, well, just about everything. While you make me feel less alone in that office of mine, you're also why I drive just a bit faster coming *from* than I do going *to* it.

Appendix A

THE VARIETIES OF NONRELIGIOUS EXPERIENCE

Interview Schedule (E-mail Version)

Thanks for taking time to respond to these questions. Note that there are no "correct" answers we are looking for and your responses to this questionnaire will be kept strictly confidential. Also, please feel free to provide as much information as you would like. In other words, we encourage you to provide specific examples in your responses, recount stories from your past, and go into as much detail as necessary to give us a thorough understanding of your experience. We are more than happy to read all of this because we want to provide the most detailed and most balanced snapshot of American atheists that we possibly can. Thanks again for helping us to do this.

BACKGROUND QUESTIONS:

1. Were you raised atheist or did you have a religious upbringing of some sort? In other words, to what degree (if any) was religion or atheism part of your family life while growing up?
2. *If raised religious*—When and why did you become an atheist? What was this transition from religion like for you, for your family, for your friends, etc.? Was this a quick transition or a slow one? Was it easy for you or difficult?
3. *If raised nonreligious*—Have you ever been drawn to religion at any point in your life? Why or why not?

THINKING ABOUT ATHEISM:

1. Do you identify yourself as an atheist? If so, what does being an atheist mean to you? And, if so, how is your life now different from before you began identifying as an atheist?
2. Why do you think most people in the United States say they believe in God, practice some form of religion, and do not identify themselves as atheists?
3. Do most people who know you—family, friends, co-workers, etc.—also know that you're an atheist? Why or why not?

4. Do you have family members who are also atheists?
5. Are most of your friends atheists? Why or why not?
6. Have you ever been treated differently by people because you're an atheist? If so, in what way(s) precisely?

THINKING ABOUT RELIGION:

1. Overall, would you say that other people's belief in God is a good thing, a bad thing, or something you're indifferent about? Why?
2. Overall, would you say that organized religion is a good thing, a bad thing, or something you're indifferent about? Why?
3. If not a religious person, do you consider yourself to be a spiritual person? Why or why not?

LIVING AS AN ATHEIST:

1. Many religious people say that belief in God provides a foundation for their morality. What do you think about this idea? As an atheist, on what do you base your morality? How do you decide what things are good or bad, whether you (or others) are behaving rightly or wrongly, etc.?
2. Many religious people consider belief in God and religious practice to be essential for raising well-rounded children with a connection to a tradition that helps them to see meaning in the world. What is your opinion about this viewpoint?
3. For many religious people, belief in God purportedly provides an explanation of how the world came into existence and why we are here. As an atheist, do you need or have answers or insights pertaining to these topics? If so, what are they?
4. For many religious people, belief in God is said to provide hope or comfort with respect to suffering in the world and to the inevitability of death. As an atheist, how, if at all, do you think through or come to terms with these things?

Conclusion: No questionnaire could possibly cover all dimensions of a topic as complex as this one. So, do you have any additional information or any further reflections that could help us to understand your experience as an atheist better? If so, please feel free to add this now.

Thanks again. Your perspective is very important to us.

Appendix B

THE VARIETIES OF NONRELIGIOUS EXPERIENCE

A Demographic Snapshot

The data here represent the 518 respondents surveyed for this study. With the exception of sixteen people who submitted surveys only, the remainder also agreed to either an in-person (27) or a telephone-based (85) interview, whereas the remainder (390) responded—either by e-mail or U.S. mail—to the questionnaire that appears in appendix A.

TABLE A.1	
	%
Sex	
Male	64
Female	36
Age	
Under 40	49
40–59	36
60 and over	15
Race/ethnicity	
African American	6
Asian/Pacific Islander	3
Hispanic/Latino	7
White	80
Other	4
Marital status	
Never married	29
Married	52

TABLE A.1 (*cont.*)

Marital status	
Partnered	6
Divorced	12
Widowed	1

Educational attainment	
Some high school or less	1
High school graduate	5
Some college/vocational school	28
College graduate	27
Some graduate or professional school	8
Graduate or professional degree	31

Employment status	
Full time	59
Part time (not primarily a student)	8
Full-time student	13
Unemployed	8
Retired	12

Socioeconomic status	
Under $50,000	39
$50,000–$99,999	35
$100,000–$149,000	15
$150,000 and over	11

Demographic region	
Northeast	17
South	21
Midwest	17
Southwest	14
West	31

NOTES

PREFACE

1 See, for example, Richard Lynn, John Harvey, and Helmuth Nyborg, "Average Intelligence Predicts Atheism Rates across 137 Nations," *Intelligence* 37 (2009): 11–15; and Satoshi Kanazawa, "Why Liberals and Atheists Are More Intelligent," *Social Psychology Quarterly* 73, no. 1 (2010): 33–57.

2 See her "Research Note: Talking about a Revolution: Terminology for the New Field of Non-Religion Studies," *Journal of Contemporary Religion* 27, no. 1 (2012): 129–39; and also Lois Lee, *Recognizing the Non-Religious: Reimagining the Secular* (New York: Oxford University Press, 2015).

3 William James, *The Varieties of Religious Experience: A Study of Human Nature* (1902; reprint, New York: Macmillan, 1961), 17.

CHAPTER 1. WELL, I'LL BE DAMNED!

1 A notable exception is sociologist Susan Budd's *Varieties of Unbelief: Atheists and Agnostics in English Society, 1850–1960* (London: Heinemann, 1977). Although a nonsociological account written before Campbell's work, I also direct readers' attentions to historian Martin E. Marty's insightful, but lesser-known, *Varieties of Unbelief* (New York: Holt, Rinehart and Winston, 1964).

2 See Elaine Howard Ecklund, *Science vs. Religion: What Scientists Really Think* (New York: Oxford University Press, 2010).

3 At about the time Campbell's book was published, secularization theory reached its zenith with such influential works as Bryan Wilson's *Religion in Secular Society* (Baltimore: Penguin, 1966); Peter Berger's *The Sacred Canopy* (Garden City, NY: Anchor, 1967); and David Martin's "Notes toward a General Theory of Secularisation," *European Journal of Sociology* (December 1969). Since then, most sociologists have questioned various aspects of secularization theory. For excellent accounts of the many issues scholars have raised, see William H. Swatos Jr. and Daniel V. A. Olson, eds., *The Secularization Debate* (Lanham, MD: Rowman & Littlefield, 2000); José Casanova, "Rethinking Secularization: A Global Perspective," *Hedgehog Review* 8 (2006): 7–22; N. J. Demerath, "Secularization and Sacralization Deconstructed and Reconstructed," in *The Sage Handbook of the Sociology of Religion*, ed. N. J. Demerath and James A. Beckford, 57–80 (Thousand Oaks, CA: Sage, 2007); and Philip S. Gorski and Ateş Altınordu, "After Secularization?" *Annual Review of Sociology* 34 (2008): 55–85.

4 Nor, I hasten to add, does my work here take a position on the so-called secu-larization debate since public expressions of atheism could point to a general weakening of religious conviction or, on the other hand, reflect just how strong normative expectations of religiosity are in a society where people would even think to identify themselves as atheists. For a subtle exploration of this issue, see Michael Ian Borer, "The New Atheism and the Secularization Thesis," in *Religion and the New Atheism: A Critical Appraisal*, ed. Amarnath Amarasingam, 125–37 (Chicago: Haymarket, 2012); and Paul Cliteur, *The Secular Outlook: In Defense of Moral and Political Secularism* (Malden, MA: Blackwell, 2010).

5 For the full text of this address, see "President Barack Obama's Inaugural Address," Obama White House, January 21, 2009, www.obamawhitehouse.archives.gov.

6 "Papa Francesco scrive a *Repubblica*: 'Dialogo aperto con i non credenti,'" *La Repubblica*, September 4, 2013.

7 Liana Aghajanian, "Intersections: Thoughts on a Sign and What It Represents," *Los Angeles Times*, April 16, 2012.

8 Bill Johnson, "Metro State Atheists," *Rocky Mountain News*, November 29, 2008.

9 Laurie Goodstein, "More Atheists Shout It from the Rooftops," *New York Times*, April 26, 2009.

10 Some lesser-known, but significant, New Atheism texts include Ibn Warraq, ed., *Leaving Islam: Apostates Speak Out* (Amherst, NY: Prometheus, 2003); Michel Onfray, *Atheist Manifesto: The Case against Christianity, Judaism, and Islam* (New York: Arcade, 2005); David Mills, *Atheist Universe: The Thinking Person's Answer to Christian Fundamentalism* (Berkeley, CA: Ulysses, 2006); Ayaan Hirsi Ali, *Infidel* (New York: Free Press, 2007); Victor J. Stenger, *God: The Failed Hypothesis* (Amherst, NY: Prometheus, 2007); Stephen Batchelor, *Confession of a Buddhist Atheist* (New York: Spiegel & Grau, 2010); and A. C. Grayling, *The God Argument: The Case* against *Religion and for Humanism* (New York: Bloomsbury, 2013). Also, writing rejoinders to the New Atheism is a veritable cottage industry at this point. Some of its more notable contributions are Amarnath Amarasingam, ed., *Religion and the New Atheism: A Critical Appraisal* (Chicago: Haymarket, 2012); Tina Beat-tie, *The New Atheists: The Twilight of Reason and the War on Religion* (Maryknoll, NY: Orbis, 2007); Christopher R. Cotter, Philip Andrew Quadrio, and Jonathan Tuckett, eds., *New Atheism: Critical Perspectives and Contemporary Debates* (Cham, Switzerland: Springer, 2017); John F. Haught, *God and the New Atheism: A Critical Response to Dawkins, Harris, and Hitchens* (Louisville, KY: Westmin-ster John Know Press, 2008); Chris Hedges, *When Atheism Becomes Religion: America's New Fundamentalists* (New York: Free Press, 2008); Michael Novak, *No One Sees God: The Dark Night of Atheists and Believers* (New York: Double-day, 2008); Terry Eagleton, *Reason, Faith, and Revolution: Reflections on the God Debate* (New Haven, CT: Yale University Press, 2009); David Bentley Hart, *Atheist Delusions: The Christian Revolution and Its Fashionable Enemies* (New Haven, CT: Yale University Press, 2009); and Alister McGrath, *Why God Won't Go Away* (Nashville, TN: Thomas Nelson, 2010).

11 See Richard Dawkins, *The Selfish Gene* (New York: Oxford University Press, 1976); and Daniel C. Dennett, *Darwin's Dangerous Idea: Evolution and the Meanings of Life* (New York: Simon & Schuster, 1996).

12 Stephen Bullivant, "The New Atheism and Sociology: Why Here? Why Now? What's Next?" in *Religion and the New Atheism: A Critical Appraisal*, ed. Amarnath Amarasingam, 109–24 (Chicago: Haymarket, 2012), 116. I learned much from Bullivant's article and its careful parsing of the factors leading to the emergence of the New Atheism, which I touch upon in this paragraph.

13 Julian Baggini, "Atheism in America," *Financial Times*, February 3, 2012.

14 Karl Marx, "Contribution to the Critique of Hegel's *Philosophy of Right*: Introduction," in *The Marx-Engels Reader*, ed. Robert C. Tucker, 2nd edition (New York: Norton, 1978), 54.

15 Richard Dawkins, *The God Delusion* (New York: Houghton Mifflin, 2006), 5.

16 Christopher Hitchens, *God Is Not Great: How Religion Poisons Everything* (New York: Twelve, 2007), 282.

17 Paul Froese and Christopher Bader, *America's Four Gods: What We Say about God and What That Says about Us* (New York: Oxford University Press, 2010), chap. 4.

18 For an extremely thoughtful exploration of nonreligious experience as something substantial in its own right and of ways to reimagine atheism beyond being reduced to a residual category, see Lois Lee's *Recognizing the Non-Religious*. Also, for an investigation of the persistent bias against the nonreligious among sociologists of religion, see Ryan T. Cragun and Joseph H. Hammer, "One Person's Apostate Is Another Person's Convert: What Terminology Tells Us about Pro-Religious Hegemony in the Sociology of Religion," *Humanity and Society* 35 (February/May 2011): 149–75.

19 Here I am indebted to Jack David Eller's essay "What Is Atheism?" in *Atheism and Secularity*, vol. 1, *Issues, Concepts, and Definitions*, ed. Phil Zuckerman, 1–18 (Santa Barbara, CA: Praeger, 2010).

20 Among other intriguing discussions of "atheistic worldviews and systems," see Andrew Skilton, "Buddhism," and Anne Vallely, "Jainism," in *The Oxford Handbook of Atheism*, ed. Stephen Bullivant and Michael Ruse (New York: Oxford University Press, 2013), 337–66; and, for Chinese society and Confucianism, see Liang Tong, "Atheism and Secularity in China," in *Atheism and Secularity*, vol. 2, *Global Expressions*, ed. Phil Zuckerman, 197–221 (Santa Barbara, CA: Praeger, 2010).

21 Joel Thiessen and Sarah Wilkins-Laflamme, "Becoming a Religious None: Irreligious Socialization and Disaffiliation," *Journal for the Scientific Study of Religion* 56, no. 1 (2017): 64–82.

22 These variations are drawn from Phil Zuckerman, *Faith No More: Why People Reject Religion* (New York: Oxford University Press, 2012), 4–7.

23 Joseph Baker and Buster Smith, *American Secularism: Cultural Contours of Nonreligious Belief Systems* (New York: NYU Press, 2015), 89.

24 See, for example, Richard Cimino and Christopher Smith, "Secular Humanism and Atheist beyond Progressive Secularism," *Sociology of Religion* 68, no. 4

(Winter 2007): 407–24; as well as Teemu Taira, "New Atheism as Identity Politics," in *Religion and Knowledge: Sociological Perspectives*, ed. Matthew Guest and Elisabeth Arweck (Burlington, VT: Ashgate, 2012), 97–113.

25 The myriad implications of this burgeoning sense of indifference are addressed in Johannes Quack and Cora Schuh, eds., *Religious Indifference: New Perspectives from Studies on Secularization and Nonreligion* (New York: Springer, 2017).

26 Quoted in Michael J. Buckley, *At the Origins of Modern Atheism* (New Haven, CT: Yale University Press, 1987), 225.

27 Quoted in Charles Bufe, *The Heretic's Handbook of Quotations: Cutting Comments on Burning Issues* (Tucson, AZ: Sharp, 1992), 183.

28 Samuel Beckett, *Endgame* and *Act without Words* (New York: Grove, 2009), 8.

29 James Thrower, *Western Atheism: A Short History* (Amherst, NY: Prometheus, 2000), 7–23. Also see Edward Jayne, *An Archaeology of Disbelief: The Origins of Secular Philosophy* (Lanham, MD: Hamilton, 2018), chap. 1.

30 Quoted in Jennifer Michael Hecht, *Doubt: A History* (San Francisco: Harper-Collins, 2003), 10; I am also indebted to this fine book for the story I tell about Anaxagoras.

31 Julian Baggini, *Atheism: A Very Short Introduction* (New York: Oxford University Press, 2003), 75–76.

32 Thrower, *Western Atheism*, 32.

33 Quoted in Michael J. Buckley, *Denying and Disclosing God: The Ambiguous Progress of Modern Atheism* (New Haven, CT: Yale University Press, 2004), 101.

34 Quoted in Alister McGrath, *The Twilight of Atheism: The Rise and Fall of Disbelief in the Modern World* (New York: Doubleday, 2004), 94.

35 Quoted in Walter Burkert, *Greek Religion* (Cambridge, MA: Harvard University Press, 1985), 313.

36 Plato, *Apology*, trans. Hugh Tredennick, in *Plato: The Collected Dialogues*, ed. Edith Hamilton and Huntington Cairns (Princeton, NJ: Princeton University Press, 1961), 8.

37 Hecht, *Doubt*, 4–44. For excellent delineations of the religions and philosophies of the Hellenistic world, see Luther H. Martin, *Hellenistic Religions: An Introduction* (New York: Oxford University Press, 1987); and Tim Whitmarsh, *Battling the Gods: Atheism in the Ancient World* (New York: Knopf, 2015).

38 Quoted in Hecht, *Doubt*, 34–35.

39 Plato, *Apology*, in Hamilton and Cairns, *Plato*, 3–26.

40 Quoted in McGrath, *Twilight of Atheism*, 8.

41 Peter Gay, *The Enlightenment: An Interpretation; The Rise of Modern Paganism* (New York: Knopf, 1966).

42 Karl Marx and Friedrich Engels, *The Communist Manifesto* (1846; reprint, New York: Oxford University Press, 1998), 6.

43 See Max Weber, "Religious Rejections of the World and Their Directions," in *From Max Weber: Essays in Sociology*, ed. H. H. Gerth and C. Wright Mills, 323–59 (New York: Oxford University Press, 1946).

44 My discussion of this theological dimension has been informed by Gavin Hyman's *Short History of Atheism* (New York: Tauris, 2010), 47–80; as well as his essay "Atheism in Modern History," in *The Cambridge Companion to Atheism*, ed. Michael Martin (New York: Cambridge University Press, 2007), 27–46.

45 See Denys Turner's reflections on this theme in his October 12, 2001, lecture delivered at the University of Cambridge and published under the title *How to be an Atheist* (Cambridge: Cambridge University Press, 2002).

46 Brad S. Gregory, *The Unintended Reformation: How a Religious Revolution Secularized Society* (Cambridge, MA: Harvard University Press, 2012), esp. chap. 1.

47 My thinking has been enhanced by José Casanova's discussion of how, rather than the inexorable decline or privatization of religion, secularization mostly correlates with differentiation, which he identifies as "a structural trend that serves to define the very structure of modernity" (39); see his *Public Religions in the Modern World* (Chicago: University of Chicago Press, 1994), chap. 1.

48 Mark Lilla, *The Stillborn God: Religion, Politics, and the Modern West* (New York: Vintage, 2007).

49 Wilfred Cantwell Smith, *The Meaning and End of Religion* (Minneapolis: Fortress, 1962), 32–44.

50 See Timothy Fitzgerald, *Discourse on Civility and Barbarity: A Critical History of Religion and Related Categories* (New York: Oxford University Press, 2007); and Brent Nongbri, *Before Religion: A History of a Modern Concept* (New Haven, CT: Yale University Press, 2013).

51 For these etymological observations, see Karen Armstrong, *The Case for God* (New York: Knopf, 2009), 87.

52 Francis Bacon, "Of Atheism," in *The Essays* (1883; reprint, Mineola, NY: Dover, 2008), 49–52.

53 James Turner, *Without God, Without Creed: The Origins of Unbelief in America* (Baltimore: Johns Hopkins University Press, 1985).

54 Ibid., 261, 267.

55 For the data in this paragraph, I draw upon Ariela Keysar, "Who Are America's Atheists and Agnostics?" in *Secularism and Secularity: Contemporary International Perspectives*, Barry A. Kosmin and Ariela Keysar (Hartford, CT: Institute for the Study of Secularism in Society and Culture, 2007), 33–39; and from Phil Zuckerman, Luke W. Galen, and Frank L. Pasquale, *The Nonreligious: Understanding Secular People and Societies* (New York: Oxford University Press, 2016), chap. 6.

56 The scholarly literature on anti-atheist bias is growing. Some of the more illuminating pieces are Marcel Harper, "The Stereotyping of Nonreligious People by Religious Students: Contents and Subtypes," *Journal for the Scientific Study of Religion* 46, no. 4 (December 2007): 539–52; Will M. Gervais, Azim F. Shariff, and Ara F. Norenzayan, "Do You Believe in Atheists? Distrust Is Central to Anti-Atheist Prejudice, *Journal of Personality and Social Psychology* 101, no. 6 (December 2011): 1189–1206; Lawton K. Swan and Martin Heesacker, "Anti-Atheist Bias in the United States: Testing Two

Critical Assumptions," *Secularism and Nonreligion* 1 (2012): 32–42; Ryan T. Cragun, Barry Kosmin, Ariela Keysar, Joseph H. Hammer, and Michael Nielsen, "On the Receiving End: Discrimination toward the Non-Religious in the United States," *Journal of Contemporary Religion* 27, no. 1 (2012): 105–27; Joseph H. Hammer, Ryan T. Cragun, Karen Hwang, and Jesse M. Smith, "Forms, Frequency, and Correlates of Perceived Anti-Atheist Discrimination," *Secularism and Nonreligion* 1 (2012): 43–67; Will Gervais, "In Godlessness We Distrust: Using Social Psychology to Solve the Puzzle of Anti-Atheist Prejudice," *Social and Personality Psychology Compass* 6 (2013): 366–77; Alan Payne, "Redefining 'Atheism' in America: What the United States Could Learn from Europe's Protection of Atheists," *Emory International Law Review* 27 (2013): 663–703; Will Gervais, "Everything Is Permitted? People Intuitively Judge Immorality as Representative of Atheists," *PLoS One* 4 (2014): 1–9.

57 Plato, *The Laws*, trans. Thomas L. Pangle (Chicago: University of Chicago Press, 1980), bk. 10.

58 This and all other biblical quotations are taken from the New Revised Standard Version.

59 While true of the American context, atheism is considerably less stigmatized elsewhere. For helpful investigations of this reality, see Samuel Bagg and David Voas, "The Triumph of Indifference: Irreligion in British Society," in *Atheism and Secularity, vol. 2, Global Expressions*, ed. Phil Zuckerman (Santa Barbara, CA: Praeger, 2010), 93–111; and Quack and Schuh, *Religious Indifference*.

60 See, for example, the Pew Forum on Religion and Public Life, "How Americans Feel about Religious Groups," Pew Research Center, July 16, 2014, www.pewforum.org.

61 Lydia Saad, "Support for Nontraditional Candidates Varies by Religion," Gallup, June 24, 2015, www.news.gallup.com.

62 Council for Democratic and Secular Humanism, "Atheists Still Remain Black Sheep of Families," *Free Inquiry* 21, no. 4 (2001): 29.

63 Penny Edgell, Joseph Gerteis, and Douglas Hartmann, "Atheists as 'Other': Moral Boundaries and Cultural Membership in American Society," *American Sociological Review* 71, no. 2 (2006): 211–34.

64 For explorations of "passing," see Erving Goffman, *Stigma: Notes on the Management of Spoiled Identity* (New York: Touchstone, 1963), 73–91; Harold Garfinkel, *Studies in Ethnomethodology* (New York: Prentice-Hall, 1967), 116; and Daniel G. Renfrow, "A Cartography of Passing in Everyday Life," *Symbolic Interaction* 27 (2004): 485–506.

65 Pew Forum on Religion and Public Life, "U.S. Public Becoming Less Religious," Pew Research Center, November 3, 2015, www.pewforum.org.

66 My analysis in this paragraph is indebted to the thoughtful reflections in Edgell, Gerteis, and Hartmann, "Atheists as 'Other.'" See also Jeremy Brooke Straughn and Scott L. Feld, "America as a 'Christian Nation'? Understanding Religious Boundaries of National Identity in the United States," *Sociology of Religion* 71, no. 3 (2010): 280–306.

67 This line of reasoning dovetails with the analysis in Peter Berger, Grace Davie, and Effie Fokas, *Religious America, Secular Europe? A Theme and Variations* (Burlington, VT: Ashgate, 2008), in which the authors explain that, in Europe, "secularist assumptions have a habit of turning religion into a problem" whereas, in the United States, "religion is not only vibrant, but welcomed as the source of essentially positive values" (45).

68 For an excellent distillation of the many studies on nonreligious Americans' moral lives in comparison to their religious counterparts, see Phil Zuckerman, "Atheism, Secularity, and Well-Being: How the Findings of Social Science Counter Negative Stereotypes and Assumptions," *Sociology Compass* 36 (2009): 949–71.

69 James Guth, John Green, Lyman Kellstedt, and Corwin Smidt, "Faith and Foreign Policy: A View from the Pews," *Review of Faith and International Affairs* 3 (2005): 3–9; cited also in Zuckerman, "Atheism, Secularity, and Well-Being," 954.

70 Christel Manning, "Atheism, Secularity, the Family, and Children," in *Atheism and Secularity*, vol. 1, *Issues, Concepts, and Definitions*, ed. Phil Zuckerman, 19–42 (Santa Barbara, CA: Praeger, 2010), 33; cited also in Zuckerman, "Atheism, Secularity, and Well-Being," 958.

71 Greg M. Epstein, *Good without God: What a Billion Nonreligious People Do Believe* (New York: William Morrow, 2009).

72 I borrow these two examples (with their accompanying quotations) from Jesse M. Smith, "Creating a Godless Community: The Collective Identity Work of Contemporary American Atheists," *Journal for the Scientific Study of Religion* 52, no. 1 (2013): 80–99.

73 Dan Barker, *Godless: How an Evangelical Preacher Became One of America's Leading Atheists* (Berkeley, CA: Ulysses, 2008), 39.

74 The classic texts here are Peter Berger, Brigitte Berger, and Hansfried Kellner, *The Homeless Mind: Modernization and Consciousness* (New York: Vintage, 1973); and Anthony Giddens, *Modernity and Self-Identity: Self and Society in the Late Modern Age* (Palo Alto, CA: Stanford University Press, 1991).

75 Michael O. Emerson and David Sikkink, "Portraits of American Life Study, 1st Wave," Association of Religious Data Archives, 2006, www.thearda.com.

76 Lydia Saad, "Three in Four in the U.S. Still See the Bible as the Word of God," Gallup, June 4, 2014, www.news.gallup.com.

77 Pew Forum on Religion and Public Life, "U.S. Religious Landscape Survey: Religious Beliefs and Practices; Diverse and Politically Relevant," Pew Research Center, June 2008, www.pewforum.org.

78 William Lobdell, *Losing My Religion: How I Lost My Faith Reporting on Religion in America—and Found Unexpected Peace* (New York: HarperCollins, 2009), 271.

79 Ibid., 170–71.

80 "Confidence in Institutions: Trends in Americans' Attitudes toward Government, Media, and Business," Associated Press–NORC Center for Public Affairs Research, March 2015, www.apnorc.org.

81 Robert Wuthnow, *Sharing the Journey: Support Groups and America's New Quest for Community* (New York: Free Press, 1994), 39.

82 Pew Forum on Religion and Public Life, "America's Changing Religious Landscape," Pew Research Center, March 12, 2015, www.pewforum.org.

83 John W. Loftus, *Why I Became an Atheist: A Former Preacher Rejects Christianity* (Amherst, NY: Prometheus, 2008), 403.

84 Robert S. Lynd and Helen Merrell Lynd, *Middletown: A Study in Modern American Culture* (1929; reprint, New York: Harcourt Brace Jovanovich, 1957), chap. 20.

85 Theodore Caplow, Howard M. Bahr, and Bruce A. Chadwick, *All Faithful People: Change and Continuity in Middletown's Religion* (Minneapolis: University of Minnesota Press, 1983), 91–95.

86 Pew Forum on Religion and Public Life, "U.S. Religious Landscape Survey."

87 Robert Wuthnow, *America and the Challenges of Religious Diversity* (Princeton, NJ: Princeton University Press, 2005), 200, 224.

88 Phil Zuckerman, "Atheism: Contemporary Numbers and Patterns," in *The Cambridge Companion to Atheism*, ed. Michael Martin, 47–65 (New York: Cambridge University Press, 2007).

89 Quoted in Raymond T. Bond, ed., *The Man Who Was Chesterton* (Garden City, NY: Image, 1960), 125.

90 "Gallup Historical Trends: Religion," Gallup, May 3–7, 2017, www.news.gallup.com.

91 C. Kirk Hadaway, Penny Long Marler, and Mark Chaves, "What the Polls Don't Show: A Closer Look at U.S. Church Attendance," *American Sociological Review* 58, no. 4 (1993): 741–52.

92 I am grateful to Ronald Aronson for bringing these surveys to my attention. See his *Living without God: New Directions for Atheists, Agnostics, Secularists, and the Undecided* (Berkeley: Counterpoint, 2008), 8–16.

93 Baylor Institute for Studies of Religion, "American Piety in the 21st Century," Baylor University, September 2006, www.baylor.edu.

94 "Religious Views and Beliefs Vary Greatly by Country," *Financial Times*/Harris Interactive, December 20, 2006, www.harrisinteractive.com.

95 Pew Forum on Religion and Public Life, "U.S. Religious Landscape Survey," Pew Research Center, 2014, www.pewforum.org.

96 Michael Hout and Claude S. Fischer, "Why More Americans Have No Religious Preference: Politics and Generations," *American Sociological Review* 67 (April 2002): 165–90.

97 See especially Max Weber, *The Methodology of the Social Sciences*, ed. Edward Shils and Henry Finch (New York: Free Press, 1949).

98 See Barney G. Glaser and Anselm L. Strauss, *The Discovery of Grounded Theory: Strategies for Qualitative Research* (Chicago: Aldine, 1967); and Kathy Charmaz, *Constructing Grounded Theory: A Practical Guide through Qualitative Analysis* (Thousand Oaks, CA: Sage, 2006).

CHAPTER 2. ACQUIRING ATHEIST IDENTITIES

1 Grace Davie, "Believing without Belonging: Is This the Future of Religion in Britain?" *Social Compass* 37, no. 4 (1990): 455–69.

2 John R. Shook, *The God Debates: A 21ˢᵗ-Century God for Atheists and Believers (and Everyone in Between)* (Hoboken, NJ: Wiley-Blackwell, 2010).

3 Steve Bruce, *God Is Dead: Secularization in the West* (Malden, MA: Blackwell, 2002), 42.

4 Jon Butler, *Awash in a Sea of Faith: Christianizing the American People* (Cambridge, MA: Harvard University Press, 1990).

5 Mark Chaves, *American Religion: Contemporary Trends* (Princeton, NJ: Princeton University Press, 2011), 6–7.

6 Michael O. Emerson, *People of the Dream: Multiracial Congregations in the United States* (Princeton, NJ: Princeton University Press, 2006), 7.

7 Jesse M. Smith, "Becoming an Atheist in America: Constructing Identity and Meaning from the Rejection of Theism," *Sociology of Religion* 72, no. 2 (2011): 215–37.

8 Stephen LeDrew, "Discovering Atheism: Heterogeneity in Trajectories to Atheist Identity and Activism," *Sociology of Religion* 74, no. 4 (2013): 431–53.

9 Zuckerman, *Faith No More*, chap. 10. Other helpful discussions of the various reasons people give for their religious disaffiliation appear in Joel Thiessen, *The Meaning of Sunday: The Practice of Belief in a Secular Age* (Montreal: McGill-Queen's University Press, 2015), esp. chap. 5; Simon Cottee, *The Apostates: When Muslims Leave Islam* (London: Hurst, 2015); and Callum G. Brown, *Becoming Atheist: Humanism and the Secular West* (New York: Bloomsbury, 2017).

10 For additional reflections concerning apostasy, see David Caplovitz and Fred Sherrow, *The Religious Drop-Outs: Apostasy among College Graduates* (Beverly Hills, CA: Sage, 1977); David Bromley, ed., *Falling from Faith: Causes and Consequences of Religious Apostasy* (Beverly Hills, CA: Sage, 1988); Edward Babinski, *Leaving the Fold: Testimonies of Former Fundamentalists* (Amherst, NY: Prometheus, 1995); Bob Altemeyer and Bruce Hunsberger, *Amazing Conversions: Why Some Turn to Faith and Others Abandon Religion* (Amherst, NY: Prometheus, 1997); Sharon Sandomirsky and John Wilson, "Processes of Disaffiliation: Religious Mobility among Men and Women," *Social Forces* 68 (1990): 1211–29; and Mordechai Bar-Lev and William Shaffir, eds., *Leaving Religion and Religious Life*, Religion and Social Order 7 (Greenwich, CT: JAI Press, 1997).

11 The classic statement here, which has been generative of a vast literature on religious conversion, is John Lofland and Rodney Stark's "Becoming a World-Saver: A Theory of Conversion to a Deviant Perspective," *American Journal of Sociology* 30 (1965): 862–75. For a thoughtful appraisal of this model, see David A. Snow and Cynthia L. Phillips, "The Lofland-Stark Conversion Model: A Critical Reassessment," *Social Problems* 27, no. 4 (1980): 430–47.

12 William James, *Some Problems of Philosophy: A Beginning of an Introduction to Philosophy* (1911; reprint, Lincoln: University of Nebraska Press, 1996), 50.

13 Robert D. Putnam and David E. Campbell, *American Grace: How Religion Divides and Unites Us* (New York: Simon & Schuster, 2010), 139. See also Chaeyoon Lim, Carol Ann MacGregor, and Robert D. Putnam, "Secular and Liminal: Discovering Heterogeneity among Religious Nones," *Journal for the Scientific Study of Religion* 49, no. 4 (2010): 596–618.

14 See Margaret R. Somers, "The Narrative Constitution of Identity: A Relational and Network Approach," *Theory and Society* 23 (1994): 605–49; and Dan P. McAdams, Ruthellen Josselson, and Amia Lieblich, *Identity and Story: Creating Self in Narrative* (Washington, DC: American Psychological Association, 2006).

15 In her important book *The Managed Heart: Commercialization of Human Feeling* (Berkeley: University of California Press, 1983), sociologist Arlie Hochschild notes, in her second chapter titled "Feeling as Clue," "In the same way that we infer other people's viewpoints from how they display feeling, we decide what we ourselves are really like by reflecting on how we feel about ordinary events" (32).

16 See Darren E. Sherkat, "Sexuality and Religious Commitment Revisited: Exploring the Religious Commitments of Sexual Minorities, 1991–2014," *Journal for the Scientific Study of Religion* 55, no. 4 (2016): 756–69.

17 Stephen M. Merino, "Irreligious Socialization? The Adult Religious Preferences of Individuals Raised with No Religion," *Secularism and Nonreligion* 1 (2012): 1–16.

18 Baker and Smith, *American Secularism*, 159.

19 Frank L. Pasquale, "The 'Nonreligious' in the American Northwest," in *Secularism and Secularity: Contemporary International Perspectives*, ed. Barry A. Kosmin and Ariela Keysar, 41–58 (Hartford, CT: Institute for the Study of Secularism in Society and Culture, 2007).

20 David Voas, "The Rise and Fall of Fuzzy Fidelity in Europe," *European Sociological Review* 25, no. 2 (2009): 155–68.

21 Legal scholar Eugene Volokh shows that this is hardly an isolated incident in "Parent-Child Speech and Child Custody Speed Restrictions," *New York University Law Review* 81 (2006): 631–733.

CHAPTER 3. MAINTAINING ATHEIST IDENTITIES

1 Steve Bruce, *Religion in the Modern World: From Cathedrals to Cults* (New York: Oxford University Press, 1996), 58.

2 Paul Tillich, *Systematic Theology*, vol. 1 (Chicago: University of Chicago Press, 1951), 205.

3 Charles Bernheimer, *Flaubert and Kafka: Studies in Psychopoetic Structure* (New Haven, CT: Yale University Press, 1982), 232.

4 For a helpful discussion of these terms, see Helen Rose Ebaugh, *Becoming an Ex: The Process of Role Exit* (Chicago: University of Chicago Press, 1988), 15–20.

5 Jamie L. Mullaney, *Everyone Is Not Doing It: Abstinence and Personal Identity* (Chicago: University of Chicago Press, 2005).

6　David A. Snow and Leon Anderson, "Identity Work among the Homeless: The Verbal Construction and Avowal of Personal Identities," *American Journal of Sociology* 92, no. 6 (1987): 1336–71.

7　Alfredo Garcia and Joseph Blankholm, "The Social Context of Active Disbelief: County-Level Predictors of Disbelief Organizations in the United States," paper presented at the meeting of the Association for the Sociology of Religion, New York, August 10–12, 2013.

8　Peter L. Berger and Thomas Luckmann, *The Social Construction of Reality: A Treatise in the Sociology of Knowledge* (Garden City, NY: Doubleday, Anchor, 1967), esp. 147–63.

9　George Herbert Mead, *Mind, Self and Society* (1934; reprint, Chicago: University of Chicago Press, 1967).

10　Bob Altemeyer and Bruce Hunsberger made a similar observation, noting that the apostates in their study tended to become secular as *individuals*—not on the basis of significant group, peer, or family influence. See their previously cited *Amazing Conversions.*

11　Stephen Bullivant, "Research Note: Sociology and the Study of Atheism," *Journal of Contemporary Religion* 23, no. 3 (2008): 363–68. As anthropologist Frank L. Pasquale put it at the outset of his thoughtful article on group-affiliated secularists in the Northwest United States and British Columbia, "The vast majority tends not to associate, at least formally or institutionally, on the basis of their secularity." See his "A Portrait of Secular Group Affiliates," in *Atheism and Secularity*, vol. 1, *Issues, Concepts and Definitions*, ed. Phil Zuckerman, 43–87 (Santa Barbara, CA: Praeger, 2010).

12　Cited in Zuckerman, Galen, and Pasquale, *Nonreligious*, 212.

13　Ibid.

14　Jacques Berlinerblau, *How to Be Secular: A Call to Arms for Religious Freedom* (New York: Houghton Mifflin Harcourt, 2012), 113.

15　See Benedict Anderson, *Imagined Communities: Reflections on the Origin and Spread of Nationalism* (New York: Verso, 1991).

16　For more on the construction of social boundaries, see Michèle Lamont, *The Dignity of Working Men: Morality and the Boundaries of Race, Class, and Immigration* (Cambridge, MA: Harvard University Press, 2000); and Michèle Lamont and Virág Molnár, "The Study of Boundaries in the Social Sciences," *Annual Review of Sociology* 28 (2002): 167–95.

17　Anthony P. Cohen, *The Symbolic Construction of Community* (New York: Tavistock, 1985), 12, 15.

18　Although he does not touch on boundary construction or the notion of an imagined community, Stephen Bullivant provides a thoughtful reminder for students of atheism to take the experiential dimension seriously in "Introducing Irreligious Experiences," *Implicit Religion* 11 (2008): 7–24. In a similar vein, Lorna Mumford notes that, among members of local nonreligious groups in London, emotional responses to specific events and experiences were often what initially spurred her respondents to reject religious faith; see her "Living Non-religious Identity in London," in *Atheist Identities: Spaces and Social Contexts*, ed. Lori G. Beaman and Steven Tomlins, 153–70 (New York: Springer, 2015).

19 Lewis Coser, *The Functions of Social Conflict* (New York: Free Press, 1956), 38.

20 Cragun et al., "On the Receiving End."

21 Even though this is a frequently referenced quotation within atheist publications (and among atheists) in the United States, its origins are not entirely clear. It is generally and most plausibly identified as a response to a question from journalist Robert Sherman at the O'Hair International Airport in December 1987; see *Free Inquiry* 8, no. 4 (Fall 1988): 16.

22 Michael A. Hogg and Dominic Abrams, *Social Identifications: A Social Psychology of Intergroup Relations and Group Processes* (New York: Routledge, 1998), 20.

23 Ibid., 74.

24 See Ann Swidler, "Culture in Action: Symbols and Strategies," *American Sociological Review* 51, no. 2 (1986): 273–86; as well as her book *Talk of Love: How Culture Matters* (Chicago: University of Chicago Press, 2001).

25 See Antonio Gramsci, *Selections from the Prison Notebooks*, ed. and trans. Quintin Hoare and Geoffrey Nowell Smith (New York: International, 1971), esp. 257–64.

26 For further discussion of how "rational actors" engage the religious sphere, see Lawrence A. Young, ed., *Rational Choice Theory and Religion: Summary and Discussion* (New York: Routledge, 1997).

27 Benjamin Beit-Hallahmi, "Atheists: A Psychological Profile," in *The Cambridge Companion to Atheism*, ed. Michael Martin (New York: Cambridge University Press, 2007), 306–7.

28 Daniel Carson Johnson, "Formal Education vs. Religious Belief: Soliciting New Evidence with Multinomial Logit Modeling," *Journal for the Scientific Study of Religion* 36, no. 2 (1997): 231–46; Darren Sherkat, "Beyond Belief: Atheism, Agnosticism, and Theistic Certainty in the United States," *Sociological Spectrum* 28 (2008): 438–59; Joseph Baker, "An Investigation of the Sociological Patterns of Prayer Frequency and Content," *Sociology of Religion* 69 (2008): 169–85.

29 Baker and Smith, *American Secularism*, 103.

30 Catherine L. Caldwell-Harris, "Understanding Atheism/Non-Belief as an Expected Individual-Differences Variable," *Religion, Brain and Behavior* 2, no. 1 (2012): 4–23.

31 Bruce E. Hunsberger and Bob Altemeyer, *Atheists: A Groundbreaking Study of America's Nonbelievers* (Amherst, NY: Prometheus, 2006), 56.

32 Hochschild, *Managed Heart*, chap. 2, app. A ("Models of Emotion: From Darwin to Goffman"). Also helpful here is Thomas DeGloma's discussion of feelings throughout his informative book on accounts of various types of personal awakening titled *Seeing the Light: The Social Logic of Personal Discovery* (Chicago: University of Chicago Press, 2014).

33 Norman K. Denzin, *On Understanding Emotion* (San Francisco: Jossey-Bass, 1984), 245.

34 See, most famously, Isaiah Berlin, "Two Concepts of Liberty," in *Four Essays on Liberty*, 118–72 (New York: Oxford University Press, 1969).

35 Charles Taylor, *Sources of the Self: The Making of Modern Identity* (Cambridge, MA: Harvard University Press, 1989), 47.

36 *In Ecce Homo: How One Becomes What One Is* (section 10), Nietzsche writes, "My formula for greatness in a human being is *amor fati*: that one wants nothing to be different, not forward, not backward, not in all eternity. Not merely bear what is necessary, still less conceal it—all idealism is mendacity in the face of what is necessary—but *love* it." See Walter Kaufmann, trans., *Basic Writings of Nietzsche* (New York: Modern Library, 2000), 714.

37 See Emile Durkheim, *Suicide: A Study in Sociology* (New York: Free Press, 1951), 246–54.

38 Eviatar Zerubavel, "Language and Memory: 'Pre-Columbian' America and the Social Logic of Periodization," *Social Research* 65, no. 2 (1998): 315–30.

39 David A. Snow and Doug McAdam, "Identity Work Processes in the Context of Social Movements: Clarifying the Identity/Movement Nexus," in *Self, Identity, and Social Movements*, ed. Sheldon Stryker, Timothy J. Owens, and Robert W. White (Minneapolis: University of Minnesota Press, 2000), 41–67.

CHAPTER 4. THE EMPIRICAL ROOT

1 Steve Fuller, "What Has Atheism Ever Done for Science?" in *Religion and the New Atheism: A Critical Appraisal*, Amarnath Amarasingam, 57–77 (Chicago: Haymarket, 2010). See also Peter Harrison, *The Bible, Protestantism, and the Rise of Natural Science* (New York: Cambridge University Press, 1998) and Rodney Stark, *For the Glory of God* (Princeton, NJ: Princeton University Press, 2003).

2 Robert Boyle, "Some Considerations Touching the Usefulness of Experimental Natural Philosophy," in *The Works of the Honorable Robert Boyle*, ed. Thomas Birch, 6 vols. (Hildesheim, Germany: Georg Olms, 1966), 2:62.

3 See Eva Marie Garroutte, "The Positivist Attack on Baconian Science and Religious Knowledge in the 1870s," in *The Secular Revolution: Power, Interests, and Conflict in the Secularization of American Public Life*, ed. Christian Smith, 197–215 (Berkeley: University of California Press, 2003).

4 John W. Draper, *History of the Conflict between Religion and Science* (New York: Appleton, 1874); Andrew D. White, *A History of the Warfare of Science with Theology in Christendom* (New York: Appleton, 1896).

5 See, for example, John H. Evans and Michael S. Evans, "Religion and Science: Beyond the Epistemological Conflict Narrative," *Annual Review of Sociology* 34 (2008): 87–105; as well as the extremely fine essays collected in Peter Harrison, ed., *The Cambridge Companion to Science and Religion* (New York: Cambridge University Press, 2010).

6 See Paul Ricoeur, *Freud and Philosophy: An Essay on Interpretation*, trans. Denis Savage (New Haven, CT: Yale University Press, 1970).

7   Charles Darwin, letter to William Graham, July 3, 1881, Darwin Correspondence Project, letter 13230, www.darwinproject.ac.uk.

8   Hitchens, *God Is Not Great*, 64–65.

9   Dawkins, *God Delusion*, 125.

10 Stephen P. Stich, *The Fragmentation of Reason: Preface to a Pragmatic Theory of Cognitive Evaluation* (Cambridge, MA: MIT Press, 1990), 62.

11 Karl Marx, "The German Ideology," in *The Marx-Engels Reader*, ed. Robert C. Tucker, 2nd ed., 146–200 (New York: Norton, 1978), 172.

12 Eagleton, *Reason, Faith, and Revolution*, 70.

13 John Hedley Brooke, *Science and Religion: Some Historical Perspectives* (New York: Cambridge University Press, 1991), esp. 33–42.

14 Charles Taylor, *A Secular Age* (Cambridge, MA: Harvard University Press, 2007); see especially his eighth chapter titled "The Malaises of Modernity."

15 Thomas S. Kuhn, *The Structure of Scientific Revolutions* (Chicago: University of Chicago Press, 1962).

16 Quoted in Peter Harrison, "'Science' and 'Religion': Constructing the Boundaries," in *Science and Religion: New Historical Perspectives*, ed. Thomas Dixon, Geoffrey Cantor, and Stephen Pumfrey, 23–49 (New York: Cambridge University Press, 2010).

17 For a helpful parsing of the humanistic and scientific strands of contemporary atheism, see Stephen LeDrew, *The Evolution of Atheism: The Politics of a Modern Movement* (New York: Oxford University Press, 2016), chap. 1.

18 Baker and Smith, *American Secularism*, 89–105.

19 Stephen Jay Gould, *Rocks of Ages: Science and Religion in the Fullness of Life* (New York: Ballantine, 2002).

20 Described in David Fergusson, *Faith and Its Critics: A Conversation* (New York: Oxford University Press, 2009), 43.

21 Blaise Pascal, *Pensees*, trans. A. J. Krailsheimer (New York: Penguin, 1995).

22 Jürgen Habermas, *Knowledge and Human Interests* (London: Heinemann, 1971), 4. See also Philip S. Gorski, "Scientism, Interpretation, and Criticism," *Zygon* 25, no. 3 (1990): 279–307; and Mikael Stenmark, "What Is Scientism?" *Religious Studies* 33 (March 1997): 15–32.

23 For an elegant and lively exploration of this question through his engagement with contemporary thinkers, see Jim Holt's *Why Does the World Exist? An Existential Detective Story* (New York: Liveright, 2012).

24 Richard Dawkins, *A River Out of Eden* (New York: Basic, 1995), 133.

25 Jürgen Habermas, "An Awareness of What Is Missing," in *An Awareness of What Is Missing: Faith and Reason in a Post-Secular Age*, by Jürgen Habermas et al. (Malden, MA: Polity, 2010), 15–23.

26 Thomas Nagel, *Mind and Cosmos: Why the Materialist Neo-Darwinian Conception of Nature Is Almost Certainly False* (New York: Oxford University Press, 2012), 115.

27 André Comte-Sponville, *The Little Book of Atheist Spirituality*, trans. Nancy Huston (New York: Penguin, 2007), 134–35.

28 José Ortega y Gasset, *Mission of the University*, ed. and trans. Howard Lee Nostrand (1944; reprint, New Brunswick, NJ: Transaction, 1992), 63.

29 I borrow most of this listing from Peter Watson's *The Age of Atheists: How We Have Sought to Live since the Death of God* (New York: Simon & Schuster, 2014), 17–18.

30 See Paul Froese, *On Purpose: How We Create the Meaning of Life* (New York: Oxford University Press, 2016), esp. chap. 3.

31 Quoted in Michael Ruse, *Atheism: What Everyone Needs to Know* (New York: Oxford University Press, 2014), 106.

32 Other books of this genre are Robert C. Solomon, *Spirituality for the Skeptic: The Thoughtful Love of Life* (New York: Oxford University Press, 2002); Chet Raymo, *When God Is Gone Everything Is Holy: The Making of a Religious Naturalist* (Notre Dame, IN: Sorin, 2008); Aronson, *Living without God*; Steve Antinoff, *Spiritual Atheism* (Berkeley, CA: Counterpoint, 2008); Eric Maisel, *The Atheist's Way: Living Well Without Gods* (Novato, CA: New World Library, 2009); Sam Harris, *Waking Up: A Guide to Spirituality without Religion* (New York: Simon & Schuster, 2014); Mark W. Gura, *Atheist Meditation, Atheist Spirituality* (Duluth, GA: InnerAction, 2015).

33 Baker and Smith, *American Secularism*, 91.

34 See especially Clifford Geertz, "Religion as a Cultural System," in *The Interpretation of Cultures* (New York: Basic, 1973), 87–125.

35 James, *Varieties of Religious Experience*, 45.

36 William Faulkner, *Requiem for a Nun* (New York: Random House, 1950), 92.

CHAPTER 5. THE CRITICAL ROOT

1 Baylor Institute for Studies of Religion, "The Baylor Religion Survey, Wave II," Baylor University, 2007, www.thearda.com.

2 While the first three fragments come from the titles or subtitles of these authors' well-known books, the fourth one comes from Sam Harris's *The End of Faith: Religion, Terror and the Future of Reason* (New York: Norton, 2005), 223.

3 Armstrong, *Case for God*, xvi.

4 Baker and Smith, *American Secularism*, 92.

5 Ibid., 93–96.

6 Ibid., 162.

7 Pew Forum on Religion and Public Life, "U.S. Religious Knowledge Survey," Pew Research Center, September 28, 2010, www.pewforum.org.

8 Pew Forum on Religion and Public Life, "Religious Landscape Study," Pew Research Center, 2014, www.pewforum.org.

9 G. F. W. Hegel, *Hegel's Philosophy of Right*, trans. T. M. Knox (1821; reprint, New York: Oxford University Press, 1967), 13.

10 Thomas Hobbes, *Leviathan* (1651; reprint, New York: Penguin, 1986).

11 Survey data cited in this paragraph and the next one come from the Pew Forum on Religion and Public Life, "U.S. Public Becoming Less Religious," 92–96.

12 Baker and Smith, *American Secularism*, 89.

13 Katja M. Guenther discusses how atheists are less critical of believers (especially less overtly devout ones) than they typically are of religious leaders and institutions in "Bounded by Disbelief: How Atheists in the United States Differentiate Themselves from Religious Believers," *Journal of Contemporary Religion* 29, no. 1 (2014): 1–16.

14 Pew Forum on Religion and Public Life, "U.S. Public Becoming Less Religious," 95.

15 Ibid.

16 For an extensive, historically rich treatment of this topic, see David Niose, *Nonbeliever Nation: The Rise of Secular Americans* (New York: Palgrave Macmillan, 2012).

17 Pew Forum on Religion and Public Life, "U.S. Public Becoming Less Religious," 95.

18 For instance, in their otherwise illuminating *There Is No God: Atheists in America* (Lanham, MD: Rowman & Littlefield, 2013), David A. Williamson and George Yancey contend that "atheism seeks to negate religion" (17). However, as we have seen here, many atheists are not particularly interested in religion, and as discussed in this chapter, those who are interested typically express more nuanced views about religion than simply seeking its negation.

19 H. Richard Niebuhr, *Radical Monotheism and Western Culture* (New York: Harper, 1960), 35.

20 Putnam and Campbell, *American Grace*, 520, 534.

21 Tom W. Smith and Jaesok Son, "Trends in Public Attitudes about Confidence in Institutions," NORC at the University of Chicago, May 2013, 10, www.norc.org.

CHAPTER 6. THE AGNOSTIC ROOT

1 See Tertullian, *Apology*, in *Tertullian: Apology; Minucius Felix: Octavius*, trans. T. R. Glover and Gerald H. Rendall, 2–229 (Cambridge, MA: Harvard University Press, 1931), 47; Augustine, *Confessions*, VII, 10, 16, cited in Catherine Conybeare, "Reading *The Confessions*," in *A Companion to Augustine*, ed. Mark Vessey, 99–110 (Malden, MA: Blackwell, 2012), 107; Pseudo-Dionysius, "The Mystical Theology," in *Pseudo-Dionysius: The Complete Works*, trans. C. Luibheid and P. Rorem, 133–42 (Mahwah, NJ: Paulist, 1987), 134; Maximus the Confessor, *Ambigua* 5, in *Maximus the Confessor*, trans. Andrew Louth, (New York: Routledge, 1996), 117; and Regis J. Armstrong and Ignatius C. Brady, trans., *Francis and Clare: The Complete Works* (New York: Paulist, 1982), 134.

2 Cyril of Jerusalem, "Catechetical Homilies," in *Nicene and Post-Nicene Fathers*, vol. 7, trans. Philip Schaff (Peabody, MA: Hendrickson, 1994), 33.

3 Thomas Aquinas, De Potentia, 7.5 ad 14, quoted in *Chasing Mystery: A Catholic Biblical Theology* (Collegeville, MN: Liturgical, 2012), 35.

4 Robert N. Bellah, "Religion and Belief: The Historical Background of 'Non-Belief,'" in *Beyond Belief: Essays on Religion in a Post-Traditional World*, 216–29 (Berkeley: University of California Press, 1970), 221.

5 See Armstrong, *Case for God*, 113–18.

6 Hecht, *Doubt*, 371.

7 Owen Chadwick, *The Secularization of the European Mind in the Nineteenth Century* (New York: Cambridge University Press, 1975), 250.

8 Thomas Henry Huxley, "Agnosticism" (1889), in *Atheism: A Reader*, ed. S. T. Joshi, 25–33 (Amherst, NY: Prometheus, 2000), 33.

9 Robert G. Ingersoll, "Why I Am an Agnostic," in *The Works of Robert G. Ingersoll*, vol. 4, *Dresden Edition: Lectures* (Lenox, MA: HardPress, 2016), 67.

10 Max Weber, "Science as a Vocation," in *From Max Weber: Essays in Sociology*, ed. H. H. Gerth and C. Wright Mills (New York: Oxford University Press, 1946), 140.

11 Harry G. Frankfurt, *On Bullshit* (Princeton, NJ: Princeton University Press, 2005), 64.

12 Baker and Smith, *American Secularism*, 23.

13 Pew Forum on Religion and Public Life, "U.S. Public Becoming Less Religious," 48.

14 Robert Wuthnow, *After Heaven: Spirituality in America since the 1950s* (Berkeley: University of California Press, 1998).

15 See Linda A. Mercadante, *Belief without Borders: Inside the Minds of the Spiritual but Not Religious* (New York: Oxford University Press, 2014); and Elizabeth Drescher, *Choosing Our Religion: The Spiritual Lives of America's Nones* (New York: Oxford University Press, 2016).

16 Ludwig Wittgenstein, *Tractatus Logico-Philosophicus*, trans. D. F. Pears and B. F. McGuinness (New York: Routledge, 1974), 90.

17 Ernest Becker, *The Denial of Death* (New York: MacMillan, 1973).

18 Pew Forum on Religion and Public Life, "U.S. Public Becoming Less Religious," 53.

19 Dylan Thomas, *The Poems of Dylan Thomas*, ed. Daniel Jones (New York: New Directions, 2003), 239.

20 In this respect, they seem to echo the sentiments of philosopher Kai Nielsen in his informative and provocative *Ethics without God* (Amherst, NY: Prometheus, 1990). "'Purpose of life' is ambiguous: in talking of it we can, on the one hand, be talking of the 'purpose to life,' or, on the other, of 'purposes in life' in the sense of plans we form, ends we seek, etc. . . . Yet, it is only the latter that are plainly necessary to make life meaningful in the sense that there are in our lives and our environment things worthwhile doing, having, or experiencing, things that bring joy, understanding, exhilaration, or contentment to ourselves or others. That we will not have these things forever does not make them worthless any more than the inevitability of death and the probability of decay robs them, or our lives generally, of their sense" (190).

21 Elizabeth Kübler-Ross, *On Death and Dying: What the Dying Have to Teach Doctors, Nurses, Clergy and Their Own Families* (New York: Routledge, 1969).

CHAPTER 7. THE IMMANENT ROOT

1 See Victor Turner, *Dramas, Fields, and Metaphors: Symbolic Action in Human Society* (Ithaca, NY: Cornell University Press, 1974), esp. chap. 1.

2 Michael J. Sandel, *Democracy's Discontent: America in Search of a Public Philosophy* (Cambridge, MA: Harvard University Press, 1996), 4.

3 Christian Smith, *Moral, Believing Animals: Human Personhood and Culture* (New York: Oxford University Press, 2003), 64.

4 McGrath, *Twilight of Atheism*, 271.

5 Aronson, *Living without God*, 39–40.

6 Jean-François Lyotard, *The Postmodern Condition: A Report on Knowledge* (Minneapolis: University of Minnesota Press, 1979), *xxiv*.

7 William Isaac Thomas and Dorothy Swaine Thomas, *The Child in America: Behavior Problems and Programs* (New York: Knopf, 1928), 571–72.

8 I borrow this distinction from Philip Kitcher, *Life after Faith: The Case for Secular Humanism* (New Haven, CT: Yale University Press, 2014), 42.

9 Alan Wolfe, *One Nation after All: What Middle-Class Americans Really Think about God, Country, Family, Racism, Welfare, Immigration, Homosexuality, Work, the Right, the Left, and Each Other* (New York: Viking, 1998), 290.

10 Taylor, *Secular Age*, chap. 15.

11 Ibid., 303–4.

12 *Euthyphro*, trans. Lane Cooper, in *Plato: The Collected Dialogues*, ed. Edith Hamilton and Huntington Cairns (Princeton, NJ: Princeton University Press, 1989), 178–79.

13 For just a sampling, see Frans de Waal, *Good Natured: The Origins of Right and Wrong in Humans and Other Animals* (Cambridge, MA: Harvard University Press, 1997); Matt Ridley, *The Origins of Virtue: Human Instincts and the Evolution of Cooperation* (New York: Penguin, 1998); Richard Joyce, *The Evolution of Morality* (Cambridge, MA: MIT Press, 2006); and Christopher Boehm, *Moral Origins: The Evolution of Virtue, Altruism, and Shame* (New York: Basic, 2012).

14 Lawrence Kohlberg, *The Philosophy of Moral Development*, vol. 1, *Essays on Moral Development* (San Francisco: Harper & Row, 1981).

15 Emile Durkheim, *The Elementary Forms of the Religious Life*, trans. Karen E. Fields (New York: Free Press, 1995), 429.

16 Quoted in Phil Zuckerman, *Living the Secular Life: New Answers to Old Questions* (New York: Penguin, 2014), 12.

17 Claude Lévi-Strauss, *The Savage Mind* (Chicago: University of Chicago Press, 1962), 16–33.

18 See Jeffrey Wattles, *The Golden Rule* (New York: Oxford University Press, 1996).

19 Nancy T. Ammerman, "Golden Rule Christianity: Lived Religion in the American Mainstream," in *Lived Religion in America: Toward a History of Practice*, ed. David D. Hall, 196–216 (Princeton, NJ: Princeton University Press, 1997).

20 Alexis de Tocqueville, *Democracy in America*, ed. J. P. Mayer, trans. George Lawrence (Garden City, NY: Doubleday, Anchor, 1969), esp. vol. 2, pt. 2, chaps. 1–9.

21 For the classic statement, see Hegel, *Hegel's Philosophy of Right*.

22 Robert Wuthnow, *American Mythos: Why Our Best Efforts to Be a Better Nation Fall Short* (Princeton, NJ: Princeton University Press, 2006), esp. chap. 1.

23 For the most comprehensive exploration of the various ways in which religiously unaffiliated parents in the United States raise their children with greater, lesser, or no exposure to religious ideas and institutions, see Christel Manning, *Losing Our Religion: How Unaffiliated Parents Are Raising Their Children* (New York: NYU Press, 2015).

24 Baker and Smith, *American Secularism*, 158.

25 Zuckerman, Galen, and Pasquale, *Nonreligious*, 126.

26 Zuckerman, Galen, and Pasquale address these and other methodological very thoughtfully in *The Nonreligious*, especially their eighth chapter titled "Secular Morality and Ethics."

27 For influential explorations of disparate constructions of moral frameworks, see James Davison Hunter's *Culture Wars: The Struggle to Define America* (New York: Basic, 1991); and George Lakoff, *Moral Politics: What Conservatives Know that Liberals Don't* (Chicago: University of Chicago Press, 1996).

28 Jonathan Haidt, *The Righteous Mind: Why Good People Are Divided by Politics and Religion* (New York: Pantheon, 2012).

29 Alasdair MacIntyre, *After Virtue: A Study in Moral Theory* (Notre Dame, IN: University of Notre Dame Press, 1981).

30 Robert N. Bellah, Richard Madsen, William M. Sullivan, Ann Swidler, and Steven M. Tipton, *Habits of the Heart: Individualism and Commitment in American Life* (New York: Harper & Row, 1985), 221.

31 Mark A. Smith, *Secular Faith: How Culture Has Trumped Religion in American Politics* (Chicago: University of Chicago Press, 2015), 214.

CONCLUSION

1 James, *Varieties of Religious Experience*, 150.

2 Ibid., 42.

3 Ibid., 390.

4 Ibid., 401.

5 Smith, *Moral, Believing Animals*, 46–55.

6 Friedrich Nietzsche, "The Three Metamorphoses," in *Thus Spoke Zarathustra*, in *The Portable Nietzsche*, trans. and ed. Walter Kaufmann, 137–40 (New York: Penguin, 1977).

7 Alain de Botton, *Religion for Atheists: A Non-Believer's Guide to the Uses of Religion* (New York: Pantheon, 2012), 12.

8 Tim Crane, *The Meaning of Belief: Religion from an Atheist's Point of View* (Cambridge, MA: Harvard University Press, 2017), 11.

9 Quoted in Taylor, *Secular Age*, 530.

10 James, *Varieties of Religious Experience*, 220.

INDEX

abortion, 65; pro-life movement, 6
Abrams, Dominic, 92–93
adaptive traits, 204
afterlife, 129, 135, 175, 188, 190
agnosticism, xiv, 14, 60, 69, 171
agnostic root, of atheism, 14–15, 168–94
agnostics, xiv, 172
Altemeyer, Bob, 103, 253n10
altruism, 204, 214–15
American atheism, 7–8, 229; New Atheism
 and, 131; presumptions about, xiii; in
 twenty-first century, 1–40
American Atheists, 3, 5
American culture, 75
*American Secularism: Cultural Contours of
 Nonreligious Belief Systems* (Baker and
 Smith), xiv
amor fati ("love of fate"), 107
Anaxagoras, 12
The Ancestor's Tale (Dawkins), 201
Anderson, Leon, 77
anger, 84–85, 101; stereotypes, 145
anomie, 109
anti-atheist bias, 247n56
apatheists, 49
Aquinas, Thomas, 18, 169
Aristotle, 14, 211
Armstrong, Karen, 145
Aronson, Ronald, 196
"Ask an Atheist" project, 25
ataraxia (peace of mind), 15
atheism: accused of, 16–17; acquisition
 frame, 47–48; agnostic root, 14–15,
 168–94; complexity of, 7–11; critical root

of, 13–14, 142–67, 194; cultural influences of, 17–18; education and, 51, 122;
empirical root of, 12–13, 115–43, 194;
empowerment and, 104; expressing,
2–3, 84, 146; as extrinsic, 16–22; freedom
and, 104–6; God and, 18–19, 166; history
of, 11–16; immanent root of, 15–16, 143,
194–225; in interview schedule, 239–40;
morality and, 22–25, 233; negative,
121; "popular view" of, 7, 39; positive,
121; presumptions about, xiii, 7–34; as
privilege, 161; public, xiii, 233, 244n4;
public expressions of, 2–3; reason and,
27, 110–11; reductionist thinking about,
6–7; religion and, 8–10; responsibility
and, 109–10, 209; revalorization of, xv;
scientific, 122–23, 165, 195, 229; stigma
of, 23–25, 146, 229, 248n59; terminology, 8, 16–17; theologian and clerical
attempts to combat, 21–22; transition to,
47–48; varieties, 228; visibility of, 4–5,
111; in West, 12. *See also* New Atheism
Atheism + movement, 233
atheist activism, 200, 233
atheist authors, xv, 131, 144; New Atheism,
 228, 231, 244n10
Atheist Film Festival, xi, xiii
atheist identities, xiii, 174; acquiring, 41–
 74; acquiring, effort in, 49–50, 58, 68;
 acquisition narratives of, 47–53, 49;
 consolidators, 48, 67–72; epiphanies
 of, 59–60, 66; formation of, 50–51;
 identity convergence and, 112; identity
 work, 77; inquisitives, 48, 53–57;

263

religion (*cont.*)
culture and, 223; dogmatism and, 156; in Europe, 249n67; foundational element of, 234; freedom of, 97, 104–5; Freud on, 117; God and, 9; Hitchens on, 127–28; influence of, 5; in interview schedule, 240; James on, 228–29; Marx on, 117; modernization and, 1–2; morality and, xiv, 23–24, 204–8; "New Age," 2; New Atheism and, 118; "new religious movements," 2; objectification of Western, 194; political engagement and, 6; politics and, 6, 51; proliferation of, 29; questioning, 108; regressive character, 195; religiosity and, 155–59; role of, 157; science and, 7, 21, 116, 122, 124–25, 128–29; science versus religion "conflict myth," xiv, 115–21; social institutions and, 96–99; "spiritual but not religious," 10, 137, 172; state and, 97–98; terminology, 120; truth and, 169; in United States, 49, 249n67; views on, influences, 73 table 2.1. *See also* organized religion; *specific religions*
religion-based moralities, xiv
religiosity, 222; personal, 156; religion and, 155–59
religious: atheists and, 80, 86–87; critical thinking and, 94–95; ethics, 222; negative experiences with, 51; nonreligious and, 231; religious institutions compared with, 159–60; unknowing and, 172
religious categories, 19–20; reframing, 191–93
religious community, 100–101
religious corruption, 28
religious culture, 75; nonreligious in, 85–86
religious diversity, 30, 51; in America, 166–67; exposure to, 64
religious education, 41, 62–64, 198–99; sexual, 51

religious experience, 128
religious groups, growth, 34
religious identities, 59, 97
religious institutions, 28–29, 159–65; atheists and, 162–63, 258n13; church-state separation and, 87, 97–98, 200; criticisms of, 166–67; influence of, 163–64; politics and, 163
Religious Landscape Study (Pew), 146
religious literacy, 95–96; of atheists, 145–46
religious pluralism, 29–30
Religious Right, 2, 33, 159
religious socialization, 50
religious tolerance, 24
religious upbringing, 73 table 2.1
Republic (Plato), 98
responders, 48, 61–67; critical thinking and, 99; difficulties, 85
responsibility, 181–85, 187; atheism and, 109–10, 209; morality and, 208–9
reverence, reframing of, 192–93
ritualism, religious, 106
Roosevelt, Eleanor, 201

Sagan, Carl, 68–69, 108
Sandel, Michael, 195
Scalia, Antonin, 210
science, 72, 73 table 2.1; for atheists, 134; Catholic Church and, 116; education, 95; faith in, 131; religion and, 7, 21, 116, 122, 124–25, 128–29; religious belief in, 141; spirituality explained by, 137–38; terminology, 120
Science and Religion: Some Historical Perspectives survey, 119–20
science versus religion "conflict myth," xiv, 115–21, 140–42, 194–95; atheists on, 229; binaries, 122, 230; myth in, 121; as narrative, 197; New Atheism and, 117–18; rationality and, 115; scientism and, 121–29; suppositions, 117–19; terminology, 120

ABOUT THE AUTHOR

Jerome P. Baggett is Professor of Religion and Society at Santa Clara University's Jesuit School of Theology (Berkeley), a member of the Core Doctoral Faculty of the Graduate Theological Union, and Visiting Professor of Sociology at UC Berkeley. He is author of *Sense of the Faithful: How American Catholics Live Their Faith* (2009) and *Habitat for Humanity: Building Private Homes, Building Public Religion* (2001).